EPISCOPATE

EPISCOPATE

The Role of Bishops in a Shared Future

Edited by C. ANDREW DOYLE

Foreword by MICHAEL B. CURRY

CHURCH
PUBLISHING
INCORPORATED

Unless otherwise noted, the Scripture quotations are from New Revised Standard Version Bible, copyright © 1989 National Council of the Churches of Christ in the United States of America. Used by permission. All rights reserved worldwide.

"Conflict Resolution for Holy Beings," from *Conflict Resolution for Holy Beings: Poems*, by Joy Harjo. Copyright © 2015 by Joy Harjo. Used by permission of W. W. Norton & Company, Inc.

Church Publishing
19 East 34th Street
New York, NY 10016

Cover design by Dylan Marcus McConnell, Tiny Little Hammers
Typeset by Newgen

Library of Congress Cataloging-in-Publication Data
Names: Doyle, C. Andrew, editor.
Title: Episcopate : the role of bishops in a shared future / edited by
   C. Andrew Doyle ; foreword by Michael B. Curry.
Description: New York, NY : Church Publishing, [2022] | Includes
   bibliographical references.
Identifiers: LCCN 2021057496 (print) | LCCN 2021057497 (ebook) |
   ISBN 9781640655539 (paperback) | ISBN 9781640655546 (ebook)
Subjects: LCSH: Episcopal Church—Bishops—History—21st century. |
   Episcopal Church—History—21st century.
Classification: LCC BX5966 .E65 2022 (print) | LCC BX5966 (ebook) |
   DDC 283.7309—dc23/eng/20220120
LC record available at https://lccn.loc.gov/2021057496
LC ebook record available at https://lccn.loc.gov/2021057497

Contents

Foreword

Michael B. Curry

I was delighted when my friend and fellow bishop, Andy Doyle, told me about this collection of essays on the episcopate. Such a compendium makes perfect sense; we are, after all, The *Episcopal* Church. And having served as a bishop for well over two decades, first as bishop diocesan in North Carolina and now as presiding bishop, I confess that I have a particular interest in the book's theme, and so I was, therefore, quick to say yes when asked to contribute this foreword.

As the age of the apostles was coming to a close in the latter half of the first century, Paul addressed one of his final letters to "all the saints in Christ Jesus who are in Philippi, with the bishops [Gk: *episkopoi*] and deacons." A baton was being passed, and yet there would be different ways in those early years of understanding what it actually meant to be a bishop.

A scholar I know well recently brought to my attention an important aspect of episcopacy noted over fifty years ago by R. P. C. Hanson in *Lambeth Essays on Ministry*, a compendium prepared in advance for bishops attending the 1969 Lambeth Conference. Hanson said that our Anglican understanding of episcopacy has what he termed both Ignatian and Cyprianic elements. He was referring here to two early church fathers, those second-generation leaders who received the baton from the apostles and wrestled with what it all meant. Ignatius of Antioch focused on the bishop's authority as chief shepherd in the diocese. Cyprian of Carthage lifted up the need for shared counsel between bishops, as those who hold a common responsibility. Even then, in those earliest days of *episkopos*, there was a lively conversation over understandings viewed at times as being in conflict and at other times as complementary.

In the centuries between then and now, there have been questions and challenges aplenty over the meaning of *episkopos*, especially in our branch of the Jesus Movement:

- At the end of the sixth century, monastic bishops in the northern and southern parts of the British Isles adapted what they knew to a new and unfamiliar local context.

- In the sixteenth century, a scholar-archbishop sought to balance the need for change with the need for continuity in the time of upheaval that was the Reformation.
- At the end of the eighteenth century, revolution gave birth to a new republic, and a church without *episkopoi* discerned what role they would have moving forward.
- In the late twentieth century, a bold African American pioneer took her place in a historic succession that for far too long had been closed to women.

In these moments, and countless others, both the idea and the reality of "bishop" in our tradition have been explored by many. The chapters you are about to read provide important additions to that ongoing conversation. I pray that by listening to the various voices, you will hear things that will both comfort and challenge you. And perhaps you then will find ways to give voice to your own thoughts and help contribute to this important part of Christian mission and ministry. God bless you. And you keep—and share—the faith.

Introduction

C. Andrew Doyle

In conversations with many in and outside the House of Bishops there has been an expressed desire to reimagine the future of the episcopate in our Episcopal Church. We are electing nine to fifteen bishops a year—the turnover is high. There is a sense of urgency to capture the moment of change as new bishops enter and begin to share their episcopacy with—and at the same time are formed by—the church they serve.

We have been in the midst of a pandemic that is now endemically with us. Church leadership and people have struggled for two years. It has been a time of adaptation and change. New questions about the role of bishop have emerged around authority. Questions have emerged also about changes in mission strategy. This has been coterminous with the desire for pastoral care from the episcopate. There continues to be a call for mission leadership. An ever so brief survey of recent episcopal elections brings the following themes to mind: congregational growth, evangelism, health, racial justice, unity amid division, and prophetic leadership. None of these is the particular gift of any one bishop, but all are shared in the priesthood of believers, of which the bishop is only one. Nevertheless, these themes indicate a desire for change, leadership, and vision.

We are also preparing for the election of a new presiding bishop. Here again arise questions concerning the role of bishop, the role of the House of Bishops, and the needs of the wider church that demand the presiding bishop's attention. Questions will inevitably arise around preaching, teaching, sacraments, and the nature of administration. The age-old debate will begin again about whether the presiding bishop can serve institutionally while continuing to serve as a bishop in a local diocese.

This collection attempts to offer to the people of The Episcopal Church some conversation starters regarding our history, our present, and the potential future role of bishop. The collection should not be seen as a solution to questions about our future. Instead, my hope is that the chapters inspire more curiosity about the ministry of bishops in The Episcopal Church. I hope that you will read the chapters in a group of discerning leaders in conversation with one another.

We are in a time of discernment. These diverse voices call our attention to our history, our unity, and our diversity in ecclesiological opinion. The collection aspires to provide the reader with a sense of what binds us together as well. Therefore, you will find common themes shared across the chapters.

The ordering of the chapters has some method. The chapter by George Sumner that started a recent conversation about the episcopate in the House of Bishops is first. I chose Bob Prichard's chapter as the next one because it gives a historical view of the episcopate and offers questions about its future. William Gregg continues the conversation as he considers the theological and practical understanding of the episcopate and what it means to do the work decently and in order while balancing history, canons, and present and future changes. Next is Bill Franklin's chapter on William White, a history piece that sits in conversation with Prichard's. Franklin also allows the reader to go deeper into one example of American episcopacy in its nascent stage. Allen Shin then takes up the topic of race within The Episcopal Church in his chapter and explores its legacy.

Katharine Jefferts Schori's chapter is a consideration of women's leadership in the Christian church of the first century to the present. It begins to expand on thoughts and questions from the previous chapters. Sheryl A. Kujawa-Holbrook invites a more particular consideration of the changes underway in the House of Bishops today and how they are affecting and may continue to affect our ecclesiology. Hector Monterroso's chapter signals a shift to topics of vision and mission. I felt as though his perspective of noncontinental US dioceses would offer a particular view of the episcopate. Bob Fitzpatrick then explores the idea of ministering within and among a people.

The collection shifts again at this point, taking up episcopate as leadership. Robert Wright breaks open the idea of leadership for us and lays a challenging foundation for future bishops. Kym Lucas then considers the role of vision and suggests that it is the community that holds the vision, and the bishop who comes alongside to help nurture it into reality. Diana Akiyama provides a forthright consideration of the challenges we face as bishops. This is followed by a consideration of authority, bishops, and General Convention resolutions by Joan Geiszler-Ludlum.

The final grouping of essays considers the future. Jennifer Baskerville-Burrows invites us into the imaginative work of relational leadership as a core component of the future episcopate. Sean Rowe considers the role that adaptive leadership will need to play for new bishops. This part of the discussion is wrapped up by Cornelia Eaton, who ponders the beauty way basket and how the episcopate may be part of the weaving of our lives with God and one another.

I believe you will find that these essays point to two emerging ideas about the future episcopate. First, I believe they point toward a church active at the margins of justice and compel us toward an episcopal presence in the world. This suggests that an embodied episcopate is a narrative-bearing vessel. In these chapters I suggest we see how the bishop is charged to speak a word of gospel to both the church and the world about what it means to be a just community. Oppression, objectification, and commodification are bred by the world of categorization and nurtured in the heart of disconnected community.[1] An embodied episcopate incarnates a just community of liberation and imprints a different relationship with God, others, and creation on the hearts of the participants. The change we see at present is a new and more diverse embodiment, and so a more reflective incarnational word is ever more available for mission.

The second theme is that of a missionary bishop. There is together a shared understanding that missionary bishops working in teams share episcopal authority and the implementation of new structures will replace the "full-time one bishop to a diocese" model. Bishops will raise up and call forth diverse clergy and lay populations focused on the mission of the new church. There will be bishops who hold positions as heads of congregations and large urban communities. There will be bishops who travel to support new ministry contexts where various creative and innovative styles of leadership are needed to propel ministry forward. There is no one solution that will define how the future church carries out its ministry. It will do all things necessary for the sake of God's mission of shalom. At the core will be missionary bishops in relationships with other orders—each taking their place in the work of an active missional church.

I hope to have brought together a few of the brightest minds across the church to help us with this very important conversation about the life of bishops within the life of the whole community of the faithful. I hope you will enjoy and be challenged by the texts collected here. Hold them in prayer, ponder them, and allow them to work on us as we elect new bishops, as we consider the presiding bishop elections, and as we contemplate how we might all work together in the life of a truly shared episcopate.

EPISCOPATE

CHAPTER 1

On the Episcopate

George R. Sumner

Setting Out the Question

Why bishops, beyond the sheer inertia of habit? What are they good for? How
has the case for them changed due to the rapidly changing circumstances of the
contemporary church? What have our answers got to do with basic questions
of identity in The *Episcopal* Church? These are the questions I want to address
in this brief chapter. At the outset, I set as my goal to offer arguments that are
equally accessible to readers with various commitments on contemporary and
controversial theological issues. I also want to recognize the valid side of the tacitly "congregationalist" assumption in much of our church life: the local congregation in worship, community, and service is most real to most members. It is against
this natural sense that the case for bishops must (and can) be made. Of course, I
acknowledge that we bishops live up to our calling fallibly; all Christian ministry,
lay and ordained, exists under the sign of forgiveness, both offered and received.

The Inherited Nonnegotiables

Let us begin with the features of the episcopate that are inherent to the calling: the nonnegotiables—features that are context independent but not content independent theologically. By this I mean that the office is comprehensible
only within the specific tradition of Christian theology, throughout which it has
borne certain theological meanings. It does not suffice to offer general reasons
for leadership in social, or specifically religious, organizations. While the church
can be helpfully studied sociologically, those features particular to the episcopate
as a tradition of explicitly Christian leadership are more pertinent. How is the

episcopate as a role in the narrative of the church in general, and Anglicanism in particular, to be understood? Going back to basics, returning *ad fontes* ("to the sources") is crucial, especially in situations that are otherwise confounding. To change the metaphor, in such a murky moment we most need the polestar.

Bishops, as our ordinal tells us, are "called to be one with the apostles."[1] In the New Testament, the apostles were witnesses of the resurrection of the incarnate and crucified Jesus.[2] First then, the office has an inherently Christological center of gravity. We are like the figure of John the Baptist in the great triptych of Gruenewald (itself a product of a time of plague), with his outsized index finger pointing to the cross.[3] Because the scriptures are the primary witness to the crucified and risen One, bishops are invariably to be its exegetes as well. Resurrection here is not a symbol for some more general concept, but points to Christ in his specific, narratively derived identity. Furthermore, the Resurrection both anticipates the End and inaugurates his eschatological reign. To be its witness is to point toward the invasion of the kingdom into time and space, the confrontation with the transcendent in Christ. The liminality and the sanctity of the episcopate are derived from the One to whom they point. In his light we are not reducible to managers or church bureaucrats (though we are those too).

Second, bishops remind us that the church is "deep and wide," by which I mean reaching back in time to the apostles and reaching out in space to the ends of the earth. Bishops are inheritors, bearers of memory, signs for the local church that they do in fact have a wider story, inheritance, family. It is worth noting that with respect to being signs of our inheritance from the apostles, as well as our share in the apostolicity and catholicity of the church, the episcopate in our church claims to partake of a wider Christian tradition. Bishops cannot be understood simply as designated functionaries or religious practitioners of our national denomination. In the same way, our appeal to scripture, our celebration of Baptism and Eucharist, and our recitation of the Nicene Creed make a claim, sometimes explicit and sometimes implicit, that we stand in a vaster company and are answerable to an older norm. We are, again, doing more than providing administration and leadership for our own membership or implementing our own rules (though we are also doing that).

To call it "the episcopate" necessarily makes a wider claim and places implied conceptual constraints on us that we may not notice: the doctrine that we have received, to which the ordinal refers, not only is from our own local formulations but also partakes of a wider inheritance of articulated belief.[4] In a similar way, our invitation to a gathering like Lambeth, while not imposing on us a superior synodical and canonical authority, symbolizes the wider global collegiality that one famous Anglican statement described as "mutual responsibility and interdependence in the Body of Christ."[5] Though there is in us Americans often the spirit of "don't tread on me," we cannot evade these wider bonds of affection inherent to the episcopal office. To be sure, the episcopate in its "rabbinic" and exegetical side will lead to disagreement, since the interpretation of the Bible is hardly uniform. At least we can say that the episcopate is an inherited and collegial ministry of fellowship and contention around the Word of God.

Third, the bishop is the chief pastor, though of course we share this role collegially with our clergy in the diocese. Shepherds protect, feed, and guide the sheep. How this is lived out varies by era and area, though the functions remain (and, in the time of SafeChurch, for example, an important aspect of guarding has been rediscovered). These three dimensions, witness to the Resurrection, representative of the church catholic and apostolic, and chief pastor, are true regardless of what the financial, educational, geographic, and other particularities of a diocese might be. Note that this third basic aspect of episcopacy has, in most cases, an element of place—one is a bishop of somewhere in particular. Hence there is inevitably a tension between the localism and the universalism of the calling, between the bishop thought of with their presbyters in one place and that same bishop with fellow bishops "from away." And at the heart of the office is that this all-too-human, walking symbol of these wider realities actually shows up, at a parish, early Sunday morning, with hat and stick, a present and embodied reminder of these wider things. Thus, in this distressing time of distance and virtuality, bishops must struggle to continue to be witnesses to the necessarily present and embodied nature of all sacramental acts.

Contextual Particularities

It is surely true that context-independent theological parameters can make non-anxious leadership more likely by alleviating the need to make it all up anew. However, we must also bring these features, like bass notes, into relationship with factors that do have more to do with our own twenty-first-century North American context. First, there is the unique history of the American episcopate: an order not derived from its (former) imperial power, with democratically elected bishops exercising authority in synod, and an episcopal house, in parallel with our secular government, that may sometimes act as a "cooling dish" in convention debate. These are features of our own kind of contextualization that are worth noting and protecting. To see bishops as per se elitist may overlook this particularly American contribution.

Second, the episcopate is being exercised in an era of disestablishment and ecclesial marginalization. We are a smaller and less wealthy church, further from the levers of power, in a gradually more secularizing culture than in the past. These trends have been accelerated by the present pandemic/recession. The prescriptions one commonly hears in the face of these challenges are sometimes diametrically opposed. Do we need to become more socially dense, better catechized, more distinct, a kind of liturgical "community of character" (as in the work of Hauerwas and Dreher)? Or is our future more diffuse, localized, and pluralist in expression (Moltmann's "total ministry" and "emerging" are examples)? Both react to the same seismic shifts, and both may overestimate how much say we have in some of the changes coming our way. The first reaction, for example, would lead one to think we need a more disciplined and traditional form of theological education, and the latter would reinforce the use of local schools of ministry of a more informal kind. But throughout, the challenge of postmodernity— conceptual, financial—faces us all. Differing responses to the same shift have more in common than one would at first see, for in both cases the bishop must find his or her voice in a situation of diminished power of various kinds (and try to grasp the kinds of freedom it allows).

Third, in a visibly fraying society we need bishops with a prophetic edge. We could have a debate about what the theological conditions for such a ministry would be. One might argue that a strong sense of divine transcendence is the main prerequisite for such a prophetic word to the wider culture, since it provides the leverage over the culture's own assumptions.[6] Some of the most trenchant social critiques in our tradition have come from theological viewpoints that were less culturally accommodated.[7] The trick is that the bishop offering critique must at the same time empathize and be in solidarity with their people. At the very least we need to recognize that the relation between this prophetic edge and one's theology of culture, as well as between the edge and pastoral identification, is not a simple or straightforward matter.

A few years ago, a priest in a suburb told me, "Bishop, we are growing because, more or less, people who come like my sermon, the band, and the Sunday school. As soon as we're batting one for three, they're gone to a church down the street. Very few are here because we are Episcopalians." The market is king! On the other hand, they have come to expect communion every Sunday. The notion that having a bishop is s a part of their ecclesial identity is a work in progress. The American democratic inheritance, functional disestablishment, and the edge are, to greater and lesser extents, what they expect in the ethos of the church they have joined, and they only need to be helped to see how episcopate relates to these too.

In reprise, those abiding features mentioned earlier ought to be entailed in all churches: Christology, apostolicity and catholicity, and koinonia are not our own possessions. So bishops are servants of things that are of the *esse*, and precisely as they faithfully subserve these, they show bishops to be of the church's *bene esse*.[8] In other words, the people in that suburban church tacitly expect certain things that make their gathering a *church*, and they may come to see the benefit of this particular kind of symbolic person who is responsible for ensuring that first things stay first, that birthrights not be sold for bowls of lentil stew. Maybe, culturally, they can come to imagine me, at least, to be "spiritual quality control."

With every calling comes a concatenation of trials and challenges. Given this mantle and context, it is not hard to locate the pitfalls, some of which I have already mentioned.[9] In our time, partisanship tinged by anger is an obvious risk. Our culture turns everything into an individual commodity, even as it valorizes novelty. The workaholic is not rare in the episcopal ranks; feeling the lack of time to study and read we may have brought with us from the presbyterate too. Sometimes we forget that the symbol that we embody precedes and exceeds us as individuals, though this ought to be a relief. For example, nearing retirement, we, like all pastors, wonder what it has amounted to and whether it was enough—the challenge of ego integration.[10] As to this last test, we must by grace grasp at the conclusion that our calling is by its nature a handing over to us and from us for a time, of testimony, symbolic personhood, and shared pastoring. Retirement is the gift of seeing how little of it is ours. All the aforementioned challenges grow directly out of the intersection of the enduring nature and the present context of this calling.

As an addendum, we can readily find all these apostolic elements and contextual features named or implied in our own ordinal in the Book of Common

Prayer of 1979. The preamble to the examination[11] comprises all three of the perennial callings of the bishop, while what we have called contextual particularities have left fingerprints in the subsequent interrogation in the sharing of the "government of the whole Church," "the support for all the baptized in their gifts and ministries," and in the "stirring of conscience."[12]

Where Does All This Leave Us?

One common thread throughout this account is inheritance, which does not exclude contestation or tension. Another is the challenge that the retrieval of the abiding meaning of the episcopate offers to contemporary construals of the episcopate as a leader/administrator of a nonprofit, say, or only a representative of a particular American, twenty-first-century denomination. While these are true, they are not enough either to sustain us or, by God's grace, to renew our church. The thread running through this whole account is what I would call the indirect pertinence of the office. By this I mean the episcopate's essential difference from the local pastorate, not just in order of magnitude but also in purpose. The bishop points away toward Christ, upward to the mysterious reality of the Resurrection, backward and outward to the apostles and our fellow churches of the nations, to the midst of society, toward features of society we may wish to avoid seeing. In each case being a contributor toward a surplus of meaning is inherent in the job. While the bishop may have a burden to worry over the perplexities of our cultural moment in many ways, this here-and-now edge is not blunted but enhanced by the office's more distant provenance and its oblique nature. The bishop learns to come alongside his or her larger flock, but as a living symbol of attention to these wider referents. In a moment in which our life may be consumed by immediate worries of survival, the retrieval of the episcopate in its indirect pertinence, ironically, may never have been more important.

CHAPTER 2

The Transformation in the Role of Bishop in The Episcopal Church since 1965

Robert W. Prichard

Introduction

In the years following the end of World War II, the bishops of The Episcopal Church took on an expanded role, which might best be characterized as CEO and evangelist-in-chief. It was a position predicated on growth in numbers and resources. After a period of stagnation in population and church growth during the interwar years, America was experiencing a baby boom, rapid growth in new suburbs, and a surge in church building. New Deal high school construction and the post–World War II GI Bill enabled former members of the military to enter college, swelling the numbers of the college educated, the demographic group in which The Episcopal Church and other mainline Protestants had tradition-ally been the most successful.[1] Since clergy were recruited from among college graduates, this growth in college population also presented the opportunity to find an adequate number of candidates for ordination, something that had trou-bled mainline denominations throughout their history. At the same time there was a revival of interest in religion, spurred on by such evangelists as Church of England preacher Brian Green (1901–1993) and Baptist William Franklin (Billy) Graham, both of whom were gathering large crowds to hear their preach-ing by the late 1940s. The nation was full of opportunity for church growth.

Bishops who were able to manage resources to establish new congregations, expand educational ministries, and recruit talented clergy led the way in what would become one of the largest periods of numerical growth in the Episcopal Church. The methods of such bishops were seen as models for others. Bishop Richard Emrich (1910–1997) of Michigan lectured about his fund-raising and founding of new congregations in the suburbs that increasingly appeared on the outskirts of large cities. Henry Louttit (1903–1984) of South Florida acquired a reputation for a rate of church planting that at one point approached a new congregation a month. John Hines (1910–1997) in Texas was also a leader in establishing new parishes in the suburbs; he was active in the formation of new church primary and secondary schools, and a new theological seminary (the Episcopal Theological Seminary of the Southwest). Dioceses electing new bishops sought candidates with experience in large congregations or in national or diocesan staff positions, those experienced in domestic or foreign missionary work, or clergy possessing a record of writing and teaching.

The national church budget was indicative of national priorities. The budget adopted by the General Convention for 1956, for example, was divided into five categories, of which foreign and domestic missionary work received the lion's share ($4.921 million for 72 percent of the total budget), followed by education and promotion ($1.102 million or 16 percent). Smaller amounts were allocated for training centers and other activities ($125,436), cooperating agencies ($50,800), and administration ($132,633.33).[2]

The location of the 1955 convention—Honolulu—was indicative of another direction of change, which would grow more important in the following decades—a slow dismantling of segregation. Protests by Black Episcopalians had moved the meeting, originally scheduled for Texas, to Hawaii to allow integrated dining and housing during the convention.[3]

An Abrupt Shift

The strategy of the early postwar years was appropriate for the baby boom years of 1946–1965. However, the birth rate slowed around 1965, and the earliest members of the baby boom generation reached college. The arrival of a large young generational cohort on the scene contributed to a change that was taking place in the nation at the time. These younger Americans of all races brought the skeptical eye of youth to the efforts of their elders and demanded immediate change in what they saw as the errors of individuals and society at large, such as denial of equal rights for racial minorities and women, government policies that did nothing for the poor, the Vietnam War, and economic cooperation with South Africa. Those calling for change at times turned violent, as in the urban riots of the 1960s. Counterviolence, which included political assassinations, bombings, police violence, and the killing of four student demonstrators at Kent State, was even more marked.

One early casualty of this changing mood was mainline church attendance, which began a long period of decline that has continued to this day. Church leaders recognized the need for new models. Under Presiding Bishop John Hines, the General Convention began a shift away from the priorities of the previous decades—foreign mission, suburban church planting, Sunday schools, church primary and secondary schools, fund-raising and tithing—and focused on empowerment for minorities (the General Convention Special Program), liturgical reform designed to make worship more contemporary, and institutional reform.

The role of bishop changed accordingly. Among the new emphases were new understandings of the relationship of bishops to the liturgy; to the recruitment, deployment, and discipline of clergy; and to prophecy and social justice. Bishops both led the way and reflected these new understandings.

Bishop as Chief Liturgical Officer

The liturgical reform that culminated in the adoption of the 1979 edition of the Book of Common Prayer (BCP) redefined the role of bishop in relationship to the liturgy. The ordination rite and the rubrics of the previous edition of the Book of Common Prayer (1928) and the canons of the church had focused on the role of bishop as the one to ordain and confirm; the 1979 prayer book expanded that role to become chief liturgical officer of the diocese. A new line in the examination section of the ordination rite explained that the bishop was called "to provide for the administration of the sacraments of the New Covenant."[4] A new rubric in the baptismal office explained that "the bishop, when present, is the celebrant, and is expected to preach the Word and preside at Baptism and the Eucharist."[5] A parallel rubric added before the Eucharist explained that "it is the bishop's prerogative, when present, to be the principal celebrant at the Lord's Table, and to preach the Gospel."[6]

Two elements contributed to this expansion of the role of the bishop. The first was the liturgical movement, best represented in The Episcopal Church by the organization known as Associated Parishes. Supporters of the movement looked back to the church of the third century as a model. That church, they understood, survived, and grew despite persecution, setting a model for the modern church, which was in an increasingly secular society. They believed that the three orders of the ordained ministry and the laity all had important roles to play in the liturgy, and that Baptism and the Eucharist were best understood as corporate events of the whole community of God. The Standing Liturgical Commission, on which members of the Associated Parishes were heavily represented, drafted new rubrics for the 1979 Book of Common Prayer, which identified the specific roles for bishops, but also for presbyters, deacons, and the laity.

There was also a practical reason for the new rubrics about bishops. Some parish laity and clergy objected to the 1979 prayer book and to the two trial books that preceded it—*Services for Trial Use* (the "Green Book" of 1971) and *Authorized Services* (the "Zebra Book" of 1973). The contemporary language would come to be a particular target of opposition led by a new Society for the Preservation of the Book of Common Prayer (1971).[7]

The new rubrics, which were clearer about the role of bishop in worship than the canons of the church at the time, made it possible for bishops to insist on the use of the new liturgies.[8] Exercising that authority was not always easy, however. At least one of the bishops of the Diocese of Virginia in the 1970s took to carrying a case of prayer book excerpts of the services of Baptism, confirmation, and the Eucharist in the trunk of his car during parish visitations, in order to counter rectors who explained that they did not have copies of the trial liturgies or the 1979 prayer book and would thus need to use the 1928 edition instead.[9] Bishops tried other approaches, such as asking for advance bulletins for their visitation services (and correcting them where needed), establishing diocesan liturgical commissions to advocate appropriate use of the 1979 prayer book, and creating guidelines about such issues as rites of initiation. Bishops were able to use their role as celebrants during diocesan conventions and parish visitations to model ways in which they believed the services in the trial liturgies and the new edition of the prayer book should be used.

This was not, of course, the first time that bishops played a key role in directing liturgical use. Bishops had been active in that role in the liturgical fights of the post–Civil War period, but they had gradually retreated from directing parish use as the result of an inability to control the ritual changes introduced by innovative parish clergy.[10] The liturgical activity of bishops of the 1970s was not simply a return to the behavior of that earlier period, however, because of an important change. The General Convention of 1967 had amended Article X of the Constitution to allow a period of "trial use" prior to the adoption of a new edition of the prayer book; before that time proposed texts could be studied but not used until adopted on second reading by the General Convention. As a result, bishops found themselves in a twelve-year period in which parishes were in the position of choosing between the use of different authorized liturgies.[11] It was a situation that called for episcopal leadership.

By the 1990s, bishops faced a different challenge. While two decades of episcopal leadership and the departure from the church of die-hard supporters of the 1928 prayer book assured the place of the 1979 edition of the Book of Common Prayer, a growing number in the church were calling for further revision of the prayer book, particularly in relation to gender. The General Convention authorized a new series of trial texts—*Liturgical Texts for Evaluation* (1987), *Supplemental Liturgical Texts* (1989), *Supplemental Liturgical Materials* (1991), and the *Enriching Our Worship* series (six volumes from 1998 to 2009); it also undertook frequent revision of *Lesser Feasts and Fasts* and the *Book of Occasional Services* and authorized the publication of liturgies for same-sex unions. Unlike the earlier period of revision from 1967 to 1985, this process of trial use did not result in the adoption of a new edition of the Book of Common Prayer; thirty-five years after the publication of *Liturgical Texts for Evaluation* the General Convention of 2022 will continue the consideration of whether and how to revise the Book of Common Prayer of 1979. Bishops have an important leadership role in the introduction and management of parallel trial liturgical materials for which there is no evident terminal date.

It is perhaps not surprising that by the early twenty-first century some in the church were making a broader claim for the liturgical role of bishop than that laid out in canons or the rubrics of the Book of Common Prayer. Bishops, according to this view, could authorize textual changes and practices not found in the Book of Common Prayer and the canons of the church. Successive bishops of California, for example, supported liturgical changes introduced at St. Gregory of Nyssa, an innovative congregation that sought to differentiate itself from other Episcopal churches. An early publication from the congregations explained that

> Whereas established congregations usually employ the new rites [in the *Proposed Book of Common Prayer*, which would become the Book of Common Prayer in 1979] to continue a Latin or English style of Anglican liturgy, St. Gregory's will choose forms that emphasize our continuity with Jewish and early Christian prayer life, which is the deepest core of our tradition. First of all, we will recover the congregational character of Jewish-Christian worship and will borrow appropriate usages from Byzantine and African Christianity to express this character fully.[12]

The congregation set a model for liturgical experimentation on a parish level. Many clergy elsewhere followed suit, emulating and in some cases exceeding the changes made at St. Gregory's. Clergy made revisions in the Eucharistic Prayers, replaced the Nicene Creed with alternate texts, and used prayer books from other parts of the Anglican Communion. A justification often made for this process was that the replacement of discrete items in the liturgy did not endanger the integrity of a common structure. This, however, was not always the case. By the 1990s St. Gregory's and many other parishes were reversing the basic ordo of the Episcopal liturgy by inviting the unbaptized to receive the Eucharist. Some made this change with the acquiescence, consent, or active support of their bishops.[13] In 2012, the General Convention stepped in, adopting a resolution from the convention's Committee on Evangelism declaring that "The Episcopal Church reaffirms that baptism is the ancient and normative entry point to receiving Holy Communion and that our Lord Jesus Christ calls us to go into the world and baptize all peoples."[14]

Liturgical innovation by bishops was often supported by appealing to sections of the Constitution and canons from the late nineteenth and early twentieth centuries. An introductory note titled "Concerning the Service of the Church," first introduced in 1892, had allowed a bishop authority to "set forth such Form or Forms as he shall think fit" for "Days of Fasting and Thanksgiving, appointed by the Civil or by the Ecclesiastical Authority, and for other special occasions for which no Service or Prayer hath been provided in this Book." Such a provision was appropriate for occasions like Independence Day or Thanksgiving, for which Books of Common Prayer prior to 1928 made no provisions. The note further allowed the bishop to authorize parish clergy to use devotions constructed from material in the Book of Common Prayer, provided Morning and Evening Prayer had been or were to be said.[15] This provision would, for example, allow a parish priest to construct a service based on recitation of Psalms and the reading of collects, something that parish clergy occasionally were doing on Holy Week.[16]

In 1904 the General Convention adopted on second reading an amendment to Article X of the Constitution related to missions to the non–English speaking. The addition, which was placed at the end of the article, declared that "nothing in this Article shall be construed as restricting the authority of the Bishops of the Church to take such order as may be permitted by the rubrics of the Book of Common Prayer or by the Canons of the General Convention for the use of *special forms of worship*."[17] An accompanying canon 42 on "the Authorization of Special Forms of Service," which was also adopted in 1904, explained what was meant by special forms. The forms were different from the devotions that had been identified in the earlier prayer book note; these were translations for congregations "worshiping in other than English" for whom there was not yet "an authorized edition of the Book of Common Prayer in such language."[18]

The expanded claim of some contemporary bishops to issue and permit worship in forms not authorized by the General Convention is certainly understandable given the General Convention's reticence to revise the Book of Common Prayer of 1979. One cannot help but wonder, however, about the long-term effect of this attitude on the nature of The Episcopal Church. The preamble of the Constitution of the church identifies two elements as basic to the Anglican Communion of which The Episcopal Church is a "constituent member": "communion with the See of Canterbury" and "upholding and propagating the historic Faith and Order as set forth in the Book of Common Prayer."[19] There are numerous American denominations that adhere to a free church liturgical tradition, but to this point The Episcopal Church's commitment to a fixed liturgy has been a distinguishing characteristic.

The Calling, Deployment, and Discipline of Clergy

Bishops of the post–World War II era devoted time to recruiting, selecting, and deploying clergy. Those who were ordained were often children of active church families, products of college chaplaincies, or active lay leaders themselves. When it came time for congregations to call new clergy, bishops often had personal knowledge of those whom they recommended to fill the vacancies. In what surely was not a unique circumstance, Episcopalians in the Diocese of Missouri referred to many new clergy recruited and deployed by Bishop Arthur Lichtenberger (bishop diocesan, 1952–1959) as his "boys."[20] Some bishops used the same language themselves; Jack Woodward (1926–2013) recalled, for example, the language with which Bishop Clinton Quinn of Texas had communicated with the dean of the Episcopal Theological Seminary of the Southwest about his possible interest in attending: "I have a boy for you."[21] The use was indicative of the close paternal relationships between bishops and clergy.

This relationship began to change in the 1970s. The General Convention sought to replace the previous system of discernment and deployment with one more like the US Civil Service. The 1970 General Convention created a new diocesan commission to oversee the ordination process (commissions on ministry), a national board to oversee deployment (the Board for Clergy Deployment), and a national board that prepared a standard national ordination exam (the General Board of Examining Chaplains) as a replacement or supplement for the diocesan exams then given. The Board for Clergy Deployment soon introduced a computerized system of clergy and parish profiles, designed to match on a national basis the skills and abilities of clergy with the needs and vision of parishes. Dioceses created the new position of clergy deployment officer to manage the complicated system.[22]

The new system was created in part to open opportunities for ordination and deployment to those who were least like the bishop's boys of the previous decades—women and minority clergy. How well the system actually worked over time is open to question, but there is no doubt that it did change the role of bishops. Bishops had less of a hands-on connection to the recruitment and replacement processes, and they were more likely to become troubleshooters who fielded complaints from those who thought the ordination and deployment processes treated them poorly. The new commissions on ministry, for example, had only advisory authority, and those whom they declined for ordination could appeal directly to the bishop for a contrary decision.

The bishops' role in relationship to the discipline of clergy also changed over time. Prior to 1868, the Constitution and canons had given dioceses the responsibility for discipline of clergy with little direction as to how that was done. After the removal of several bishops by dioceses and unsuccessful attempts to remove others, the General Convention of 1868 provided a list of offenses for which bishops and other clergy could be disciplined and an outline for procedure. These were expanded, particularly in 1904. The end result by the middle of the twentieth century was a system that gave bishops broad discretion as to how they dealt with errant clergy, while protecting them from what they perceived to be frivolous charges. For example, the canons in effect in 1982 limited the persons who could complain about ordinary misconduct of a bishop to either three bishops or ten or more adult communicants, and they limited members of the court that would hear such complaints to fellow bishops. If the matter concerned doctrine, ten bishops diocesan (or bishops otherwise exercising jurisdiction) were needed for a complaint, and two-thirds of the House of Bishops had to consent to a trial.[23] Not surprisingly, few bishops were convicted of misconduct, though some were prevailed upon to resign by the threat of trial and public exposure. Priests and deacons were given less protection; the 1982 canons left the process for presentment and trial to the individual dioceses, though they did lay out a process for courts of review.[24] Bishops often simply moved or suspended clergy accused of misconduct, reasoning that a full-scale trial would embarrass the church and violate the confidentiality of the person who complained.

The realization in the 1990s that approaches of this sort had often been used to excuse sexual abuse in The Episcopal Church and in other denominations and that secular courts were increasingly willing to impose huge fines on offending institutions led to a demand for reform. Female clergy and the Church Insurance Agency led the way in advocating a new understanding of best practices in relationship to clergy misconduct. The General Convention revised its canons on discipline in 1994 and again in 2009. Among notable changes, these revisions allowed a single layperson to bring charges against either a priest or bishop and advised the appointment of an advocate to assist complainants.[25]

The 2009 changes were the first to provide concrete definitions and standards for clergy sexual behavior. These included a ban on "physical contact, bodily movement, speech, communication, or other activity sexual in nature" by a member of the clergy with "an employee, volunteer, student or counselee . . . in the same congregation as the member of the Clergy, or a person with whom the member of the clergy has a pastoral relationship."[26]

The complex revised process left bishops with a role very different from the largely pastoral role of the mid-twentieth century. One indication of the complexity of the revised process is the difficult-to-find link for Title IV (the Discipline Canon in The Episcopal Church) structures and procedures on The Episcopal Church's website. It displays information on thirty different components of the disciplinary system.[27]

During roughly the same period, the General Convention was persuaded to give the presiding bishop greater authority over other bishops, no doubt a result of cases of episcopal misconduct and the abandonment of The Episcopal Church by a number of bishops. Two important changes were made in the canons. Canon IV.17 (2009) gives the presiding bishop the authority over individual bishops that a bishop diocesan has over priests and deacons.[28] In addition, the canon concerning the "abandonment of this Church by a bishop" (canon IV.9 in 2006, which became canon IV.16 in 2009) dropped the requirement that "the three senior bishops having jurisdiction in this Church" consent to the presiding bishop's suspension of a bishop suspected of abandoning the church.[29]

This more complicated structure, adopted for the best of reasons, has further complicated the life of bishops, who now need to police clergy dating patterns and attend to a complicated—and frequently changing—structure, even if their intent is only to find ways to ignore it. It is not uncommon for bishops to say that dealing with Title IV matters is the most time-consuming and least enjoyable part of their ministry.

The Bishop as Prophet

Prominent progressive bishops of the second half of the twentieth century, such as James A. Pike (1913–1969) of California and John S. Spong (1931–2021) of Newark, popularized the idea of bishops as prophets. As they understood it, their role as bishops was to function in very public ways as critics of the institution they served. They argued that by doing so, they represented the ideas of people on the margins of and outside the community of faith. Bishops who embraced this understanding exercised their prophetic ministry in a number of ways. Pike's *Time for Christian Candor* (1964) labeled the doctrine of the Trinity as "excess luggage" that the church would do best to drop. In 1974 a trio of retired bishops—Daniel Corrigan, Robert Dewitt, and Edward Wells—ordained eleven women deacons to the priesthood, although they did not have jurisdiction over them, and the women had not secured permission of their standing committee. In 1989 Spong ordained a gay man, who was vocally opposed to fidelity to a single partner, despite appeals to refrain from the ordination by the presiding bishop and his council of advice.

Progressive bishops, however, did not have a monopoly on making claims for prophetic inspiration. By the 1990s bishops of a more traditional bent were considering prophetic actions of their own. From 2007 to 2012, five such bishops and their diocesan conventions—Pittsburgh, San Joaquin (California), Fort Worth, Quincy (Illinois), and South Carolina—took the prophetic step of leaving The Episcopal Church.[30] Since that time, several other bishops have made the personal decisions to depart from The Episcopal Church as individuals, while not attempting to bring dioceses with them.

The idea of bishops as prophets has become so common in The Episcopal Church that it hardly seems exceptional today. It is, however, a departure from much of the history of Christianity. The New Testament authors understood prophets as coming from the margins rather than as institutional religious leaders. Mark tells us that the crowds regarded John the Baptist as a prophet (Mark 11:32). Luke identified Agabus, a man not otherwise known as a leader (Acts 11:28), and the four daughters of Philip (Acts 21:9) as prophets. Paul (1 Cor. 12:4–11) regarded prophecy as a charismatic gift given by Spirit to whom it will, and he listed it as distinct from the gifts of teaching and of leadership (1 Cor. 12:28).

The ordinal of the Book of Common Prayer of 1979 makes no claim that the bishop is a prophet. Rather it understands the call to become a bishop as a call to "guard the faith, unity, and discipline of the Church; to celebrate and to provide for the administration of the sacraments of the New Covenant; to ordain priests and deacons and to join in ordaining bishops; and to be in all things a faithful pastor and wholesome example for the entire flock of Christ." The ordinal does, however, call upon bishops to "encourage and support all baptized persons in their gifts and ministries," which would presumably include prophecy, and to regard the "heritage" they have received as including the faith of prophets.[31]

Bishops for the Coming Decades

For what then should The Episcopal Church look in future bishops? If one anticipates challenges and patterns of the sort that we have seen in the past fifty years, one might look for the following qualities in a candidate for ordination:

1. A gift of administration. Even though the membership of The Episcopal Church has decreased significantly since 1965, it would be hard to argue that the administrative load on bishops has gotten any lighter. Bishops today contend with a complex set of procedures and expectations that have been put into place since 1965, and they cope with them with fewer staff members. Dealing with administrative expectations with limited resources requires gifts that not all possess. We might emulate the Roman Catholic Church, which often chooses leaders from among those who have earned graduate degrees in canon law, who presumably know how to function appropriately within the guidelines and in conjunction with the various agencies and bodies within that church. The problem with following this approach in The Episcopal Church, of course, is that no Episcopal institution in the United States offers a degree in canon law, and the one most widely known program in the Anglican Communion—Cardiff University's LLM program—is more suited to those interested in the United Kingdom than in the United States. To make this approach feasible, institutions of higher learning in the United States would need to offer one or more programs devoted to Episcopal canon law.

2. Ability as liturgical leaders. The Episcopal Church might focus on the role of bishops as liturgical leaders, introducing, explaining, and implementing liturgical revisions on which the General Convention agrees. This would require a level of self-discipline and a willingness to forgo individually authorizing liturgical innovation, which is not found in all current members of the House of Bishops. It is not clear, moreover, that the General Convention will reach any consensus about revision in the near future. Indeed, one might ask whether the failure of the General Convention to reach a decision about prayer book revision over the past thirty-five years is itself a decision.

Has the General Convention abandoned the idea of a fixed liturgy already? The answer is not self-evident. It is worth asking, for example, whether the extended period of parallel liturgical use is a temporary strategy, like the conventions through 2000 calling for acceptance of diverse views on sexuality, which were followed by a narrowing understanding of acceptable policies that could be held by members of the episcopate.[32] Liturgical leadership is important, but it is difficult without more clear leadership by the General Convention.

3. Open to alternative understandings of prophecy. There is no question that bishops who have embraced the idea of prophecy in the last half century have made major changes in the life of the church, bringing both changes in long-held policies and division. It may, however, be time to rethink this approach, recalling that for much of the history of the church prophecy was understood as the gift of outsiders without institutional power. Perhaps we should look for candidates who understand the actions of previous prophets as part of the heritage of the faith and order of the church (as the prayer book ordinal suggests) and who recognize that prophecy can be a gift of the laity, without claiming to be prophets themselves.

One could argue that the genius of The Episcopal Church through much of its history has been the ability to present the faith in light of both significant reforms and the church's long history. The quip credited to Bishop William Lawrence of Massachusetts (1850–1941)—that he "recalled the introduction of things in his youth that were now being attributed to the twelve apostles"—is not an entirely bad thing.[33] The Christian faith is both ancient and contemporary, and a presentation that highlights both aspects can be very attractive. It is, however, most convincing when the rate of change is measured.

Preparing leaders for the challenges of the past is not a sufficient preparation for the challenges of the future, however. One might also ask, what things are we leaving undone in our institutional life today? What will we need to do in the future that we are not doing in the present? The current presiding bishop has provided one example by modeling emphases of the past that we might well revisit: evangelism, lively preaching, and deep engagement with scripture.

CHAPTER 3

Episcopacy and "Things Done Decently and in Order"

William O. Gregg

> . . . but all things should be done decently and in order.
>
> *1 Corinthians 14:40*

Defining the Terms

If one did not know better, they might be tempted to think that this English rendering of Paul's words was crafted by a proper Victorian Anglican. They certainly express a core idea associated with the Anglican tradition in its people, its institutions, and the Book of Common Prayer. The point here, however, is not to get lost in the weeds of satire and caricature, but to reflect on the substance of what Paul was saying to the Corinthians then and to us now regarding the church and specifically bishops.

The church in Corinth was not always a decent and well-ordered assembly. Paul admonishes the congregation sternly about numerous things. The context of Paul's admonition in 1 Corinthians 14:40 was speaking in tongues and claiming to prophesy during the liturgy. Apparently, the liturgy was not infrequently thrown into indecency and disorder by persons speaking or purporting to speak "in tongues" (*glossolalia*) and/or prophesying. Paul was opposed to neither, but they were to be done to edify the congregation, not disrupt its worship, and hence, not to be edifying.

The core of the problem was not the substance but the timing and manner of delivery. By disrupting the worship, the one prophesying or speaking in tongues displaced the proper focus of the liturgy, worship of God. The order of the liturgy forbade neither prophesying nor speaking in tongues. Rather, the order was to give focus so that the worship of God was well ordered and decently done.

Decent here, I think, is about doing the order of liturgy in an appropriate, proper manner so that the people participating in the liturgy effectively render their sacrifice of praise and thanksgiving to God that culminates in the breaking of the bread according to the apostles' teaching and the instruction of Jesus.

To do anything or all things "decently and in order," then, is about both what is being done and how it is being done, for the benefit of the people of God who were participating and maintaining a proper focus on God, whether in liturgy or some other form of assembly or work of the community. In this context, we see the interaction of structures and processes and our theological understandings of the triune God, the church, and human beings that give the structures and processes theological content and meaning. This meaning forms the foundation for how we live faithfully in the world. Paul's admonition to the Corinthians, and to us, is that liturgy, and by extension, the life of the community, the church, and daily life, done decently and in order is fundamentally relational among people and between God and God's people. Good order empowers the people to sustain an appropriate focus on the purpose and meaning of what is done, and, in the case of liturgy, on the people's sacrifice of praise and thanksgiving to God. It is this focus that brings worship into its deepest relational dimension with God, who is the ultimate focus of all worship. Out of this liturgical focus comes the focus of daily life on God as the ground of living decently and in order.

Doing good order decently is also ultimately about the dynamic relationship between God and God's people. "Decently" addresses the dimension of doing order in a dynamic, personal[1] manner. It is also a way of respect, awe, and love of the One worshipped. "Decently" is a qualitative aspect of good order and of the relationship that is being engaged. As already noted, the relational dimension functions on the level of person to person as well as person to God and God to person. The "decent" dimension of good order gives the character, texture, and expression of the commitment and relationship being celebrated. "Decently" is the expression of value: this act, this liturgy, this living is important, has inherent value, is personal, and therefore needs, indeed must, be done carefully, precisely, correctly, and with dignity and respect both for God's people and for God. Decently done order, then, is an act of love toward God and God's beloved. It signifies that God's coming to us in our worship is God's act of love. The liturgical moment is a thin place of grace.

Constitution and Canons of The Episcopal Church

The Constitution of The Episcopal Church (2018 rev.) and the canons are the fundamental implementing documents for the life and work of The Episcopal Church. The Constitution, together with the Book of Common Prayer (a constitutional document), forms the framework within which holy orders function. The canons of Title III articulate the ways in which ordained ministry is created, authorized, and enacted. Title IV addresses the ways in which The Episcopal Church establishes and maintains appropriate discipline and responds to multiple forms of misconduct among clergy.

The episcopate is addressed as a part of the structures and processes established for The Episcopal Church to do the work God is giving it decently and in order. A fundamental assumption of the Constitution and canons is that the life and work of the church must be properly ordered on organizational, theological, and scriptural grounds. Without right order, the participation of the church in the *missio Dei* cannot be decently or effectively done. Hence, the bishop and the office he/she holds must be rightly ordered and decently done as their part in the rightly ordered and decently done life and work of the church as a whole. What the Constitution and canons make clear is that the heart of the episcopate is the relationship of the people of God with the Father through the Son in the Spirit. This heart of the episcopate comes to fruition in the development of the abilities and capacities of a man or woman through a process of discernment that includes preparation intellectually, spiritually, physically, and psychologically. The context of this process is the church and the individual bishop. While complex, this process underscores the importance of doing things decently and in order in matters of great importance and value for the individuals coming to ordination and already ordained as well as for the church as a whole. This context of process, structures, faith, and values inheres in the office of the bishop, precisely as the bishop is responsible for overseeing the life of the church in all its parts rightly ordered and decently done.

Biblical Foundations

In addition to the text from 1 Corinthians, scriptural evidence of the value and role of doing all things decently and in order is plentiful. In the two creation stories of Genesis,[2] God reveals God's self as a God of order in the process of creating. Creation is an ordered reality, an οικονομία, reflecting God's own self-ordered being and acting. The creation is, then, also done decently—that is, rightly in form and substance and righteously (ordered) both in terms of its own internal relationships among its parts and in terms of relation to and relationship with God the Creator.

The connection between living decently and in order is further reflected in the patterns of relationship between God and Israel in the several covenants, beginning with the Ten Commandments. Covenants were designed to define the relationship of Israel and God, and thus provided both structures and processes that made it possible for God's people to live creatively, generatively, and faithfully with God. In doing so, God's people received blessing from God as manifested in their prosperity and well-being. The pattern recorded was one of making covenant, keeping covenant, breaking covenant, call to repentance (by a prophet), failure to accept the call to repentance, judgment, repentance, forgiveness, and restoration articulated in a new covenant. This process is always bookended by being in right relationship with God as manifested in acting and living decently and in order. The external consequences of breaking covenant were the concrete manifestations of a broken relationship resulting from not acting and living decently and in order.

Keeping covenant was essentially about right relationship (righteousness). Here we find a fundamental, dynamic dimension of living/doing "all things decently and in order." The manner and structures of the covenant relationship sustain the right relationships (righteousness) both with God and among human beings. The biblical context is about more than etiquette. Doing things and living decently and in order are about the personal dimension of life with God, and in the Christian context, of life in the Spirit through the Son with the Father. Decently and in order is a way to describe both how we are with God and how God is with us. Decently and in order is a way to describe how we are to act and live with one another that is grounded in relationship with God and effected sacramentally in our Baptism. In each instance, the relationship in form, substance, and manner is personal precisely because it is characterized by how we give ourselves to each other as the Father through the Son in the Spirit gives God's self to us.[3] Decently and in order, in terms of episcopacy, can be understood as fundamental to the nature of the order of the church and the ways in which that order is exercised.

When we look at the pattern of action and consequences in Jesus's ministry, there is clearly a pattern of restoration manifested in the renewal or restoration of life done decently and in order. The healing stories illustrate the restoration of individual right relationship as, for example, the healing of the centurion's daughter, or blind Bartimaeus, or the woman with the hemorrhage. There are examples of restoration of right relationship at the social and personal levels, as we see in the story of Zacchaeus or the healing of the ten lepers. From a biblical perspective, to do things decently and in order has the power to heal, to restore, and to create and sustain health and wholeness in God's beloved and among God's beloved.

When we look at the lessons assigned for the ordination of a bishop, we find further indications of the qualities and actions of the office executed decently and in order. The ordination lessons chosen from Isaiah suggest that episcopacy exercised decently and in order is characterized by action in the public realm for the social, economic, and physical well-being of God's people with God. Isaiah 61:1–8 begins, "The Spirit of the Lord is upon me," which is cited by Jesus in his sermon in the synagogue in Nazareth (Luke 4:18). Isaiah 42:1–9, one of the "Suffering Servant" passages, emphasizes God's call to the one to be ordained and consecrated a bishop and that God will be present and active with the bishop in his/her ministries. Things done decently and in order, then, are marked by God's call, God's presence and activity, and acting for and with God's people for their good. The Epistles, from Hebrews 5:1–10 (ongoing prayer to God understood precisely as a priest after the Order of Melchizedek), 1 Timothy 3:1–7 (bishop as model of a person and life done decently and in order), or 1 Corinthians 3:4–9 (knowing who and whose one is), speak to the health and wholeness of the bishop in him-/herself and his/her life that are necessary for the exercise of a faithful life and the office of bishop done decently and in order. The appointed Gospels, from John (John 20:19–23 and 17:1–9, 18–21) and Luke (Luke 24:44–49a), focus on the divine context. The passages from John emphasize Jesus's prayer for God's beloved called and sent to proclaim the gospel and the mutual indwelling of God in and through the ones sent, and they in God. The Emmaus Road story in Luke focuses on the sacramental presence of Christ in the Eucharist, relating to the sacramental roles of the bishop as chief priest and pastor. The lessons, then, hold up to the new bishop and the church the multilayered nature of episcopacy as sacramental, symbolic, pastoral, and publicly active grounded in right relationship with God and God's people. The lessons may be understood as a scriptural amplification of the Summary of the Law, which the people of God, with God's help, daily incarnate.

Decently and in Order as Manifested in the Office and Work of the Bishop

If we apply the idea of doing "all things decently and in order" to the episcopate, what theological perspective and insight for the office and work of a bishop would result? From the perspective of the New Testament, what we now call a "bishop" was named ὁ ἐπίσκοπος,[4] whose principal ministry was to oversee the life and work of the church. The passage of time and development of the church as an institution have made the work of oversight broader, more complex, and more complicated.[5] In these days, we understand that all forms of ministry are grounded in scripture (with the practical defining of the ministry of the apostles and the creation of the diaconate in Acts 6, the emergence of ὁι πρεσβύτεροι [elders, priests] and ὁι ἐπίσκοποι) and in the tradition of the church as it developed across time and adapted to new contexts, conditions, and circumstances. Moreover, especially since the publication of *Baptism, Eucharist, and Ministry* in 1982,[6] we have come to see all ministry, lay and ordained, as sacramentally derivative of Baptism through which all are explicitly incorporated into the body of Christ. In the sacrament of Baptism, we are released from the ultimate consequence of sin, marked as Christ's own forever, and sealed by the Holy Spirit.

Turning again to Paul and 1 Corinthians, we begin our life as ordered in Christ as a necessary part of Christ's body, the church. In this context, the emergence of holy orders and the distinction between lay and ordained ministries may be seen. The church engages a process of self-ordering, through the Spirit, as Christ's body. The purpose by the church was to discern how to undertake the life and work of God in the most efficient and effective ways. Paul's insight about doing all things decently and in order, therefore, is grasping for a clearer graphic form—and suggests a natural process of development. In this sense, what the tradition has developed is a natural discovery of how to implement God's revelation in creation and the experience of how relationship with God works: decently and in order.

However, Paul was not simply addressing a relational insight. He was also making an important ecclesiological point, one that Luther, for example, would use in explaining why orders were necessary for the church. That is, good order was and is necessary for the church to be able to function faithfully and effectively in the life and work we enter through Baptism and in which we are sustained by the Spirit for the proclamation of the Word, and the right celebration of the sacraments, especially the Eucharist. Good order is of the *esse* of the church.

The specific question here is, again, "What is the relationship between 'doing all things decently and in order,' and the office and praxis of episcopacy?" The primary text for defining the office of bishop is to be found in the Book of Common Prayer (1979) in the liturgy for the ordination of a bishop.[7]

The liturgy for the ordination of a bishop is a celebration of Holy Eucharist within which the church ordains (and consecrates) a new bishop. Liturgically, The Episcopal Church orders the episcopacy within its baptismal origin by ordaining a bishop in the context of the meal, which sustains the faithful as we live "the new life of grace"[8] into which we are washed, marked, anointed/sealed, and fed. The good order of the church is grounded in the good order of its prayer and sacraments. Thus, the liturgy is both the "decent" context and demanding of this act of God in and through the church being done decently—that is, properly and with solemn dignity according to the prayer book.

The liturgical setting also affirms that this ordaining is of the church as a whole. The stakeholders, present actually and symbolically, are the whole body of Christ: the one, holy, catholic, and apostolic church. Therefore, the doing of an ordination of a bishop decently and in order affects the good order and decency of the whole church and its capacity to be an effective instrument of God's work in the created order. What constitutes good order and decency in the ordination of a new bishop and defining who a bishop is and what the life and work of the bishop are is clearly articulated step by step as the liturgy moves forward to the prayer ordination and consecration of the new bishop and the climax of the liturgy in the Eucharist.

First the church, represented by the electing diocese and "trusting in the guidance of the Holy Spirit," presents to the presiding bishop or designee "to consecrate [this priest] as a bishop in the one, holy, catholic, and apostolic Church."[9] The new bishop is elected out of the good order of the church in the proper manner, as further affirmed by the reading of the various canonical testimonials. The consent of the church is further affirmed by those in attendance when they are asked to do so and declare that the ordination and consecration should proceed.[10]

The bishop-elect then publicly commits him-/herself to doing all things decently and in order in the declaration of belief in the Old and New Testaments as the Word of God, and to conform to the doctrine, discipline, and worship of The Episcopal Church. The declaration is confirmed by signing the document together with witnesses.[11]

In the Examination the church declares,

> You are called to guard the faith, unity, and discipline of the Church; to celebrate and to provide for the administration of the sacraments of the New Covenant; to ordain priests and deacons and to join in ordaining bishops; and to be in all things a faithful pastor and wholesome example for the entire flock of Christ.[12]

The bishop exercises this ministry by faithfully overseeing the life and work of the church in its love and service of God's beloved. In this context, the church invokes the Holy Spirit "to consecrate *him* a bishop in the one, holy, catholic, and apostolic Church."[13] This ministry is exercised in the larger context of the church catholic, with "your fellow bishops" in the tradition of the church.[14]

We see in the progression of the liturgy that order, decently enacted, inheres in the external structures, actions, and prayers, and so also in the essence of the office of bishop. The ground of this order decently done is faith in the triune God, manifested in this liturgy by calling upon the bishop-elect to lead the assembly in the Nicene Creed. This act identifies not only the theological core of episcopacy but also the dynamic that orders the life and work of the church and each Christian. "We believe in God" is both source and ground for the ways in which we live our lives in response to God's calls to us. This order decently done inheres, therefore, in the very nature of the church and each member of the body of Christ, and therefore, in holy orders given by God through the church. Moreover, the ordering of a person as bishop is clearly the work of the Holy Spirit, a pneumatological event—effectively expressed in the prayers singing the hymn *Veni creator Spiritus* and the ritual act of laying on of hands. Ordering a new bishop is not merely an institutional act.

The sacramental foundation of the ordering of the life and work of the church in a decent manner is reflected in the role of bishop as ordinary. It is the bishop within whom is the authority for ordering the extension of his/her authority to preside at the Eucharist, baptize, absolve, and bless to the priests of the church, and extending, when necessary, the authority to baptize to both deacons and laypersons. The ordinary orders—that is, structures—the life and work of the church, specifically in ordering men and women as laypersons (Baptism), priests (with other priests also laying on hands), and deacons (laying on of hands reserved to the ordinary), and ordaining and consecrating bishops (with at least two other bishops). Functionally and theologically, the "order" of the church is structurally of the essence of the office of bishop, and that order is extended through his/her ordering members of the church for their particular participation in the body of Christ for God's mission (*missio Dei*) in the whole created order (*οἰκονομία*).[15] Again, as noted earlier, doing things "decently and in order" is ultimately focused on relationship, beginning with God, and, much in the way Richard Hooker understood "law," developing from God to humans and creation or from humans and creation to God in a network of functional holy relationships well and effectively lived.[16]

Leadership Well Ordered and Decently Done

The bishop diocesan is the primary leader of a diocese, the "chief priest and pastor." She or he has the responsibility as the embodied symbol of the unity of the church to gather God's people, to cast the vision of God's call to the diocese with clarity as an invitation to the diocese to respond to this call, to oversee its implementation, and to equip the saints (clergy and lay) to take their part with joy, delight, thanksgiving, and wonder in their love and service of God's beloved in the name of Jesus and the power of the Holy Spirit. As a chief priest and pastor, the axiom "decently and in order" speaks directly to the bishop's ministry of calling, equipping, and sustaining right relationships (righteousness) within the diocese in order to maximize effective participation by all God's beloved in the *missio Dei*.

However, this is not to say that this work of overseeing right relationship is the bishop's alone. We are one body and therefore we are all responsible for doing all things decently and in order, gathered around the bishop.[17] Decently done order, decently done leadership, is always grounded in our Baptism, which formally and explicitly relates us to God and one another in a particular way—that is, as the body of Christ,[18] decently ordered from Christ, who is the head. Hence, the leadership of the bishop in terms of doing all things decently and in order is biblically, theologically, and canonically grounded sacramentally in Baptism as lived in the particular form of his/her life as a bishop in relationship with the other parts of the body of Christ.

I think that arguably the ideal of this hierarchical model of how leadership works to promote ecclesial life lived decently and in order may be found in St. Benedict's *Regula*.[19] There is a delicate balance in the *Regula* between clear, decisive, accountable leadership and a highly participatory process of discerning and determining the life and work of the household in order for the monks and nuns to live their vows efficiently, effectively, and faithfully. The *Regula* is emphatic that the role of the abbot is one of service of God for and to the household. Order is sustained in the context of relationship with God and the community. There is a clear understanding of authority and power, responsibility, and accountability, what each is, what each is for, who has it, and what its purpose is. No one in the household is without some degree of power, authority, responsibility, or accountability. The abbot is responsible and accountable for the household, and therefore, to God and the people of the household. Authority and power are for service to God and especially the household as well as others, for their support, encouragement, building up in faith the members and therefore the whole household, and the living of one's vows (whether Benedictine or, in our case, our baptismal vows).[20] Benedict was particularly concerned that the good order of the house was organized around the praying of the Daily Offices in balance with daily work.[21] The goal of the *Regula* is to create a healthy community of love that faithfully and effectively lives the new life of grace of Baptism.

In terms of a bishop, the center of the life of the diocese, for him-/herself and all people, lay and ordained, is also the life of prayer balanced with daily work. This life includes the Daily Offices and Eucharist, as well as the reading and study of scripture and theology, and engagement of other resources that will create and sustain the life of faith and the ministries of the body of Christ individually and corporately. The bishop, as an abbot or abbess, is responsible for seeing that the daily prayer and work of the diocese is accomplished. This responsibility is fulfilled in the course of attending to the administrative work of the institution as well as the oversight of staff, clergy, parishes, and missions, and the participation of the diocese in public life. Life done decently and in order requires the bishop to know him-/herself, what his/her part in the body is, the functions and roles of the bishop, and the relationship of bishop to all the other parts of the body. Thus, to do things decently and in order requires both an acute self-awareness and a deep awareness of the whole context, the whole household, the whole body. To live as the church requires that the body, in an Episcopal system, understand the hierarchical relationships properly with a mature sense of discipline, commitment, and obedience in the Spirit, through the Son, with the Father.

What Jesus did, and what Benedict did, following Jesus's example, was to create a well-developed community capable of doing its life and work in an ordered and decent manner with appropriate and effective structures, processes, and relationships characterized by clarity of purpose, meaning, roles, responsibilities, and accountabilities that empowered the community with strength, courage, direction, and effectiveness.[22] In the present context, we may think of the office of bishop and the office of abbot/abbess as parallel positions of leadership and responsibility, as specified in the liturgy in which they are created. Neither office is about raising someone above everyone else in the community. Neither office is about someone being "better" or "more important" than the rest of the community. The office is about service in love, oversight that sees that the work of each part is done well, leadership that guides, inspires, gives direction, and articulates meaning, and always the office is about working with the whole body in cooperation and collaboration for effective participation in the *missio Dei*. All these qualities and dynamics are clearly grounded in and focused on the triune God in whom all things live and breathe and have their being. It is here that I would argue we find the intersection of tradition, flexibility, creativity, and open-ended generativity and change. Here we find the axiom of the Chicago-Lambeth Quadrilateral, "locally adapted" and practically applicable. Theologically, this phrase opens the doorway for the episcopate but also for the whole life and work of the church, to explore the role and work of the Spirit moving in and through the church in a process of discerning how and to where the bishop and the church are being called. This movement of the Spirit renews, enlivens, sustains, changes, and creates life within and through the church. The church's leaders, particularly its bishops, inspired by this spirit navigate the sometimes fragile, turbulent, and challenging waters of living our baptismal vows.[23]

Doing All Things Decently and in Order in a Fractalized World

What "decently and in order" may come to mean as we move forward may seem for many overwhelmingly unclear at best and impossible at worst. Many experience these new realities as we continue to live in the COVID pandemic as extremely difficult on every level of life: religious, social, economic, health and health care, education, individually, family, professionally, and the list goes on. For many, this level of disruption and disorder brings to mind the dynamic image of fractals. Physicists assure us that fractals are not chaos, appearances to the contrary. They are simply massive events of nearly no order at all. But there is order, however rudimentary, and therefore, there is hope and possibility. We still call that experience "chaos." The days of the pandemic have seemed to be more and more chaotic. There is definitely an absence of doing all things decently and in order, in spite of the best efforts on the part of some. Individuals and systems that had been steady and reliable seem to have imploded or exploded. It feels like living in the middle of a fractalized world in which many people feel fractalized as well.

That said, the physicists also assure us that fractals are moments of creative possibility and new opportunities. Fractals are inherently moments of great hope, moments for renewal and new life. Fractals, theologically, are a holy invitation to transformation, a kind of dying to old life and rising into new life, of becoming new wine in new wineskins, of bringing forward the very best of who we have been and to become who we are to be going forward, at least for a season. I think that we find ourselves as a society, as a church, and as bishops in a fractal moment through which will emerge a new understanding, a new defining, and a new praxis of doing all things decently and in order. This fractal moment will, I suggest, bring us to a new and deeper understanding of the ministry of the bishop that will creatively and generatively promote and sustain the capacity, vision, and will of the church (as institution and as individuals in community) to do all things decently and in order. The possibility is that the renewal of the episcopate as it emerges out of this fractal moment will include revisions of our understandings and practices, and revisions of the ordinal. This new emergence may call us to shed former, even cherished, understandings and practices of episcopacy. Going forward may necessitate the creation of new and of as yet unthought-of understandings of episcopal practices. At the heart of this time of renewal, creation, and transition, the work of the bishops and God's people together is to be faithful, to be open to the movements of the Spirit, to listen carefully with the ear of our heart for God's voice, to discern together the deep work of the Spirit in and through us institutionally and individually. A fractal moment is never a permanent moment. It is always a moment of potential in transition to a new realization of that potential. It is the gateway into a new thing to be done decently and in order, with God's help. This moment for us really is a moment of renewed hope and possibility to create, with God's help, a new order and a new practice of decency that is deep, rich, holy, and faithful.

Conclusion

It is the challenge and opportunity of bishops precisely as chief shepherds, pastors, and priests to lead with wisdom and care God's beloved into our future. This moment calls for the bishop to exercise careful, thoughtful, and faithful leadership that invites creativity and generativity from all the dioceses in which s/he serves. Moving forward decently and in order will, I think, call for weaving together the very best of who we have been, letting go of who we no longer are or can be, and being faithfully open to the work of the Spirit within and through us to become who God is calling and equipping us to be. We are, in this sense, in something of the same position Abram and Sarai found themselves in as they began their journey to become Abraham and Sarah. For us, the energy of this fractal moment comes as the still, small voice heard with the ear of the heart that says: "Come. Have I got an adventure for you. Come. And we shall go together to the new place where you will both continue to be my beloved and become new and renewed as my beloved. Come."

A moment of anxiety, certainly. A moment of risk, certainly. A moment that takes our breath away, yes. But not a moment for which bishops are unequipped (even when one does not yet know this). The bishop is to be the chief adult in the room, and that will take hard, focused, and intentional work. It will take the willingness to model thoughtful, effective leadership. It will take the will to actualize new ways of thinking about and distributing the work, new systems, new structures, and new processes. It will take a commitment to God and God's people to succeed *and to fail*, and to learn from both. Emerging from this fractal moment will require plenty of both success and failure, but neither will be wasted time or effort if received as bearers of grace.

This renewal of things done decently and in order will be born in the very heart of episcopacy and in the heart of each bishop. Some things will look and sound and be as they always have been. The creation of new things and ways done decently and in order will also be born in the very heart of episcopacy and of each bishop. Some things are only now beginning to take form—the ways we gather, celebrate liturgies, and are present for and with each other. Technology is impacting how we gather and what it means to be present in person, sacramentally, and spiritually. How we gather and celebrate our liturgies is taking new forms. How we care for one another, love one another, serve one another is in a creative process of rising anew from our fractal moment into a new order. We as the church must wrestle with what it means and how it will be to do all things decently and in order.

As Peter said to Jesus at the Transfiguration, "It is good for us to be here" (Matt. 17:4). And as Peter and the apostles learned, so the bishops will learn, with God's help, what it is to be transfigured in Christ through the Spirit in these days and going forward, to live and work, pray and serve, love and shepherd, decently and in order, with God's help. So it is that we invoke the Holy Spirit to make a man or a woman a bishop among us in Christ's one, holy, catholic, and apostolic church:

My *brother/sister*, the people have chosen you and have affirmed their trust in you by acclaiming your election. A bishop in God's holy Church is called to be one with the apostles in proclaiming Christ's resurrection and interpreting the Gospel, and to testify to Christ's sovereignty as Lord of lords and King of kings.

You are called to guard the faith, unity, and discipline of the Church; to celebrate and to provide for the administration of the sacraments of the New Covenant; to ordain priests and deacons and to join in ordaining bishops; and to be in all things a faithful pastor and wholesome example for the entire flock of Christ.

With your fellow bishops you will share in the leadership of the Church throughout the world. Your heritage is the faith of patriarchs, prophets, apostles, and martyrs, and those of every generation who have looked to God in hope. Your joy will be to follow him who came, not to be served, but to serve, and to give his life a ransom for many.[24]

Sacramentally, ecclesiologically, spiritually, missiologically, and organizationally, the capacity of the church to do all things decently and in order emanates from the bishop. With God's help, the bishop is empowered by the Spirit to lead, to shepherd, and to gather God's people to love and serve God in their love and service of God's beloved. With the bishop, the people of God create, promote, and sustain holy work, well done, in right relationships with God and among God's people. With the bishop, the church is created, called, and empowered to do all things decently and in order.

CHAPTER 4

Bishop William White's "Opinions" on Episcopacy, Race, and Ecumenism

R. William Franklin

O f the first four bishops of The Episcopal Church, William White (1748–1836) is the only one who can be said to be the real leader of the church from the American Revolution into the fourth decade of the nineteenth century. The bishops and deputies of the General Convention after 1800 looked to him as a father figure, our George Washington.[1]

White served as curate and then rector of the united parishes of Christ Church and St. Peter's in Philadelphia. They were numerically the largest Anglican congregation in the most populous city of the thirteen colonies. On February 4, 1787, he was consecrated first bishop of Pennsylvania by the archbishops of Canterbury and York and two other English bishops at Lambeth Palace. Eight years later he became presiding bishop, until 1836. He is the only Episcopalian to have served as both the president of the House of Deputies and the presiding bishop, a distinction commemorated by a joint worship service of the two Houses of the General Convention on July 17, 2021.

White occupied a position that made him a leader. He came from an affluent Philadelphia family. He earned a place alongside the intellectual elite of his native city: Franklin, Hamilton, Washington, and Madison. He was a patriot. At one time during the Revolution, White was the only Anglican priest who remained in Pennsylvania. On the Fourth of July, 1776, he removed prayers for the king from the liturgies of his parish, for which he could have been executed as a traitor to the Crown. It was not surprising that he was called to serve as the chaplain to the

Continental Congress, and then chaplain to the US Senate from 1777 to 1800, when the US capital was moved from Philadelphia to Washington.

His revolutionary spirit was made manifest in a number of progressive church moves. In 1794 the bishop welcomed St. Thomas African Episcopal Church into the Diocese of Pennsylvania. St. Thomas was the first Black congregation of any American denomination, and it flourished long before there were any separate Black American denominations.

In 1804 Bishop White ordained the first Black priest in The Episcopal Church, the lay leader and then deacon of the St. Thomas Church, Absalom Jones, fifty-eight years old, a former slave, who had worked years to purchase his freedom. To broaden the racial embrace of Episcopal clergy, White made the unprecedented move to dispense Jones from the requirement of Episcopal priests to be examined in their mastery of Latin and Greek.[2]

In 1824 White ordained at St. Thomas African Episcopal Church the second Black Episcopal priest, again with a suspension of the Latin and Greek language requirement for ordination. He was William Leavington, who in 1827 founded St. James' Church in Baltimore, whose later rector would be Michael B. Curry, the first Black presiding bishop of The Episcopal Church.[3]

A second area of White's initial revolutionary spirit was in ecumenism, in building close relationships with other American denominations. Methodism had begun as an evangelical movement within the Church of England. Yet its founder, John Wesley, a priest of the Church of England, broke unity in 1784 by ordaining Thomas Coke as a "superintendent" of the Methodist mission to America. The Methodists were organizing a denomination separated from existing American Anglican congregations. Amid the aftermath of the American Revolution at their 1784 "Christmas Conference" in Baltimore, Thomas Coke and Francis Asbury claimed the title of "bishop" and set about founding congregations with a threefold order of ordained ministry—bishops, elders, and deacons—yet grounded within the framework of the Methodist "Book of Discipline," not Anglican canon law nor the Book of Common Prayer, and without a concept of bishops ordained in continuity with the apostolic succession. Methodists and Episcopalians were going their separate ways.

Seven years later, in 1791, Thomas Coke approached William White in Philadelphia about conversations toward reunion. Coke proposed a "Methodist Society in the Protestant Episcopal Church" as a means toward the reunion of the two bodies. Coke met privately with White, and White considered a reunion scheme in which Episcopal bishops would ordain two Methodist bishops for a Methodist group within The Episcopal Church. White was particularly attracted to the idea that through this proposal a large number of Black Methodists might come into The Episcopal Church.

Yet not one other Episcopal or Methodist leader came forward to support this scheme. The conversations foundered also because Coke was insistent that Methodist clergy be dispensed from the Greek and Latin language proficiency requirements of The Episcopal Church.[4]

Before 1820, White joined in other ecumenical enterprises with several denominations, including the Philadelphia Lutherans. The Philadelphia Bible Society was organized in December 1808. It was a work of several Christian churches together, and White served as first president of the society. He vigorously supported the efforts of the society to distribute Bibles that contained no commentaries reflecting the theologies of specific denominations. Like King James I in 1611 launching the King James Bible, he saw making widely available the shared common text of the Bible as an instrument toward Christian unity. A sacred text without specific denominational doctrinal notes, made available to all, would heal the denominational divisions of the new United States.[5]

The most daring contribution of William White to the future of American Anglicanism came in the publication of his short pamphlet *The Case of the Episcopal Churches in the United States Considered.* It appeared in 1782, while the American Revolution was still raging. Here White addressed two issues: the structure of a postrevolutionary Episcopal Church and the shape of episcopacy in a republican nation, or what to do if there could be no bishops.[6]

When *The Case* emerged in August 1782, it was not known that Great Britain and the colonies were soon to embark on negotiations that would end the war and free the thirteen colonies from the Crown. More and more churches were closing, and a majority of clergy were fleeing to Canada and Great Britain.

In these fraught circumstances, on what basis could White outline a structure for an American Anglican Church that was a radical break from earlier English tradition? He did this by basing his ecclesiology on two principles: first, that authority in the church could no longer rest on the Crown, and second, that authority in the church could rest upon the sovereignty of the people. He must incorporate the ideology of the American Revolution into an understanding of church authority based on the sovereignty of the people, not the sovereignty of a monarch. In the newly freed thirteen colonies, Anglicans might now form a church no longer based on state establishment and its privileges, which was the model of the then-current European ecclesiologies. He called for the reorganization of the church around republican principles. Ultimate church government would be founded on the authority of a federal "convention" made up equally of elected priests and laymen, a convention in which power would be exercised by votes, in democratic fashion.

And yet this revolutionary democratic model was actually based on earlier church history. White states in *The Case*, "In the earlier ages of the church, it was customary to debate and determine in a general Concourse of all Christians in the same city; among whom the bishop was no more than president . . ."[7]

"Conciliarism" is a theory of authority in the church that is the outgrowth of the role that councils ("conventions," in White's terminology) played in the ancient church. Conciliarism as a coherent movement was the work of German, French, Spanish, and Italian canon lawyers in the thirteenth century. In the face of the rising claims of the monarchical authority of the bishop of Rome, these canon lawyers launched a counterargument: that ultimate authority in the church is lodged not with one episcopal figure but in a corporate body, a council, that is representative of the whole body of Christ. The ideals of conciliarism lived on in the movement of Christian humanism in the Renaissance and then into the sixteenth century to influence the Reformation and aspects of the evolution of the Church of England.

Based on this ancient precedent of government by representatives, White sketched out for republican America his proposal of the American Church as a corporation governed by elected representatives. He gave American republican expression to the conciliarists' concept of ultimate authority over the church vested in a convention ("council") made up of the elected representatives of the *congregatio fidelium*—elected priests and laity and, after 1789, elected bishops.

White foresaw the introduction of laity into the government of the church as the restoration in the New World of a very ancient principle. His studies of early church councils convinced him that the laity was represented in ancient ecclesiastical councils. Church authority was vested in ancient times in councils, not in bishops alone.[8]

However, bishops and ordination were the second issue with which White grappled in *The Case* of 1782. There had been no Anglican bishops in America. The bishop of London exercised episcopal authority from abroad. There was active opposition to the introduction of bishops into the colonies. In the context of a continuing revolutionary war and an uncertain future relationship with the Church of England, White did not believe that bishops were absolutely necessary for the church. Bishops were a *bene esse*, a good thing, but not an essential institution, not of the *esse*, the essence, of the church. Until communion with the Church of England could in some way be re-established, White was willing to allow a presbyteral form of ordination to provide conditional ministers for America. He writes in *The Case*,

> I am still of the opinion that in an exigency in which a duly authorized ministry cannot be obtained, the paramount duty of preaching the gospel, and the worshipping of God on the terms of the Christian Covenant, should go on, in the best manner which circumstances permit. In regard to the episcopacy, I think that it should be sustained, as the Government of the Church from the time of the apostles, but without criminating [*sic*] the Ministry of other Churches; as is the course taken by the Church of England.[9]

White is supporting here, for a period, presbyteral ordinations that interrupt apostolic succession, so that the gospel might still be rightly preached and the sacraments duly celebrated. Until relations with the Church of England could be fully restored, in America three priests would now ordain, rather than a bishop. He called for the election of a "superior order of clergy"[10] (still a priest, though now also a superintendent or overseer) to supervise the clergy and parishes of a region. This would involve a conditional ordination to oversight, similar to a conditional Baptism in dire circumstances.

In *The Case* White argues that when bishops could be restored, their selection should be based on the principle of the Revolution: the sovereignty of the people. Bishops, "superior clergy," should be elected by the clergy and the laity together. As in the case of the authority of conventions based on the ancient concept of conciliarism, White supported the concept of popular elections of bishops as based on ancient practice: "even in the city of Rome, the privilege of electing the bishop continued with the people to the tenth century; and near these times there are resolutions of councils, that none should be promoted to ecclesiastical dignities, but by election of the clergy and people."[11] This was a progressive republican ecclesiology of the episcopate, a complete break for a new nation with the ways of the Church of England in choosing its leaders.

And yet for White a role for the episcopate, even though not essential, would be for the good for an Anglican Church now independent of Great Britain. In his *Memoirs of the Protestant Episcopal Church* White writes,

> The expedient [of temporarily suspending episcopal government] was sustained by the plea of necessity, and by opinions of various authors of the Church of England, acknowledging a valid ministry under circumstances similar to those of the existing case. . . . Although reference was had to the position of the Church, that "from the Apostles' time, there have been in the Church of Christ, the three orders of bishops, priests, and deacons," nothing was said in proof of the fact; because it was not questioned in this Church; and because argument to the effect would have been indiscrete.[12]

So William White did indeed believe in three orders of ministry and that bishops continued the apostolic succession in a church, but under the circumstances, the Church of England could not transfer the office of bishop, and through it, the apostolic succession, under such circumstances in which consecration of a bishop by the Church of England required an oath of loyalty to the English monarch, impossible while the Revolutionary War continued. However, also under the given circumstances, White believed valid gospel ministry could continue without the requirement of three orders of ministry or the apostolic succession continuing.

The historical context suddenly shifted in 1783, when the colonies and Great Britain signed a peace treaty ending the war and recognizing the independence of the thirteen colonies. In March 1783 Samuel Seabury was elected bishop by ten priests in Connecticut, and in November 1784 he was consecrated as the first American bishop by bishops of The Episcopal Church of Scotland (which was not then in full communion with the Church of England). In 1784 William White presided at a gathering of Episcopalians from Middle Atlantic and Northeastern states who proposed a meeting of a governing General Convention of The Episcopal Church in Philadelphia in 1785. White presided over this first meeting of the General Convention, which accomplished:

1. Drafting of a constitution for the American Church, presbyterian in character;
2. Inviting the church in each state to elect its own bishop, who would confirm new members, ordain clergy, and serve on an ex officio basis at each future meeting of the General Convention;
3. Drafting of an American version of the Book of Common Prayer;
4. Devising a plan to have the newly elected American bishops consecrated by bishops of the Church of England.

In 1786, Pennsylvania, New York, and Virginia elected bishops, while the English Parliament passed laws allowing English bishops to consecrate them. White was elected in Pennsylvania and subsequently sailed to England for consecration into the historic episcopal succession, which he now affirmed as a necessary link outside the United States to ensure the validity of future American episcopal orders. On February 4, 1787, William White and Samuel Provoost, of New York, were consecrated as bishops by the archbishops of Canterbury and York and two additional English bishops.

As bishop, White presided over the next General Convention, in 1789, which met in his own Christ Church in Philadelphia. This convention:

1. Promulgated a constitution that granted to the General Convention sovereign authority over what were called the state conventions, and only later dioceses, a constitution that gave the convention the power to create new dioceses, promulgate and interpret canons for the church, promulgate and revise an American Book of Common Prayer, and set up courts for the trial of a bishop.
2. Defined in the area of the episcopate.
3. The validity of Seabury's Scottish consecration.
4. Created a separate House of Bishops, which provided the bishops with their own legislative community and possessed the right to originate legislation and to veto legislation;

5. Enhanced a more prominent place for the episcopate and for the Book of Common Prayer in the identity of The Episcopal Church than either had in White's *Case*:

   a. A similar principle of both the Constitution and the canons was the centrality of the place of the office of bishop and the Book of Common Prayer;

   b. No person could officiate in an Episcopal church without episcopal ordination and no prayers could be used in an Episcopal church that were not to be found in the Book of Common Prayer.

In all of this work White's greatest achievement in the final eleven years of the eighteenth century was to reconcile the two factions of The Episcopal Church—Connecticut and the New England states with the Middle Atlantic and the Southern states—into a moment of ecclesiological and liturgical unity in America, through the exercise of his great political and pastoral skills, honed in Philadelphia in the crucible of the days of the Revolution and the US Constitutional Convention. As the collect for the Feast of William White on July 17 states, God "endowed him with wisdom, patience, and a reconciling temper, that he might lead your Church into ways of stability and peace."[13]

White wrought unity out of what were essentially two warring Episcopal Churches: one in Connecticut—Scottish, High Church, and Tory; the other, Middle Atlantic and Southern—English, latitudinarian, and patriotic. Bishop Seabury and his people considered the bishop of New York to be a lazy deist who spent his days on his country estate studying botany and translating the Italian poems of Torquato Tasso into English. Bishop Samuel Provoost and the Episcopalians of New York considered Samuel Seabury to be a traitor to the United States, worthy of prosecution because he served the British Army through the long Revolutionary War. By 1800 three of the first Episcopal bishops were dead. White alone was left to lead the church into the first thirty-six years of the nineteenth century.

There were challenges. White must preserve the unity he had wrought in 1789, preserving the unity of Anglicans as one body, as well as the European heritage of Anglicanism, while continuing to build an American denomination linked in the public mind to the enemy nation, Great Britain. Out of an American population of four million there were now only ten thousand members of the new

Episcopal Church. The Episcopal Church began to divide into two parties, a High Church Party, focused on New York City and the Diocese of New York, stressing The Episcopal Church's difference and necessary isolation from other Protestant denominations, and a Low Church Party, focused on absorbing the evangelicalism of the Second Great Awakening, as well as a closer association with the Calvinist theology of the Presbyterians and the Princeton Theological Seminary.[14]

The evangelical Second Great Awakening, and the de-emphasis on the academic training of ordinands, led to the rapid rise of the "popular denominations." The Baptists flourished in this environment, and by 1840 the Methodists were the largest US denomination, claiming 34 percent of American church membership. The old colonial denominations, like the Episcopalians, the Presbyterians, and the Congregationalists, advocating a learned ministry and occupying a similar social profile, remained static. The Episcopal Church continued to be haunted by the popular linking of episcopacy with tyranny and continued to be tarred by anti-British fury during the War of 1812 and after.[15]

This made an impact on William White. He had been at the heart of national affairs during the Revolution and the first days of the republic. He now withdrew more into a conservative cocoon after the US capital moved from Philadelphia to Washington, DC. He stayed behind in Philadelphia and retreated into a more cautious stance on race, had no involvement in the burgeoning abolitionist movement, withdrew from cooperation with other denominations, and projected a more constrained Episcopal Church profile.

Race is the first example of this constrained profile. Even though he ordained Absalom Jones in 1804, as the first Black priest, White later insisted on an agreement that Absalom Jones's congregation could not send clergy or lay deputies to the Pennsylvania diocesan convention, nor could the congregation be involved in any way in the normal privileges of diocesan life. St. Thomas African Episcopal Church was effectively segregated from the diocese. In addition, in 1816 White became a member of the American Colonization Society, which worked for the voluntary removal to Africa of free American Blacks. This plan, which White supported, cut to the heart of American racism—assumptions about African Americans' inferiority, and the inability of Black Americans to take their part fully in civic life and in church life.[16]

In a similar way White took steps to increase the individual authority of the presiding bishop, with a parallel de-emphasis on the role of clergy and lay elected members of the General Convention. After 1800 the presiding bishop was granted the authority to issue on his own pastoral letters on behalf of the whole church, to summon on his own special meetings of the convention, and always to serve as chief consecrator at all ordinations of bishops. From 1820 the presiding bishop gained another title, serving as the president of the Protestant Episcopal Missionary Society in the United States. White, in his addresses to the House of Bishops, stressed that bishops must move beyond simply ordaining, confirming, and making parish visitations. They were urged to take their place at the heart of diocesan life, always presiding at diocesan conventions, issuing regular pastoral letters that were to inspire vitality in diocesan life.[17]

White recognized that much more must be done in the new century to clarify the theological principles of The Episcopal Church. The 1789 General Convention had adopted the Book of Common Prayer and a constitution. White urged that the General Convention become more precise and well defined in the area of its doctrine. The General Convention must identify the body of doctrine that defines its character to shape better a concerted response to the divisions being wrought in America by the Second Great Awakening by officially adopting "Articles of Religion" and by creating a required course of ecclesiastical study for those seeking ordination.

White was convinced that the identity of The Episcopal Church was adrift and that the solution was to place clear limits on an acceptable Episcopal ecclesiology that stood in marked contrast to the theological realm of the rest of American Protestantism. He did this first by convincing the General Convention to adopt an American version of the Thirty-Nine Articles of the Church of England (1571) on September 12, 1801, rewriting article VIII, "Of the Creeds," omitting article XXI, "Of the Authority of General Councils," and altering article XXXVI, "Of Consecration of Bishops and Ministers."[18]

In 1804 White prepared for adoption by the General Convention a "Course of Ecclesiastical Studies," to be required of all ordinands in The Episcopal Church, a common course of study for all clergy. To White this list marked the boundaries of acceptable Episcopal theological opinion that could not be transgressed by clergy.[19]

In 1846 there was published a collection made up of selections from Bishop White's addresses and letters from the first thirty years of the nineteenth century that precisely defined his opinions about contested theological points, titled *Bishop White's Opinions on Certain Theological and Ecclesiastical Points Being a*

Compilation from the Writings and in the Words of The Rt. Rev. Wm. White, D.D., by a Protestant Episcopalian, published by Henry M. Onderdonk and Co.[20] The Onderdonks were a High Church family who produced High Church bishops of New York and Pennsylvania, who were faced with ecclesiastical trials in the House of Bishops in the 1840s as part of the growing conflict between the High Church and Low Church parties in The Episcopal Church.

The *Opinions* is the most detailed collection of the more reactionary writings of Bishop White as a compendium for the benefit of the younger clerical and lay members of the General Convention. The extracts cover a wide variety of topics: original sin, the plan of salvation, good works, evangelism and evangelical preaching, the relation of the Bible to the church, tradition, the meaning of the term "catholic," the sacraments, baptismal regeneration, and clergy insubordination. Three topics illustrate White's move from bold progressive leadership to cautious withdrawal:

a. "Of Uniting with Professing Christians Exterior to the Protestant Episcopal Church: Question: Is not disunion the result of acting with spurious liberality? White: Of all mistaken expedients for the increase of Union, there cannot be any one of them more delusive than the prospect here contemplated; professed to be for the combining in worship of bodies of Christians, now disjoined. Instead of this, it tends to the opposite effect of dividing our Church, as existing in its present forms, and into how many separated and perhaps hostile Communions, it is impossible to foresee."[21]

b. "Question: Is there a danger of being too sensitive to the feelings of those who dissent from us? White: There is the opposite danger being so sensitive to the feelings of those who dissent from the distinctive principles of our Church, that such, their discrepancies, ought never to be presented to congregational view; which, we are told, should be limited to what are contended to be the only essential doctrines of Christianity assented to by all who deserve the name of Christians. In contrariety to this it is here maintained to be inconsistent with ministerial fidelity, to keep back purposely, any truth believed to be contained in Scripture; although the time of propounding it, and the question of its pertinency are points subjected to the determinations of Christian prudence."[22]

c. "Question: Is it true liberality for Churchmen to join in religious exercises, when all distinctive principles are lost sight of? White: It was expressed to be a specious but delusive profession of liberality, inviting us to join in religious exercises, and in religious instruction whether delivered orally, or through the channel of the press; in which it is understood, that all distinctive principles are to be lost sight of."[23]

It is clear in the *Opinions* that the two fundamental distinctive principles of The Episcopal Church, never to be lost sight of, are the centrality of episcopacy and of the apostolic succession. There should be no compromises on these points:

> Question: Does Christian charity to all who differ, involve any yield-ing of conscientious points of difference? White: There are some indeed, who to show how much they soar above illiberality of religious senti-ment, would throw down every barrier dividing our communion for some others in visible administration, because they think the existing differences of no importance. Among the objections to such a plan, it is not the least, that it tends to the disturbance of peace and charity; while the securing of these is its professed object. And such must be the effect, unless these mistaken promoters of unity can persuade one of two par-ties, whom they may at any time aim to reconcile, to give up the point which they think invalid in Christian verity. So far as there have been attempts to draw The Episcopal Church into this plan, liberal as some conceive, the design has uniformly exacted the sacrifice of the prominent characteristics of our system.[24]

The centrality of the episcopate was a chief characteristic of the system. White admits that for many Americans the office of bishop is connected with immoderate power, monarchy, and foreign influence. He launches a High Church defense of episcopacy: there are three orders of ordained ministry, not one, as Protestant denominations attest. Episcopacy is even of divine institution by Jesus and His apostles. In section 9 of the *Opinions*, "Of Episcopacy," White begins by quoting the preface to the ordinal in both the American and the English Books of Common Prayer: "It is evident unto all men, diligently reading Holy Scripture and ancient authors, that from the Apostles' time there have been three orders of Ministry in Christ's Church—Bishops, Priests, and Deacons." And then he quotes Richard Hooker's *Laws of Ecclesiastical Polity*, Book 7, page 5: "Wherefore let us not fear to be herein bold and peremptory, that if anything in the Church's government, surely the first institution of Bishops was from Heaven, was even of God: the Holy Ghost was the author of it."[25]

In answer to the question, how should we act in regard to the episcopacy, this is White's answer in an address at the General Theological Seminary in 1828, quoted in the *Opinions*:

> In regard to the Constitution and government of the Christian Church, we affirm, that "from the beginning there have been the three orders of Bishops, Priests, and Deacons," and that it is "evident from Scripture, and from ancient authors," meaning the writings of the early Fathers. If the fact be as is stated—and we ought to be supposed sincere in the profession of it—is it not sufficiently important to induce us to adhere to and not by any act to imply the nullity of, what claims so high an origin.[26]

In chapter 10 of the *Opinions*, "Of Apostolical Succession," White makes four points about the essential connection of the doctrine of apostolic succession to episcopacy:

a. The doctrine is fundamental to identity: "Is Apostolical Succession essential? White answers: To justify the candidate [for ordination] in believing that he is called according to the will of Christ, he should be convinced, after due enquiry, that the Church to which he looks for ordination, is a true Apostolic Church, deriving its authority from that founded by the Apostles. For since they did confessedly found a Communion, and since it did confessedly transmit its ministries, there seems no possible right to the name of a Christian Church at present, but in succession from the original established body."[27]

b. White did not intend to be against apostolic succession in *The Case*: "Question: Did Bishop White, in his pamphlet, entitled 'The Case of the Episcopal Churches in the United States Considered,' consent with those who were adverse to the Apostolic origin of Episcopacy? White answered: To those who, being adverse to the apostolic origin of Episcopacy, have considered him (Bishop White) as having consented with them in opinion; he (Bishop White) is ready to declare, on every suitable opportunity, that the contrary was intended to be implied, and that it is obvious, according to his conceptions, on the face of the performance."[28]

c. The concept of three orders of ordained ministry cannot be surrendered for the sake of church unity: "Question: Is Episcopacy a constituent part of our Church? White answered: But you think the Episcopal Church might have continued to have three orders, although giving up the succession; and this would have led to the Union with other Churches; that is, she might have given up what she conceives to be a constituent part of her institutions, and coeval with her holy religion: in the mere doing of which I see little ground of Union with others; but much ground of disunion with herself."[29]

d. The doctrine of apostolic succession sustains Christian peace, not division: "Question: Is Apostolic Succession essential to the peace of the Church? White's answer: We hold up the Succession of the Ministry, as a principle clearly deducible from Scripture, and essential to the peace and government of the Church. Again, we affirm the necessity of succession from the Apostles."[30]

Conclusion

What is the relevance of White's story for this moment in the history of The Episcopal Church? We are also living, like White, through a great moment of almost revolutionary change. We are coming to terms with a continuing pandemic health crisis, with the enduring legacy of white supremacy, with a deep political division that has threatened the peaceful transfer of presidential power, and with a divided Christian church. White's solution to Episcopal identity at a time of crisis was to turn inward. In the midst of the American Revolution he had stood on the side of change, an ecclesiology that focused on the ultimate authority of the laity and the ordained together in the General Convention. In the nineteenth century he clung to the authority of bishops. In the eighteenth century he contemplated cooperation with other denominations. In the nineteenth century he clung to a church of three orders of ordained ministry and the apostolic succession. He first made gestures toward racial justice by ordaining two Black priests. But then, for all practical purposes, he moved toward an affirmation of white supremacy in allowing the segregation of the Diocese of Pennsylvania and advocating the resettlement of free American Blacks to Africa. Concerned about the growth of the "popular denominations," he did nothing to expand the class identity of The Episcopal Church.

Perhaps he was wearied by his own advancing age or exhausted by nearly six decades of unceasing effort to establish The Episcopal Church in a new American form. Or he may have been daunted by the religious and political populism he saw emerging in the Jacksonian era of the maturing American republic.

Surely, we can identify with White's exhaustion as we struggle through our own era of pandemic, protest, political division, attacks on our institutions, and acknowledgment of the racism and injustice in which our own church has been complicit. And surely we must at the same time confront White's racism and classism and neglect of those unlike himself, even as we recognize those same failures in other revered leaders of The Episcopal Church.

We find ourselves at a moment when some of our people are terrified by the demographic decline of our church and by the growing financial peril of under-resourced dioceses and of many congregations. William White's life is both an inspiring example and a cautionary lens through which to examine our current crisis.

Could both Whites be right for us, the revolutionary White and the reactionary White? Who are the leaders, now and in the past, with the vision to see the immediate crises and the issues beyond them, and the skill to deal with both? How will we as bishops redefine our role, as White urged, beyond simply ordaining, confirming, and making parish visitations?

We need leaders and structures to respond to the needs of today, as White so courageously saw in the days after the Revolution. And we need the long view that he took in his later years, of the apostolic episcopate and the understanding of our roots in church history, to ground us in our faith and stand the test of time.

CHAPTER 5

Episcopate, Race, and Unity of the Church

Allen Shin

Introduction

In the aftermath of the Civil War, guarding the unity of the postbellum Episcopal Church was the most urgent crisis and a messy business facing the bishops and the church. In 1861, the southern dioceses seceded from the North by organizing the Confederate Church and electing Bishop Stephen Elliott of Georgia as its presiding bishop. The 1865 General Convention managed to achieve the reunion, which was completed with the Diocese of Virginia voting to rejoin the old church in May 1866.

Unity can be engineered by human efforts; communion cannot. This unity certainly did not reflect true communion from the perspective of African Americans and their allies. So long as African American congregations and their members were excluded from full participation in the life of the church on all levels, true communion was but a faint glimmer on the horizon. The unity of the church continued to be a critical issue in The Episcopal Church in terms of the status of African Americans throughout the reconstruction and Jim Crow eras. A century would pass from the 1865 reunion before we saw a beginning step toward some semblance of communion of races in The Episcopal Church.

The election of John Melville Burgess as the first African American diocesan bishop in Massachusetts in 1968 was the milestone that nudged The Episcopal Church on a path toward communion in terms of racial justice and equality. It opened the doors to more African American bishops. Although there was still a long journey ahead toward the Beloved Community of Jesus, the Burgess election put The Episcopal Church at least on the right path of racial justice.

In the middle of this century-long struggle for racial equality is Bishop Edward Thomas Demby, the first African American bishop of The Episcopal Church on American soil. This is a brief study contrasting the unity of the church that was restored at the 1865 General Convention and Bishop Demby's vision of the unity of the church, which was deeply tied to his own episcopate and his fight for racial integration in The Episcopal Church.

The Cost of Reunion

Despite their desire to remain loyal to the worship and beliefs of their church, African American leaders realized that without the respect of whites, unity alone was valueless.[1]

Gardiner Shattuck, in his book *Episcopalians and Race*, makes the poignant observation above on the reunion of the postbellum Episcopal Church from the African American point of view. It is no secret that the cost of the reunion of the southern and the northern dioceses was largely borne by African American Episcopalians, for the reunion was achieved by keeping the whole issue of slavery and the status of the African American Episcopalians out of the discussion at the 1865 General Convention and leaving it to the dioceses to legislate on the issue.[2]

During the Civil War, although the southern dioceses seceded and organized their own Confederate Church, many bishops of the South and the North maintained their personal relationships with each other. From a systems point of view, their communications would make an interesting study on the importance of staying connected as it laid the ground for the reunion when the time came. An example of this was Leonidas Polk of Louisiana, whose behind-the-scenes political maneuvers are the subject of Robert Crewdson's study.[3] In his letter to Horatio Potter of New York, Polk wrote, "If we must separate, it must be to follow our nationality and not because we have differed on any point of Christian doctrine or religious duty."[4] Even though the southern dioceses had, in fact, seceded, he was careful to make the distinction between separation and division and to couch the separation in the political language of "nationality" rather than any theological or moral principles. "Separated but not divided" was the euphemism of the day that kept The Episcopal Church from a complete schism and enabled the subsequent reunion. One significant sign of this, as Crewdson notes, was that the General Convention, which met in New York in 1862, "never recognized the withdrawal of the southern dioceses and included them in its roll call."[5]

Many northern bishops were also sympathetic toward the southern bishops' dilemma and willing to compromise for the sake of peace and unity of the church. Most influential among them was John Henry Hopkins, bishop of Vermont (1838–1868) and presiding bishop (1865–1868). As a senior bishop in the House of Bishops he had great influence among the northern bishops and played a critical role in the process of the reunion. In his study of Hopkins, James Donald portrays a bishop who held on to the racist view of slavery while at the same time speaking of the abolishment of slavery in its natural course.[6] Hopkins wrote a treatise on the biblical justification of slavery in 1861, in which he also suggested that the institution of slavery would die a natural death someday. Thus, he concluded, "it belongs to the Slave States themselves to take the lead in such a movement. And in the meanwhile, their legal rights and their natural feelings must be respected, if we would hope for unity and peace."[7] Felder Dorn attempts to give a fair assessment of Hopkins but ultimately acknowledges that "he never came to grips with the root evil of slavery. It was his greatest failure."[8]

Soon after the war ended in May 1865, Hopkins began his political engineering of the reunion.[9] On June 22, he proposed to the northern bishops for their approval his letter, inviting the southern bishops to the October General Convention in Philadelphia. While the northern bishops were all in favor of the eventual reunion, most disapproved of his proposed letter. The northern sentiment was that since the southern dioceses seceded from the church of their own accord, they should make the first move for reunion. Alfred Lee of Delaware insisted that "full fellowship should not be restored to any southern churchman until he had shown the proper spirit of contrition."[10] Some even expressed hostility toward the southern dioceses. Bishop A. Cleveland Coxe of Long Island called it "the Confederate Church lunacy."[11] The public sentiment in the North was just as hostile. The *Philadelphia Episcopal Recorder* advocated hanging the southern bishops and clergy for having sponsored the secession movement.[12] The southern bishops were just as hostile toward the North. Bishop Green of Mississippi and Bishop Thomas Davis of South Carolina supported the idea of a permanent Southern Episcopal Church. Having failed to get the approval of the fellow northern bishops, Hopkins sent his own personal letter to the southern bishops, inviting them to the October Convention and assuring them of the greetings of "kindest feelings."[13] The southern bishops were not ready to admit that the establishment of the Confederate Church was a schismatic act. They were simply separated by circumstance but not schismatic. Hopkins agreed with them that the southern dioceses acted legally and wisely.

Hopkins's letter inspired at least two southern bishops and some southern delegates to attend the October Convention. In his study on the Episcopal reunion, Henry Rector focuses on two southern bishops in attendance at the 1865 General Convention—Bishop Henry Champlin Lay (Arkansas and the Southwest territories, 1859–1869; Easton, 1869–1885) and Bishop Thomas Atkinson (North Carolina, 1853–1881). While the other southern bishops preferred to postpone a decision on the question of reunion for a while, Bishops Lay and Atkinson decided not to wait and traveled to Philadelphia in October 1865.

There were, however, considerable barriers that needed to be resolved for the reunion to happen at the convention.[14] The first issue was Polk of Louisiana's military service as lieutenant general in the Confederate Army. Although he had died by the time of the convention, any condemnation or slur on Polk was a delicate issue for the southerners and could have derailed any hopes of reunion. No direct reproach was pronounced on Polk by the convention. But a resolution that forbids military service by any member of the clergy was passed, looking toward the future.[15]

The second issue was Bishop Lay's episcopal designation. He had been appointed missionary bishop of the Southwest territories but resigned from the position to remain in solidarity with the other southern bishops. The churches in Arkansas elected him as their bishop in 1862, even though Arkansas had not yet been recognized as a diocese. At the 1865 convention, the House of Bishops recognized him in his former position as missionary bishop of the Southwest territories. He most likely welcomed this redesignation since very little was left in Arkansas after the war.

The third issue was the episcopate of Richard Wilmer of Alabama, who had been elected as bishop in 1861 and consecrated in 1862 without the consent of the northern bishops and their dioceses. Moreover, he was at the time under house arrest for the pastoral letter to his clergy, in which he forbade them from praying for the president of the United States. Needless to say, his pastoral letter became a contentious issue, especially in the House of Deputies. The bishops tried to calm the hostility by securing his assurance that he would not send such a pastoral letter again and by passing a resolution that read, "We do hereby express to the Bishop of Alabama our fraternal regret at the issue of his late pastoral letter, and assured confidence that no further occasion for such regrets will occur."[16] His election was eventually approved by the convention. There was the question of the validity of Bishop Charles Quintard's election in Tennessee during the war years and also of his service in the Confederate Army. But his election was also confirmed by the convention, and he was consecrated at St. Luke's Church in Philadelphia on October 11, 1865.

The most contentious issue of the convention was the theme for the service of thanksgiving for the reunion and the subject of the House of Bishops' pastoral letter to the church. Bishop George Burgess of Maine proposed various themes for thanksgiving, one of which was "for extension among all classes of men the condition of freedom and social improvement—in other words the abolishment of slavery." His motion was quickly tabled.[17] Sensing that tabling the motion had to do with the northern bishops' desire not to offend the southern bishops, Burgess approached Bishop Lay and inquired as to what of the resolution he found offensive. Lay replied, "I trust in God that freedom may bring to the colored race all the blessings you anticipate; but wiser than men, I, and northern man at that, honestly doubt whether freedom will prove to them a blessing or a curse. Why should this House commit itself in a matter wherein it has no authority?"[18] Burgess, then, proposed an amended resolution without the extension of freedom clause that Lay found so offensive. The amended resolution was passed. On the morning of October 17, the service of thanksgiving was held at St. Luke's Church with a prayer that included this general wording: "thou hast healed our divisions and restored peace to our land and the fellowship of thy church."[19] The dissenting group of bishops and deputies, led by Charles P. McIlvane of Ohio, held a separate service in the evening of that day at the Church of Epiphany, with a prayer of thanksgiving for the restoration of "national authority, concord and peace throughout the land" and for the "deliverance of the land from involuntary servitude."[20]

Then came the mess regarding the pastoral letter. There was considerable political jockeying among bishops about who would be charged to write the pastoral letter. Hopkins indicated that he wanted nothing to do with the letter unless he was in charge. McIlvane of Ohio, however, had already written a draft pastoral letter, which he read aloud to the House. It included a eulogy for President

Lincoln and words declaring the end of slavery and a call for aid to those "who have been delivered from that yoke of bondage."[21] After McIlvane's reading of his draft letter, William Whittingham of Maryland moved not to accept his draft as the pastoral letter, and it passed. Horatio Potter of New York moved that there should be no pastoral letter, and the bishops agreed. Hopkins, then, stood to read his draft pastoral letter, which included an eloquent tribute to Alonzo Potter, Horatio Potter's predecessor and brother. Kemper moved to accept this letter, but it was defeated as the bishops had already voted not to send out a pastoral letter. No pastoral letter was sent out to the church, and it was just as well given the division among the bishops on this issue.

The reunion was accomplished. The southern bishops were pleased with the outcome, and the northern bishops breathed a sigh of relief. Bishops Lay and Atkinson sent a letter "To our brethren in the southern dioceses," encouraging them to join in the reunion with the northern bishops. In his letter to the southern bishops, Lay wrote that "they are content with the assurance that we render for conscience sake allegiance, honest and sincere, to the Government of the United States and will teach others so to do."[22] The letter is revealing of the fact that the reunion was achieved at the convention by not discussing the moral or political issue of slavery and by not requiring the southern bishops to address the issue at all. So long as they gave allegiance to the government of the United States, the ecclesiastical unity was simply a matter of fraternal vote. The principle that had led the southern dioceses to separate was the same that argued for their return— it was only a political separation, not an ecclesiastical schism, and the church ought not to meddle in the secular politics.

The unity of the church was, thus, preserved but not without dissent. Seven northern bishops wrote a statement of dissent on the thanksgiving service, which had downplayed the cause of the war and omitted any mention of the emancipation of slavery. Their statement is worth quoting here.

In the decision of the House of Bishops with reference to the Day of Thanksgiving for the restoration of peace and to other important subjects, the ground has been taken, that, for the sake of more complete conciliation, no sentiment should be expressed by this House, or this convention, or this Church, in any collective capacity, on subjects of such importance and so dear to all of us as the re-establishment of the National union and the emancipation of the slaves.

The House of Bishops unquestionably loved this country and its unity, and they could not approve the system of human bondage, but they will seem to have adopted as the position henceforth occupied by this Church, on which is consistent with indifference to the safety and unity of the Nation, and to the freedom of the oppressed.

This is a position which, as the undersigned believe, should not be maintained by any branch of the Christian Church in the United States, whether in the present or any future generation. To signify that it was not accepted by all on this occasion, and that those who did not accept it believed it to have been accepted at all, only because an extreme desire for conciliation and unanimity prevailed for the hour, the undersigned have prepared this document, with perfect and cordial respect for their brethren, but under the consciousness of a great duty to the inseparable interests of their beloved Church and Country.

Philadelphia, October 24, 1865

Charles P. McIlvane	Bishop of the Diocese of Ohio
Alfred Lee	Delaware
Manton Eastburn	Massachusetts
George Burgess	Maine
Henry W. Lee	Iowa
Gregory T. Bedell	Asst. Bishop of Ohio
Thomas H. Vail	Kansas[23]

I have belabored the above details of the 1865 General Convention to show how the system of the convention and The Episcopal Church at the time chose to put the unity of the church above all else, even at the cost of racial justice. Crisis can be an opportunity for change. But the system has tendency to resist change by adapting to ways to preserve the status quo. In preserving its unity, The Episcopal Church system managed to preserve the culture of racism and white supremacy in its DNA, which it had inherited from the prewar period. Underneath the thin surface of unity was a lingering sense of betrayal and unfinished business. In the following decade The Episcopal Church would see an exodus of African Americans from the church. According to Gardiner Shattuck, "thousands of African Americans abandoned their membership in The Episcopal

Church and other white-controlled denominations, while the African Methodist Episcopal Church, the African Methodist Episcopal Zion Church, and black Baptist churches experienced astounding growth."[24]

Unity does not always reflect communion, and this reunion fell very short from the perspective of the African Americans. Communion is foremost and fundamentally God's gift. Participation in this gift of grace requires a confession of sin and a resolve for amendment of life, neither of which took place regarding the sin of slavery by the bishops and the church at this convention. So long as the emancipation of slavery was swept under the rug and not celebrated; so long as the national sovereignty of the United States was not prescribed; and so long as the Southern Church was not held accountable for its part in the war, the unity achieved at the convention was but a thinly veiled gentlemanly fraternity and perpetuation of white supremacy. There was no resolution or prayer of unity in the House of Bishops before or after the closing service, and ill feelings lingered on as the bishops departed. This reunion was at best a hesitant beginning of a long journey ahead toward the true unity of the church. In the middle of this journey was Bishop Edward Demby.

Making Bricks without Straw: Demby's Episcopacy and Struggle for Racial Equality

All that he did or failed to do reflected on the black clergy of the Episcopal Church with repercussions for their future. Thus, he stayed for twenty-one years. He coped. He suffered. His destiny was to make a proverbial silk purse out of the sow's ear, and in many ways, he accomplished it. Like Christ whom he faithfully followed, Demby bore it all without complaint.[25]

With these words Bishop Herbert Thompson (Southern Ohio, 1992–2005) captures the essence of Bishop Demby's moral disposition and has given him the recognition he deserves in the history of The Episcopal Church. Whatever the personal cost he had to bear, Demby remained unwaveringly committed to his vision of racial integration and equality in The Episcopal Church. He saw racial integration, not segregation, as the way of guarding the unity of the church in the long run and thereby preserving the integrity of his own episcopate as a bishop of the whole church and not just of the segregated African American congregations. In the most critical moment and time, he helped to set The Episcopal Church on the right course in its journey toward racial justice, which the segregationists in the church—whites out of indifference or racist motives and Blacks for the expediency of gaining independence from white paternalistic control—were trying to bend backward.

Edward Thomas Demby V was born on February 13, 1869, in Wilmington, Delaware, serendipitously the same day as the Feast of Absalom Jones. His parents, Edward Thomas Demby IV and Mary E. Anderson, were freeborn African Americans who established themselves in the middle-class African American community in Philadelphia. Edward Demby Sr. had a Roman Catholic background and worked as a brick mason and a lay minister of some kind. Mary Anderson had a Protestant upbringing and worked as a housemaid. She instilled in their children the virtues of self-reliance, sacrifice, leading by example, and education, all of which Demby exemplified in his life. Michael Beary offers a thorough biographical background of Bishop Demby,[26] from which I would like to highlight a few important aspects.

In his memoir, Demby mentions his West Indian heritage on the maternal side without further details for verification. Beary observes an influx of West Indians to the United States, especially those aspiring to priesthood due to the racial politics in the West Indies. The Anglican Church in the West Indies remained solidly white on the clerical level while the laity was almost entirely Black. With the African American exodus after the Civil War, The Episcopal Church was faced with a severe shortage of Black clergy to minister and evangelize the African American population. It was an alarming trend, given the fact that "in the Colonial period and in the early days of the Republic the vast majority of Black Christians in America were Anglicans."[27] According to Harold Lewis, "scores of West Indian students came to the United States at the invitation of American bishops to study for ordination and serve black parishes both in the South and the North."[28] Lewis not only talks of West Indian Anglicans as missionaries to African American Episcopalians but also of their "high church" influence on African American liturgical culture.[29] Beary observes that "the number of black Episcopalians increased from approximately fifteen thousand at the turn of the century to about forty thousand by 1930, primarily due to West Indian immigration."[30] Although we cannot verify it with any detail, the West Indian lineage for Demby must have been a matter of some importance and pride.

Education seems to have been of utmost value and the highest goal for Demby. He was first tutored by his maternal uncle, Eddy Anderson, at his private school at Ezion Methodist Episcopal Church in Philadelphia. From his uncle's academy, Demby's educational journey took him to a series of elite Black academic institutions that included Howard Divinity School, Payne Theological Seminary in Wilberforce, Ohio, and National University (the University of Chicago). In the process he was ordained in the African Methodist Episcopal Church and was called to be the dean of Paul Quinn College in Waco, Texas, in 1894, at the age of twenty-five. During these years, he also supported his own education by tutoring, as his family did not have the means.

While at Paul Quinn College, Demby converted to The Episcopal Church. It is not clear when he became interested in The Episcopal Church. He was confirmed by Bishop John Spalding of the Diocese of Colorado, who became his mentor and friend. What inspired Demby's conversion to The Episcopal Church was the doctrine of apostolic succession and the Anglo-Catholic movement that was sweeping through the church at the time.[31] He held historical tradition in high regard as a validation of the church's orthodoxy and showed a high church inclination in the matters of worship. His emphasis on the historic apostolic succession and the catholic ecclesiological outlook formed a foundation for his deep commitment to the unity of the church and racial integration in his episcopal tenure.

One telling incident that testified to his high regard and determination for education occurred around his ordination examinations. White examiners regarded the Black ordinands as intellectually inferior and did not test them in certain areas of academic rigor. Demby insisted that he be tested in all areas like his white counterparts. He wanted to take the opportunity to disprove the notion of Black intellectual inferiority. He also reasoned that "should I ever be elected as a bishop in the church, it could not be said that I did not take a complete examination."[32] He scored in the ninetieth percentile in all areas of the examination, which amazed the examiners. Bishop Thomas Gailor of Tennessee duly ordained him to priesthood in 1899 with great fanfare at St. Paul's in Mason, where he had been serving as the deacon in charge since 1896.

After St. Paul's, Demby was called to a series of significant African American congregations—St. Augustine's in Kansas City, Missouri, St. Michael's in Cairo, Illinois, St. Peter's in Key West, Florida, and Emmanuel in Memphis, Tennessee. In all these churches, the education of African American children was central to his ministry, which led to building parochial schools and industrial schools everywhere he served. This is also the reflection of his high value of and personal commitment to education, and in every place his ministry was a big success. St. Peter's Key West under his charge grew to be the second largest African American Episcopal church, St. Philip's in Harlem being the largest. It was at Emmanuel Church, Memphis, however, where his priestly gifts and leadership skills bore the fruits of ministry that gained him the admiration even of his bishop and the white Episcopalians. He was also actively involved in elite fraternal societies and charitable enterprises in Memphis and, according to Beary, "was himself a drawing card" for many organizations.[33]

Influenced by the Anglo-Catholic tractarianism, publishing pamphlets was also the centerpiece of his ministry. At Paul Quinn College, he published a book under the aegis of the college, titled *A Bird's Eye View of Exegetical Studies: The Writings of St. Paul and St. James*. At St. Peter's Key West, he published several pamphlets—*My Companion: A Booklet on the Sacrament of Prayer and Penance*, *The Devotions of the Cross*, and *The United States and the Negro*, which was his speech on the anniversary of the emancipation, condemning Jim Crow. This pamphlet foreshadowed his later struggle for racial integration. At Emmanuel Church in Memphis, he continued to publish evangelistic teaching tracts, around which he created a society, called "The Guild of One More Soul."

During these years of ministry, Demby suffered several personal tragedies in his life. While serving in Tennessee, he married his first wife, Polly Alston-Sherill, who tragically died not long after the wedding. This prompted his move to Kansas City, where he met his second wife, Nettie Ricks, the only daughter of a prominent Black family in Cleveland, Ohio. In 1903, his father suddenly died while he was bedridden with illness himself. Unable to attend the funeral, he became depressed and grieved for a long time. The Dembys moved to Cairo, Illinois, a commercial river town with a large African American population. At Key West, they suffered the death of their first and only child, Thomas Benjamin Demby, two weeks after his birth. This was followed by another tragic event, the death of Nettie's mother. Meanwhile, two storms swept through Key West twice, and the church had to be rebuilt each time. In 1907, Demby became chronically ill, and the couple decided to move back to Tennessee for respite. But he was soon called to serve at Emmanuel Church in Memphis. While these tragedies took a personal toll on him, Demby endured the pain and persevered through each tragic event, coming out stronger for the next big thing. The success of Emmanuel Church led to his appointment as archdeacon for colored work in the Diocese of Tennessee, which would set the stage for his later election to the episcopate.

Demby's arrival in Memphis coincided with the growing sentiment for segregation in the Diocese of Tennessee. White Episcopalians in the diocese campaigned to remove Black representation from the diocesan convention. Jim Crow had gained a strong foothold in the country and the church, and segregation increasingly became the way of life. Beary observes that "by 1920, black congregations in the South were disenfranchised or organized into separate convocations with little or no representation in the diocesan level."[34]

One alarming effort for segregation in the church happened in 1883. Bishop William Green of Mississippi gathered his southern colleagues at Sewanee to discuss the status of the African American Episcopalians in the South. They proposed a resolution to the General Convention in 1883 that read, "In any Diocese containing a large number of persons of color, it shall be lawful for the Bishop and Missionary Convention of the same to constitute such population into a special Missionary Organization under the charge of the Bishop."[35] It came to be called the Sewanee Canon. While it sounded benign on paper, it was designed to allow the dioceses to legislate the segregation of African Americans and to keep the African American congregations under white control.

Alarmed by this, Black leaders, led by Alexander Crummell, organized themselves to defeat the resolution. This was the beginning of the Conference of Church Workers Among the Colored People (CCWACP), which later evolved into the Union of Black Episcopalians. At the convention, the Sewanee Canon was approved in the House of Bishops but defeated in the House of Deputies. It seems that white supremacy and the need to appease the southern bishops were still deeply entrenched in the systemic culture of the House of Bishops. In 1889, the CCWACP, led by George Bragg, called upon the convention to define the status of the African American Episcopalians. The convention sidestepped the issue of segregation in favor of leaving it to the dioceses to legislate their own policy.

In 1904, the CCWACP proposed the formation of an African American missionary district with its own bishop. This proposal actually had precedent in the 1874 General Convention. Faced with the declining ministry to African Americans, the Diocese of Texas broached the topic and proposed the election of a suffragan bishop "for supervision of freedmen." Bishop Wittingham of Maryland, then, proposed the creation of special missionary districts and bishops for colored work. A committee was commissioned to study the issue. In 1877, the committee reported that "it was inexpedient to take any action on providing bishops exclusively for different races and tongues."[36] The missionary district plan was defeated in 1904, just as it was in 1877.

When the CCWACP and its allies proposed the missionary district plan again in 1907, Bishop William Brown of Arkansas, a committed segregationist and racist, was determined to stop this as the plan included the election of an African American bishop in The Episcopal Church.[37] Arkansas had become segregated under his oversight. At the Arkansas convention in 1902, Brown proposed a canon to "constitute a Convocation of Afro-American Episcopalians and submit its actions to the Annual Convention of the diocese for review," with no seat or vote in the convention.[38] The Arkansas decision was not well received outside the diocese, and the CCWACP quickly censured the diocese. At this point, Brown made the smartest political move he could have made. Recommended by the CCWACP, he appointed George McGuire, Rector of St. Thomas, Philadelphia, as the archdeacon of the newly constituted Afro-American Convocation.

At the 1907 Convention, Brown made a plea for an autonomous "Negro Episcopal Church," essentially a separate African American denomination. The convention rejected Brown's proposal out of hand, and the missionary district plan also failed. However, the suffragan bishop plan was adopted in a less ambitious form. The new suffragan bishop, if elected by any diocese, was entitled to a seat in the House of Bishops with the right to the floor but no right to vote. Seeing the racist intentions of Brown, George McGuire left Arkansas for good and accepted a call to St. Bartholomew's, in Cambridge, Massachusetts. This put the kibosh on Brown's plan and ended his Arkansas experiment. In 1921, McGuire would leave The Episcopal Church altogether to found the African Orthodox Church and become its first bishop.

In the meantime, the debate over the suffragan plan raged on in the South. Brown declared that the new suffragan would be no more than a glorified archdeacon and continued to advocate for a separate Black denomination. George Bragg also disparaged the Black suffragan plan, calling it a "suffering bishop" or a "dummy bishop."[39] The white Episcopalians perceived the suffragan plan as an encroachment upon Jim Crow segregation and white supremacy; the Black Episcopalians perceived this plan as an extension of Black servility and dubbed the Black suffragan a "puppet bishop."[40]

In 1911, the Diocese of Arkansas entered a new chapter with the election of James Winchester to succeed William Brown. Winchester grew up on the family-owned plantation in Maryland, with many slaves working on the farm. He exemplified genteel white paternalism toward Blacks, which was characteristic of a southern aristocrat. He believed in Christianity's power to enhance race relations and promoted Black ministries when he deemed it appropriate and beneficial for everyone. George Bragg noted that Winchester was a friend to Black ministries.[41]

In 1914, Winchester appointed the Rev. Daniel E. Johnson as archdeacon for colored work in the Diocese of Arkansas. Johnson in many ways paved the way for the election of a Black suffragan bishop in Arkansas. He challenged white members of the diocese to spend more to support Black ministries, and with Winchester's blessing, made an appeal for a Black suffragan bishop. At the 1916 General Convention, the Black missionary district plan was proposed again by some southern bishops and was defeated again. Afterward, George Kinsolving of Texas conferred with Bragg and the CCWACP representatives on the idea that the suffragan plan needed to be attempted before any further legislative progress could be made for a missionary district plan. The CCWACP gave their grudging consent.

In early 1917, the bishops of the Southwest territories, led by Winchester of Arkansas, approached Edward Demby about the suffragan bishopric for the colored work in the Southwest. Demby declined the invitation. The optics of being recruited by white bishops without consultation with the national African American leaders and organizations would put him in an impossible situation. Winchester, then, nominated three other candidates—Hutchins Bishop of St. Philip's, Harlem, George Bragg of St. James, Baltimore, and James Russell of Southern Virginia. Russell and Demby were the two candidates chosen for the special election convention in December 1917. Demby was elected unanimously on the first ballot, and this time he accepted the call. North Carolina quickly followed suit with the election of Henry Beard Delaney as its suffragan bishop for colored work. Demby was consecrated on September 29, 1918, and Delaney on November 21.

Although two Black bishops had been previously elected—James Theodore Holly for Haiti in 1874 and Samuel David Ferguson for Liberia in 1885—the postbellum Episcopal Church was unable to elect Black bishops on American soil until the election of Demby and Delaney. Supporting the mission and evangelism in the overseas missionary districts of Liberia and Haiti had its origin in the American Colonization Society (ACS), which assisted the US government in setting up a colony in Africa for the freed former slaves. The growing number of free people of color made the slave owners anxious, and they welcomed the emigration and even the repatriation in some instances of the free Blacks to the West African colony. The culture of racism and white supremacy made it easier to elect Black bishops to support the overseas mission in Africa than the mission to African Americans on American soil.

Harold Lewis notes that Demby and Delaney were not the choice of "the Negro establishment" of the time, and they were regarded with skepticism by the Black churchmen, because they were found by the white establishment to be "safe candidates" who "remained in their place."[42] Lewis's observation, however, is revealing not so much of Demby and Delaney but of the culture of racism and white supremacy in The Episcopal Church at the time. While three more Black bishops were subsequently elected for Haiti and Liberia, four decades would pass before the third African American bishop would be elected in The Episcopal Church on American soil—namely, Bishop John Melville Burgess in the Diocese of Massachusetts. This led Lewis to aptly observe that "the black suffragan scheme began and ended with [Demby and Delaney]."[43]

In his first report to the Arkansas convention in 1919, the new suffragan bishop laid out the vision and the plan for his ministry, which included a church orphanage, a training school for Black missionary priests, a parochial school, and a church hospital, and put a price tag of $250,000 on the work. He then declared that "within a few years the work that we now have will be self-supporting," and went on to state that "a separate Colored American Episcopal Church in America. No, never! The Episcopal Church must remain one, and united, apostolic and catholic."[44] As naïve as his speech was, it showed the virtue of self-reliance and a deep commitment to racial integration. The early years of his ministry were more a question of survival than of success.

Demby himself would describe his episcopal ministry in the February 1928 issue of *Arkansas Churchmen* with these words:

> For the most part in Arkansas, I have been making bricks without straw, building single-handed with patience and faith with the belief that some liberty-loving churchmen concerned in the extension of the church among the colored people will ere long hear and respond to the Macedonian cry.[45]

This captured the sense of his work at its core. With the allusion to Exodus 5, Demby poignantly painted his episcopacy. For him it felt like slavery even six decades after the emancipation.[46] Not only was he given no housing and stipend for his episcopal ministry but also he had to raise his own funds for the ministry he was called to carry out. The reference to the Macedonian cry in Acts of the Apostles 16 was his own cry for help.

His salary was paid by subscriptions from various dioceses, which amounted to $3,000 in 1921 and $2,400 in 1922. He had to accept the fact that fund-raising had to be part of his work, although he was never at ease with it. To give his work a higher profile, he turned to publishing a pamphlet, called *The Mission of the Episcopal Church among the Negroes of the Diocese of Arkansas*. He drove home the point that the African Americans in the Southwest were in dire need of the mission and ministry of The Episcopal Church, which was no less important than the missionary work overseas, and he cried aloud his own Macedonian cry for help. Contributions began coming in with greater regularity. His speaking engagements doubled and quadrupled in the following years, which essentially became the source of income for his stipend and ministry. Beary summed up: "Demby was called to do a great deal with very meager resources and look good while doing it."[47]

In the meantime, the missionary district plan was put on the agenda of the General Conventions throughout the 1920s and 1930s.[48] And The Episcopal Church did what it does best—commissioning a committee to study the issue and report back. At each convention, the missionary district plan was reported to be a bad idea, and at each convention it was set aside for further study. Every time the missionary district plan was proposed, it was on some level a direct challenge to Demby's own ministry, putting him and his work under greater scrutiny. In the 1934 Convention, the challenge became more personal in nature. The committee reported that there was no consensus among the African American Episcopalians regarding the missionary district plan and questioned the idea of a Black bishop altogether, because there was "some limitation in the Negro which makes him ineffective in the episcopate."[49] It was a subtle attack on the only Black bishop at the time (Delaney had died in 1928). This overtly racist statement undermined Demby's credibility and made a cruel folly of his already challenging circumstance. With the stock market crash of 1929, the appropriated budget for his ministry fell from $9,800 in 1930 to $3,800 in 1936. His stipend fell from $3,000 to $1,800.

His greatest ecclesiastical challenge, however, came during the episcopal election debacle in Arkansas in the 1930s. Beary devotes more than two chapters to the messy election process in detail.[50] I will focus on the pain that Demby had to suffer in the process. With Bishop James Winchester's resignation in 1931, Edwin Saphore, the suffragan bishop at the time, effectively became the bishop-in-charge. The 1931 convention had a special significance for Demby and the Black clergy of the diocese as they constituted a quarter of the clergy vote. Because the episcopal election was the only time they were allowed to vote in Arkansas, the Black clergy held quite a lot of political clout. Saphore appointed Demby to read the Epistle in the convention Eucharist, which was a significant recognition of Demby. This special convention failed to elect a bishop and the second special convention was scheduled for May 1932 at St. Paul's Church in Newport.

Saphore again appointed Demby as the Epistle reader for the Eucharist. Since St. Paul's was a segregated congregation, the vestry of St. Paul's practically ordered their rector, the Rev. William Holt, to strike Demby's name from the list of those assisting in the Eucharist. Holt wrote a letter to Demby, which could only have infuriated him: "There is no objection to the [colored] convocation sitting in the church and voting, I hear, but there might be some feeling about the two races taking Holy Communion together. I have a beautiful chapel, which I use frequently, in the church crypt; would it be agreeable to you to celebrate for your people there? I will be present with you and assist you in the celebration."[51] Demby sent a rather convoluted reply of a polite "No," which was misconstrued by Holt and his party as an agreement. As the Eucharist was about to begin, Demby and the Black clergy quietly entered the main nave and were seated in the back pew. When the procession began, Holt and his party were alarmed by the imminent danger of an integrated communion but there was little they could do. After the white members had received communion, Saphore and Holt waited for the Black clergy to come up for communion. But they did not. So Saphore and Holt invited them up. Demby did not move and told the other Black clergy to stay put.

The election took place between two candidates, John Williamson, dean of Trinity Cathedral, and William Witsell, rector of Christ Church, Little Rock. Williamson was elected at the eleventh ballot. What unraveled from here on was ecclesiastical politics in one of its ugliest forms. The Black clergy had been humiliated and Demby had to rise to their defense. Urged by Bishop Capers of South Carolina, Demby composed a letter about the humiliating incident, questioning the integrity of the election convention altogether.[52] Was he being played by Capers? Or was this a calculated move on his part? More letters of accusations and rebuttals went back and forth among the players on both sides. On August 4, 1932, Tom Wood, the chair of the Executive Council of Arkansas and a member of Trinity Cathedral, read some of these correspondences to the cathedral congregation. Open conflict began. The Colored Convocation, which met at St. Philip's, Little Rock, passed a resolution in support of Bishop Demby: "We regard this act of Bishop Demby as an example of rare courage in the face of certain peculiar conditions existing in this section of our country."[53] The resolution was a subtle challenge to the culture of white supremacy that lay behind the incident. The convocation also wrote a letter of thanks to Bishop Capers for his support of Bishop Demby.

The *Arkansas Democrats* downplayed the race issue of the incident and reported that "persons who refused to be quoted have said that the objection to Dean Williamson's election was the result of dissatisfaction of supporters of certain other candidates."[54] The newspaper was really pointing the finger at Witsell. The genteel white paternalism disdained bringing attention to an African American, be it a bishop, and to the Black discontent with the racist status quo. The race issue was swept under the rug, and Witsell became the target. The controversy would be called the "Witsell Conspiracy." Demby was spared of being scapegoated for the debacle.

Not all African American clergy, however, supported Demby. Holt circulated a response, which contained a letter of the Rev. E. J. Lunon, the dean of AME seminary, Shorter College, in Little Rock, in which he weighed in with a personal criticism of Demby: "The effect of Bishop Demby's attitude is to perpetuate the old fallacy of the colored people seeking to mingle with the whites at the expense of their racial pride and self-respect. Bishop Demby would force his way among the whites."[55] Capers wrote a rebuttal, pointing out the fact that Holt had raised the color line by trying to arrange a separate service in the name of avoiding the color line and said that "[Dean Williamson's election] has created a disastrous division in the diocese and therefore his election should not be confirmed."[56] The issue now turned into one of race relations by both sides. This further undermined Demby as he was now seen as trying to bring down the Episcopal election on the grounds of racial discrimination. The controversy raged on with divisions on every side. Williamson's election was never confirmed, and the controversy would not be settled until April 1935, when the Arkansas convention elected Saphore as its bishop.

Saphore, however, had to retire in 1937 due to health issues. At the 1938 Arkansas convention in April, the election of a new bishop was once again deadlocked, this time between Williamson and the Rev. Arthur McKinstry from Texas. On the second day of the convention, Witsell convinced the two candidates to withdraw, and Edward Eckel of Oklahoma and Claude Sprouse of Kansas City were nominated. When Sprouse was elected on the fifth ballot, the convention immediately rose to sing the doxology. But Sprouse declined, putting a damper on their joy. Yet another special election had to be scheduled for June. Thankfully, at this special election Bland Mitchell was elected resoundingly on the first ballot. For his consecration in October 1938, he designated Bishop Demby as the Epistle reader. Demby wept at this gesture, for he had not had a role in the convention Eucharist since October 1931. Mitchell apparently said, "Bishop Demby, we are all brothers in Christ."[57] Demby was now ready to depart in peace. He retired in February 1939. Demby recalls the whole event with these words in his memoir:

> I was requested at one convention to take the Negro clergy and delegates in the basement of the church for their communion while the Caucasians would make theirs in the upper part of the church. I was

to be the celebrant assisted by the rector of the parish, and the acting bishop would be the celebrant in the main body of the church assisted by some of the Caucasian clergy. I refused to have anything to do with such doings, and then my hell on earth began, and to say I did not get scorched would be prevarication.[58]

The 1940 General Convention was the final battleground for the missionary district plan. Beary offers a pretty good account of this.[59] The bishops for the first time acknowledged the failure of segregation and the cost borne by the African American churches but were sharply divided on the remedial course of action. Coming into the convention, the missionary district plan had strong support from many bishops and the African American deputies. But Demby was unwavering in his principle that one does not segregate to integrate and that integration was the only acceptable theological solution. The legislation proposed to the General Convention would allow African American churches to secede from their dioceses, form a missionary district, and elect its own bishop. The proponents of this legislation pointed out how it could stimulate the growth of African American Episcopal churches, particularly in the South. On the day of the vote, Demby was asked to speak on this issue. This was the first time he had ever been allowed to speak in the House.

For twenty-two years I have been sitting in this House of Bishops, and this is the first time I have spoken; the problems brought before you have not been concerned, for the most part, with Negroes, but this matter does. If the request of the Fourth Province for a missionary district for Negroes is passed, it will be the greatest setback to our Negro work it has ever had. . . . We want Negro bishops, but as suffragans working as assistants of the diocesans, helpers of the diocesans.[60]

This speech turned the tide, consolidating those who might have been on the fence about the missionary district plan to get behind Demby. Beary aptly observes that "he, more than anyone else, ended the long campaign for the missionary district plan."[61] The 1940 General Convention was, in Beary's words, "the death knell of ecclesiastical segregation in the Episcopal Church," and began the process of desegregation of the diocesan conventions in the southern dioceses. The Diocese of South Carolina was the last diocese to integrate African

American delegates into its convention, in 1953. That same year Sewanee admitted its first African American seminarians, the last Episcopal seminary to do so. In an ironic way, the bricks without straw for which Demby labored all his life became the foundation for a new Episcopal Church, rising on the horizon.

In 1945, Demby was invited to confirm a large class of confirmands at the Church of the Ascension, a white Episcopal Church in Lakewood, an affluent suburb of Cleveland. He had been invited to give talks in the white churches or read the Epistle at the diocesan convention before. But this was the first time, I believe, the brown hands of an African American bishop were laid upon the heads of white children for confirmation in the history of The Episcopal Church. I wonder what went through his mind and what he was feeling at that moment. It must have taken all his strength to fight back the tears, for this was a monumental moment of affirmation not only of his work for racial integration and equality but also of his own episcopate. He was recognized and accepted by the people of this white congregation as a bishop of the whole church on that day. Communion is not a thing or a moment but a journey, an eternal journey of grace of which few are privileged to get momentary glimpses. All who were present in that confirmation service got a glimpse of this grace of communion that day.

Then, at the 1946 General Convention, the suffragan bishops were given the right to vote in the House of Bishops. This was the final moment of triumph for Demby, in his struggle for both racial equality and the integrity of his own episcopacy. He was now truly a bishop of the whole Episcopal Church. As a person of color in the House of Bishops, I am deeply aware of the fact that I stand on the shoulders of this unsung hero of the church.

After his wife, Nettie, died in early 1957, he breathed his last breath on October 14 of the same year. The virtues of self-reliance, sacrifice, leading by example, and education, which were instilled in him by his mother, served him well as he persevered in his lifelong struggle for racial integration and equality. Bishop Edward Demby is commemorated along with Bishop Henry Delaney on April 14 in *Holy Women, Holy Men*.

Loving God, we thank you for the ministries of Edward Thomas Demby and Henry Beard Delaney, bishops of your Church who, though limited by segregation, served faithfully to your honor and glory. Assist us, we pray, to break through the limitations of our own time, that we may minister in obedience to Jesus Christ; who with you and the Holy Spirit lives and reigns, one God, now and for ever. Amen.[62]

Conclusion

History is essentially an interpretive and meaning-making enterprise and is often told by the winners and the majority in power. If the stories and the perspectives of the oppressed are marginalized and silenced, such history cannot be meaningful to everyone, even to the majority in the long run, for the interpretation and the meaning of such history remain incomplete and shallow. If history is to be meaningful for everyone, the forgotten and untold history must be continually excavated, curated, and added to the history we already have. History, thus, is an ever-unfinished task; there is always a story that cries out to be told and be reckoned with. The story of Bishop Edward Thomas Demby is a story that needs to be told and be reckoned with, if we are to gain a fuller knowledge of the history of race relations in this church.

The history of race relations in The Episcopal Church, seen from the perspective of the episcopate, is fraught with decisions that might have been well intentioned at the time but are unpalatable in hindsight. White supremacy and the unity of the church were unfortunate ideological bedfellows at the 1865 General Convention and many instances since. Unity is important to what it means to be a church for sure. But it is often uncritically assumed and accepted as a guiding principle of the decision-making process in the life of the church. Not all unity reflects true communion, and not all unity leads to Beloved Community of Jesus. Christ crucified is not a therapy for Christian well-being but God's call to deep transformation and the living water for healing and new life. The church must risk being crucified for the resurrection of a new humanity of love, justice, and mercy. It is only by dying to injustice that we rise to justice, by dying to hatred that we rise to love, and by dying to pride and greed that we rise to mercy and compassion.

The COVID pandemic has exposed a syndemic of multiple crises, not the least of which is the crisis in race relations. More studies have been done, more books have been written, and more workshops and conversations have taken place online on this issue during these pandemic months than any other period in the past. Yet, liberation from the grip of the culture of white supremacy and systemic racism feels far from reality for African Americans and many other people of color. It even feels as though we have taken a few steps back since the civil rights movement. It has been exhausting and heartbreaking for me to witness the visceral outbreaks of racial violence against African Americans, Asians, and other people of color. I believe we are experiencing a collective trauma of sorts. The biggest challenge for the church in the days ahead, I believe, is the work of healing and repairing traumatized communities, particularly in race relations. Crucial to this work of healing and repairing is the leadership of the bishops, who embody the symbol of unity of the church. This is a heavy mantle to bear particularly at this moment in history. It is my hope that this small contribution may sow some seeds of contemplation for the ongoing work of healing and repairing broken race relations and traumatized communities.

CHAPTER 6

Women Leaders Enable Leadership by All

Katharine Jefferts Schori

The world has always had honored women leaders. Some led and oversaw large communities: Cleopatra and Hatshepsut in ancient Egypt; Nzinga Mbandi, the seventeenth-century queen of what is now Angola; several matrilineal/matriarchal indigenous tribes, including the Hopi and Haudenosaunee; and the recent tenure of Wilma Mankiller as principal chief of the Cherokee Nation (1985–1995). Biblical prophets like Huldah and Miriam, Esther and Vashti are remembered for their leadership, courage, and clarity. Shiphrah and Puah led "from below," subverting Pharaoh's genocidal plans with creative nonviolence. In eras of nearly exclusive male public leadership, women still found opportunities to bring greater justice to their communities, succoring the poor, weak, and dispossessed.

The world has also long repudiated, banished, and even executed women who moved "above their station." Think of the medieval "wise women," healers and herbalists like Hildegard of Bingen, some of whom were branded "evil" or "witches" for their trouble. Patriarchal systems have always found ways to keep women out of what is judged "male territory," territory marked with vitriol and violence. Men maintained command and control of their game, while many women are still expected to stay out of the public sphere, particularly as the world waits to see how the Taliban will govern.

Women's leadership in the church is not new. The first witnesses to the Resurrection were women, who spread the news to the wider community. There are multiple examples of women's ecclesial leadership in the early church, in the gospels as well as Acts of the Apostles. Female deacons were appointed to minister to and with women, just as male deacons were appointed to serve men;

wealthy women like Phoebe and Lydia supported local congregations; in spite of Paul's proscription,[1] women were speaking their good news aloud and were named apostles—for example, Mary Magdalene and Junia; and many were martyred for their open claim on the gospel. There is dispute (predictably) about a ninth-century Italian mosaic depicting Theodora Episcopa, who some scholars believe functioned as a bishop.[2] Significant archaeological finds indicate the liturgical leadership of women, including some showing pallia[3] worn by Mary, mother of Jesus, and her cousin Elizabeth.[4] Italian frescoes (late fifth or early sixth century) appear to show women as liturgical leaders and preachers, ostensibly bishops.

Women monastics (*ammas* or desert mothers—e.g., Amma Syncletica) led and guided groups of ascetics (both female and male) in the fourth and fifth centuries. Medieval abbesses were effectively ordained, at times clothed with miters and given crosiers, like some of their brother abbots.[5] There are multiple examples of mitered abbesses who exercised quasi-episcopal authority over not only the nuns in their charge but also the local clergy and laity,[6] continuing in some places into the nineteenth and early twentieth centuries.[7]

Double monasteries, with both male and female congregations, developed at least as early as the fourth century. They were forbidden by II Nicaea (787), but re-emerged in the twelfth century, particularly among Benedictines and Bridgettines. Columbanus (540–615) preferred abbesses as leaders of twin monasteries and encouraged the practice.

Brigid of Ireland (d. 524) founded a double monastery at Kildare, governed together by abbesses and abbot-bishops for generations, the abbess having oversight of all Ireland's monasteries. Scholars believe Brigid was ordained as a bishop, although some accounts ascribe it to an error by the ordaining bishop. Women's ecclesial oversight (*episcope*) and leadership continued to be robust in Ireland until the Synod of Kells-Mellifont forbade it in 1152.[8]

Women's monastic orders, and powerful abbesses, continued in Britain until the dissolution of the monasteries (1536–1541) under Henry VIII. Although expelled from their former properties, some, like the Benedictines at Nunnaminster, managed to live together in community until their remaining members died.[9]

A Roman Catholic academic theologian has summarized the evidence of women's ordination in the Middle Ages and concludes that yes, they clearly were ordained and functioned in their designated offices, even if later male clerics anachronistically denied the legitimacy of women's orders based on the male clerics' later theology and practice, rather than the women's own.[10]

The Emerging Anglican Communion

Women's leadership in the British-American colonial era, and far beyond the days of Revolution, was an essential part of the active lay ministry, which sustained and grew the Anglican and later Episcopal congregations. Clergy were rare visitors to most congregations, and laymen officially "governed" them. Women generated much of the churches' financial support, with widow's mites, quilt raffles, and church suppers.[11] Yet the world has often failed to recognize that even in communities segregated by gender, women develop and exercise leadership in their own sphere—as abbesses, mothers superior, deaconesses, female Church Army workers on the frontier, and The Episcopal Church Women. Without them The Episcopal Church would likely not exist today.

Women of color were the pioneers in presbyteral and episcopal ordination.[12] The first Anglican woman ordained priest, Florence Li Tim-Oi, served valiantly in Macao during World War II, but blowback across the communion led her to relinquish her license at war's end.[13] Barbara Harris, of blessed memory, was the first woman bishop in the Anglican Communion. Elected in 1988 and consecrated in early 1989, she was threatened with violence, reviled, ridiculed, and worse. "Blessed are you when people revile you and persecute you and utter all kinds of evil against you falsely on my account. Rejoice and be glad, for your reward is great in heaven, for in the same way they persecuted the prophets who were before you."[14]

In the decade after Bishop Harris's election, seven more women were added to The Episcopal Church's House of Bishops, as well as ninety men. During the first decade of the second millennium, seven women and eighty men were elected. From 2011 to 2015, five women and thirty-one men were added; from 2016 to 2020, twenty women and twenty-three men joined the House. As of September 2021, six women and no men have been elected as bishops this year. There has been significant impetus toward gender parity in this office, yet it has reached only 15 percent women among all living Episcopal bishops. Among active bishops, women now comprise 27 percent of the whole.

Varied Ecclesial Processes in the Worldwide Anglican Communion

Women have yet to be ordained to all three orders in a majority of the provinces of the Anglican Communion. Three provinces permit women to be ordained only as deacons; eleven provinces ordain women only as deacons and priests; and twenty permit women as deacons, priests, and bishops. Four provinces do not ordain women at all.[15] Today women bishops are functioning in twelve provinces;[16] eight more provinces permit them but have not yet consecrated a woman.[17]

The challenges seem to be centered in conservative cultural norms, sometimes masquerading as theological dicta and "tradition." Once ordination to the diaconate is permitted, it seems to take roughly thirty years before a province permits or ordains women as bishops.[18] When women have visible leadership roles in mixed-gender segments of society (including the church), the roadblocks begin to recede. Female judges, attorneys general, principals of educational institutions and business concerns, and political leaders begin to normalize the leadership of women in sacred contexts as well.

Some ecclesial contexts require more levels of consent to ordinations than others. A few provinces, like the Church of England, appoint bishops rather than electing them at the local diocesan level. The extraprovincial dioceses, like Cuba until its return to The Episcopal Church, may have less onerous processes for designating bishops. The Metropolitan Council, which oversaw Cuba from 1966 to 2020, was able to nominate two female bishop candidates to the Diocesan Synod, who affirmed their appointments in 2007[19] and 2010,[20] respectively. They were the first two women bishops in Latin America, and were joined by a woman bishop in Brazil in 2018.

The Church of England, after laborious and contentious debate, authorized the ordination of women bishops in 2015. Bishops in that province are appointed, rather than elected, and the Crown Appointments Commission quickly began to name women to episcopal posts at nearly the same rate as men.[21] That province also changed the manner in which bishops represented the nation in Parliament, decreeing that women would take each open post as Lords Spiritual[22] during the first decade of women's episcopacy.

In 2018 the wider Anglican Communion was surprised to discover that the archbishop of Juba (South Sudan) had quietly ordained a woman bishop in late

2016. The Rt. Rev. Elizabeth Awut Ngor is the assistant bishop of the Diocese of Rumbek.[23] South Sudan's lay church leaders are nearly 50 percent female, there are women clergy in nearly every diocese,[24] and women have been strong leaders in all areas of the Sudanese church throughout the long conflict between Sudan and South Sudan.

In contrast, provinces that have an electoral process for naming bishops have seen a much slower growth rate in women's inclusion. The Episcopal Church lamented the results for quite a few years before insisting that the selection process begin with anonymity. Names and identifying characteristics are now elided from initial selection materials in an attempt to reduce bias around gender, race, and other characteristics. That has had a remarkable effect and has produced a significant number of episcopal election slates that have been majority women or women only. This obviously represents a critical mass of experienced and well-qualified women priests.

Several models have emerged, both in The Episcopal Church and elsewhere, seeking to provide coaching, support, and networking for women discerning ministries in larger church contexts, such as deans of cathedrals, diocesan staffs, large-parish rectors, churchwide ministries, and bishops. The first one began under the leadership of June Osborne, then dean of Salisbury Cathedral in the Church of England (now the bishop of Llandaff, in Wales), seeking to equip English women clergy for larger spheres of leadership. Dean Osborne partnered with the Rt. Rev. Mary Gray-Reeves, then bishop of El Camino Real, to develop the empowering and equipping work in The Episcopal Church, in a program called "Beautiful Authority." The Rev. Helen Svoboda-Barber started WEEL (Women Embodying Executive Leadership) in a later and similar endeavor, and both have made major contributions to women's readiness for episcopal leadership, including women of color. This movement in general not only seeks to help women navigate the road to election as a bishop, but also specifically recognizes the necessary shifts in leadership models—generational, theological, practical, and contextual—that will serve God's people in the next quarter of the twenty-first century.

Diversity and Inclusion in The Episcopal Church

The Episcopal Church is broad and diverse, in spite of stale caricatures. Still largely a white church in the United States, the fastest-growing demographics are in the overseas dioceses,[25] and communities of color across the church. The church is increasingly committed to racial reconciliation and contextual evangelism. The gospel is universal, yet it is understood and experienced in incarnate persons and communities, each with differing gifts, wounds, laments, and vocations.

The increasing breadth and depth of nontraditional bishops (i.e., other than white, male, heterosexual, English dominant, university educated) mean the gospel is incarnated in far greater variety, and far more communicable to the diversity of humanity. Most people from nondominant populations[26] cannot become what they have not yet seen, imagined, or experienced. An example: a mother and young son who regularly attended a small, rural Episcopal church with a female priest went to a large metropolitan church for the first time. As the service began, the little boy exclaimed, "Mommy, mommy, can boys really be priests?!"[27]

The evangelical focus of the Lausanne Covenant[28] challenges the "whole church to take the whole gospel to the whole world," yet a richer and deeper understanding may be had when Christians seek to discover where the gospel is already at work in ways never before imagined. The living gospel is discovered anew as new members of the body of humanity and creation participate in giving thanks for God's creativity, using their gifts of curiosity and compassion, and loving what God has done, is doing, and will do long after we have returned to the dust.

The current expansion and diversification of the House of Bishops are not just about increasing numbers. The greatest salience of these shifts is the expansion and diversification of ministry—the ways in which neighbors are loved and served. Creative leadership is the spark, and its variety has much to do with varied origins, experiences, and social locations.

Current examples include TikTok ministry;[29] "Wild Church" in Northern Michigan;[30] refugee ministry;[31] neighborhood "little pantries" providing shelf-stable food and hygiene items—and/or books for all ages;[32] First Nations Kitchen,[33] an indigenous feeding ministry in Minneapolis; retiring the medical debt of neighbors;[34] HIV ministry in Honduras;[35] and solidarity with migrant workers in Saipan.[36]

The wider world should expect greater health and possibility when leaders have direct experience of their communities' hopes and suffering. That experience usually resides in a far greater demographic range than has been typical in this church. The Episcopal elections we've seen in the last decade bear testimony to the work of the Spirit in bringing gifts of experience, location, new life, and creativity to the gospel work at hand.

Since January 2010, this church has elected twenty-nine women as bishops, including seven Black women (one Haitian), one Asian American, one Latina, and twenty white; and fifty-seven men, including five Black (one Haitian), six Latino, one Asian, one Asian American, and forty-four white.[37] At least two LGBT bishops are included. This cohort is just reaching the level of roughly one-third women (and one-third of the women are women of color), which is the threshold at which systemic cultural norms begin to shift.[38] The House of Bishops as a whole is still well below that level, even among the group of active bishops. The male bishops elected in the last decade are only about one-quarter men of color. The rate of electing women and minority bishops began to significantly increase in 2016–2017, with four women (one Black) and thirteen men (six of color) elected in those two years.

Since January 2016 (up to September 2021), election rates have been essentially equal by gender, and are approaching the demographics of the United States,[39] with twenty-four women (nine of color, one LGBT) and twenty-five men elected (nine of color, one LGBT). Most of the women (eighteen; seven of them of color) were elected in 2020 and 2021.

Women bishops and bishops of color are represented at about the same rate as in the (US) business world.[40] Their representation is similar to that in the political sphere, at least in the United States, and it's clear that nondominant political leadership makes a significant difference to underserved populations.[41]

The Episcopal Church has not elected many disabled bishops, although a significant percentage has become disabled during their active ministries. Accommodations continue to be made in physical access to church spaces, in some contexts for vision and hearing challenges, and in access to sign-language interpretation and real-time translation services, yet there is a great deal more to do. Leaders who understand and experience these life conditions are an important gift to the whole community. Addiction can also be disabling, and the church and wider society have robustly benefited from the leadership of bishops in recovery.

Theological Realities

The body of Christ has many parts, each with gifts differing, and an essential part of the body's vocation is to image God. The variety of God's creation means no one individual or clan, sect, species, gender, or pride-filled dominance group can bear the fullness of the divine image. It takes the whole creation to begin to approach that fullness. Attempts by any one group or part to quash or quell the others are sinful limitation or repudiation of God's own delight in variety and possibility. We (creatures, human beings, Episcopalians) cannot grow and live into our vocation(s) without experiencing and delighting in what God has wrought. Humility (our humble origins in soil) and appropriate pride in the indwelling spirit within us enliven and evoke a creative tension. Dismantling the rigid systems of domination, precedence, and narrow privilege is essential to the holiness, healing, and wholeness of our communities, whether they are the House of Bishops or the local school board or the kindergarten playground. We are created to need one another—and when we begin to recognize the love of God for each and every one, we (individually and corporately) begin to reveal the image of God, as power-filled evangel.

The presence of women, people of color, and nondominant populations in leadership ministries brings gifts that aren't those of the "usual suspects" in the C-suite or at the boardroom table. People who have long had to function in the shadows learn essential skills for navigating and surviving systems of dominance—gifts like compromise, collaboration, subtle and creative diversion, and many others! Such gifts can begin to dismantle supremacy systems, like dethroning the playground bully. There's a wonderful story about a small boy who had been repeatedly threatened, robbed, and pummeled by a bully on the school bus. One day the smaller one blew his nose into his hand, walked up to the bully, and said, "I'd like to shake your hand." End of torment.[42]

Jesus taught his disciples creative and nonviolent ways to dethrone the proud and empower the oppressed. The charismata of healing and caring are often located in nondominant groups, who have had no other option. That is the core truth of Alcoholics Anonymous—those who know the traumas of addiction are the most helpful aids to healing. Who has often been culturally, historically, and biologically slotted to care for the weak? Who are the traditional caregivers of children, the poor, aged, and infirm? Who but women, women and men of color, immigrants, those who are themselves poor? Yet those carers and caregivers are imaging the God who became weak that we might be strengthened.

The expanded diversity in leadership this church is beginning to experience will change us all. Those skills learned in "weakness" are precisely what a proud community needs—the "soft skills" of recognizing and celebrating diverse gifts, of claiming the gifts in *all* the people, in liturgy that truly becomes the work of all the people. We might note that the Episcopal Preaching Foundation is training laypersons to preach, some fifty years after women had to cover their heads in church and were never permitted to read scripture or pass the chalice or share in congregational governance and oversight. Yet many of those excluded women exercised transformative ministry in feeding the hungry and forming young Christians and building relationships with people in overseas "mission fields."

Those "soft" skills are migrating toward new norms for effective ministry in community. Collaboration, inclusion, and diversity are expected and celebrated (albeit not yet by all). As women, and women of color, and LGBT people become more visible in leadership spaces, more of the *anawim* and the marginalized also begin to access those spaces—and the functioning of those systems continues to be transformed. Allies, partners, validators, and encouragers help to grow that presence—and prophets (gentle and not) continue the critical reconstruction of Beloved Community.

This kind of transformation is always partial. We will see women who operate like "good old boys," and we'll see old boys subverting the shifts, for brokenness is equal opportunity. Domineering ploys, infidelity, impostor syndrome, overfunctioning, self-promotion—each one of us has wounds to be healed, and gifts to be used, and opportunities to grow. We need all God's children to walk the way toward the Beloved Community. Shalom shall abound when

All God's creatures got a place in the choir . . .

sing(ing) a song of the hope the present has brought us . . .

. . . marching upward to Zion, the beautiful city of God![43]

CHAPTER 7

Women and the Episcopacy

Insights for Ecclesiology

Sheryl A. Kujawa-Holbrook

Women have been eligible for election to the episcopate since January 1, 1977, when the decision by the General Convention allowing them to be ordained to the priesthood and episcopate became effective. It was twelve years before Barbara C. Harris was ordained suffragan bishop of the Diocese of Massachusetts in 1989.[1] At the time of Harris's election, women in the episcopacy were a greater controversy across the Anglican Communion than ordination to the priesthood.[2] Thirty-three years is not a long time to assess the impact of women on the episcopacy and Episcopal ecclesiology. Sociologists and theological educators suggest that women's entry into the ordained ministry represents the most significant transformation in pastoral leadership in the twentieth century, if not since the Reformation.[3] As a denomination, we have formally "studied" women's ordination since 1919, informally since 1855, when the diocese of Maryland "set apart" the first two deaconesses.[4] "While it is less so now than in the past, the traditional male-oriented societal patterns, customs, and thought-forms are still dominant. Sexism runs very deep in our history and culture," stated the late Pamela P. Chinnis, the first woman president of the House of Deputies.[5]

Why Gender Still Matters

Gender matters because institutional sexism is at the core of social relationships, as well as ecclesial, political, and economic structures. In sociological terms gender is considered a fundamental structure of inequality. Restrictive gender roles hurt all people by limiting human potential. Throughout the history of The Episcopal Church women needed the structural support of male allies to effect institutional change. Historically, women were most recognized for impact in local communities, while the hierarchical culture of The Episcopal Church remained largely unchanged. Throughout the history of women's ministries an underlying bias dictated that it is women's role to serve, but not to exercise institutional authority through direct governance. This assumption was directly challenged by two recent phenomena. First, from 2006 to 2015 the two highest offices in The Episcopal Church, the president of the House of Deputies and the presiding bishop, were both held by women. Second, the current escalation in the numbers of women elected to the episcopacy. Recent research on women's ordination by scholar Valerie Bailey Fischer argues that women in senior leadership are *not* a modern phenomenon, especially when the authority of women in the early church and medieval abbesses is considered. Rather, the movements of the nineteenth and twentieth centuries were a "renewal" of ancient practice confirming that women governed ecclesial communities since the inception of Christianity.[6]

Though women bishops are visible throughout The Episcopal Church, and while record numbers of women are being elected to the episcopacy, the data suggests that gender equity is not the norm. Although recently ordained women bishops do not report the hostility experienced by the first generation of women bishops, they do report experiences of institutional sexism, racism, and homophobia. One historic thesis about ordained women is that the numbers are consistently rising, but the institutional impact is negligible, mostly because women are in lower- and midlevel positions. As record numbers of women are elected to the episcopacy, this thesis significantly changes. "Ultimately gender matters because diversity in all forms of ministry holds both a transformative potential not only to imagine one's vocation, but to question the assumptions that we and others make, and to struggle for a future where children and youth across a spectrum of gender, race, and other traits can develop and share their gifts for leadership naturally in a church that welcomes them," writes sociologist and leading scholar of women's ordination Paula Nesbitt, in a report for the Executive Council Committee on the Status of Women. "When we come to a time when this is our lived reality, gender shouldn't need to matter."[7]

Nesbitt contends that greater gender equity is an opportunity for transformation as leadership opens to the whole spectrum of social identities. The greater diversity in ministry, the less likely we are to limit our mission and vision. Greater diversity in ministry is an opportunity to expand the public voice of the church.[8] Nesbitt also makes a connection between greater diversity and institutional survival. Given predictions that by 2050 most mainline denominations will be extinct, she posits the question, "How much is the Episcopal Church worth keeping?" Nesbitt argues that if we want to survive for continuing generations, then leaders in the dominant church culture need to listen and respond to the needs of local communities and the world.[9] The marginalized, including women bishops, have relational and adaptive leadership skills to offer the evolving church.

There are various interpretations of the impact of women bishops. Some argue that growing numbers of women bishops force the church to be more egalitarian, while others are concerned that it will trigger a backlash. Some predict that the feminization of the clergy, now extended to the episcopacy, means that the office of bishop loses status. Others suggest that greater numbers of women in the episcopacy are a sign of demise; The Episcopal Church is dying, the money is all gone, so we might as well let women give it a go. Some feminist scholars, like Elisabeth Schüssler Fiorenza, argue that "women are church and have always been church" and we should be cautious about prioritizing ordination lest we perpetuate clericalism while accepting inequality in a patriarchal church. Women were the first witnesses to the resurrection, are most of the fully baptized members, and account for most churchgoers—so how could the church exist *without* women? There are also hopeful voices, including many Episcopal women bishops, who believe that despite the challenges of clericalism, the increasing numbers of women elected to the episcopacy are a sign of renewal that will ultimately transform the church.[10]

While many view an increasing number of women elected to the episcopacy as positive, though long overdue, evidence of institutional resistance is also apparent. Though the Diocese of Kansas became the first diocese to organize an Episcopal election with all women nominees in 2018, with the Diocese of Montana following in 2019, in the years since the election of Barbara C. Harris in 1988 there were many years when no women were elected at all—namely, 1990, 1991, 1994, 1995, 1999, 2000, 2004, 2008, and 2009. Valerie Bailey Fischer questions if the stagnation is a symptom of backlash, or at least ambivalence about electing a critical mass of women.[11] Women have been ordained in equal numbers as men since the early 1990s, yet this shift did not impact higher levels of church leadership until now, nor do the demographics reflect the overall membership of The Episcopal Church.[12]

Women Bishops by the Numbers

There is no single source for statistics related to women in the episcopacy in The Episcopal Church. How the number of women bishops is framed in relation to the entire House of Bishops, or as a subset of active bishops, determines the percentage of women overall. Alastair So-Schoos of the Church Pension Group reports that there are currently thirty (26 percent) women and eighty-five (74 percent) men who are considered active bishops in The Episcopal Church. Another nine (5 percent) women and 168 (95 percent) men are retired bishops. Between 2016 and 2020, eighteen (46 percent) women and twenty-one (54 percent) men were consecrated. So-Schoos comments that the recent trend indicates that more women are being ordained into the episcopate than in previous periods, and that greater numbers of male bishops are succeeded by women at the time of retirement. "In the coming decade, we will be able to see whether or not the trend in the last five years will hold."[13]

This trend is confirmed by Todd Ousley of the Office of Pastoral Development by tracking episcopal ordinations as well as nomination and election processes. He predicts that the numbers of women ordained to the episcopate from 2016 through (anticipated) 2021 are equal, and notably, that the final slates (committee and petition nominees) are 49 percent women and 51 percent men. "I posit that the balance on nominees is a sign that intentionality in the nomination process is paying dividends and that distribution is also representative of a shift in electing conventions which we have long suspected would be the last hurdle on diversity," says Ousley.[14] He believes that the shifting demographics of the House of Bishops are important beyond statistics. "This is an issue of doing the right thing, the just thing, and reflecting the fullness of the whole people of God. That's the deeper call."[15] In comparison, the Office of Pastoral Development reports that about 28 percent of all active bishops and bishop-elects are people of color, about 8 percent higher than the general population of the United States.[16]

Chilton Knudsen, one of the senior women in the House of Bishops, reports that there are forty-three women in the House of Bishops as of August 2021, counting recent elections (and not yet consecrated) in the dioceses of Chicago, South Carolina, Pittsburgh, and Iowa. This number represents almost one-third of active bishops, a tipping point for gender ratios. Obviously, forty-three women in the episcopate are a less significant percentage of the total House of Bishops, at about 14 percent when active and retired bishops (312) are counted together.[17]

Denominational data reports an ongoing gender gap in compensation and professional mobility for women clergy that is shrinking yet persistent. The 2019 Episcopal Clergy Compensation Report indicated that women comprise 40 percent of the clergy, with men comprising 60 percent, with an overall compensation gap of 13.5 percent. The same report indicates that while equal numbers of women and men serve as associates, assistants, curates, and in specialized ministries, the largest opportunity gaps are in the categories that relate most directly to the episcopacy: senior clergy (485 men and 154 women) and solo clergy (1,601 men and 953 women).[18]

Contextually, the trends related to gender equity in the United States are regressive and have an impact across institutions. For example, the Global Gender Gap Report 2021, published through the World Economic Forum and the United Nations, ranks the United States thirtieth on the gender equity index out of 156 countries in 2021, down from a ranking of twenty-third in 2020. The Global Gender Gap Index considers four factors in the rating: economic participation and opportunity, educational attainment, health and survival, and political empowerment. The data reveals the many contrasts experienced by women in the United States. Under the category of economic participation and opportunity, the United States ranks first among countries for the percentage of women in professional and technical fields, but sixty-fourth in wage equality. In educational attainment the United States ranks first in overall literacy and enrollments in secondary and tertiary education, but seventy-ninth in elementary education. In the health and survival category, the United States ranks first in terms of survival at birth, but ninety-ninth in overall life expectancy. Lastly, in terms of political empowerment, the United States ranks the highest for women in government positions but sixtieth in the number of women in the legislature.[19]

Though not focused directly on gender equity in the church, the data suggests that The Episcopal Church operates within a national context where women and girls face ongoing injustice, discrimination, and violence. Although the United Nations declared gender equality a basic human right foundational to a peaceful and sustainable world, and while some progress has been achieved, women continue to be underrepresented in all levels of leadership. Importantly, the United Nations reports that what progress has been made could easily be reversed by the effects of the COVID-19 pandemic, as women bear a disproportional share of the negative impact of the virus in all categories.[20]

Systems of Support and Potential Backlash

The shift in the numbers of women in the episcopate did not occur without direct systemic intervention. Mary Gray-Reeves, the former bishop of the Diocese of El Camino Real, and the current managing director of the College for Bishops, along with other senior women clergy developed Beautiful Authority in 2011 for networking and formation. The program was founded, in part, because young women clergy were confronted with many of the same issues experienced by the first generation of women clergy, an indication that The Episcopal Church had not significantly shifted in attitudes since ordination became a reality.[21]

At the same time Helen Svoboda-Barber, rector of St. Luke's, Durham, and a professional coach, and the late Steffani Schatz, canon to the ordinary of the Diocese of California, started the Facebook networking group "Breaking the Episcopal Glass Ceiling" for women clergy. Svoboda-Barber continued the work by creating Women Embodying Executive Leadership (WEEL), a program offering networking support and group discernment for women called to the episcopate or another form of senior leadership. Participants from WEEL actively encourage others to consider senior leadership roles and participation on standing committees and bishop search committees. Svoboda-Barber encourages diocesan search committees to gain expertise in antibias practices early in their decision-making processes. She is also an organizer of Leading Women, a joint initiative of The Episcopal Church and the Anglican Church of Canada for women discerning a call to senior leadership. "I am thrilled with the diversity, not just gender, but also people of color and LGBTQ folks," said Svoboda-Barber in 2019. "It's not that women are better than men, but we [The Episcopal Church] will be much better when our House of Bishops is more diversified."[22]

Paula Nesbitt cautions us about potential backlash once the number of women bishops reaches a tipping point of 30–33 percent, the same percentage of active women bishops compared to the number of active male bishops currently in the House of Bishops. (If we count all bishops, active and retired, the tipping point has not yet been reached.) At this critical juncture the number of active women bishops in the House of Bishops is large enough to transcend tokenism and to have sufficient power to impact institutional change. Nesbitt argues that this level of equitable power sharing is more likely to incite hostile backlash than any other gender-conscious goal or practice.[23]

For example, Nesbitt points to the late 1980s as a period in Episcopal Church history when backlash against gender equity revealed anxieties over changes in traditional church culture. "A series of accommodating changes that overwhelmingly affected female clergy, such as conscience clauses, flying bishops and alternative pastoral care arrangements, and prohibitions in some dioceses about interims being called as rector, served to limit women's opportunity and authority even though their competency in the priesthood and then the episcopate was both demonstrated and officially accepted."[24] Similarly, Nesbitt adds that resolutions devised to limit the number of suffragans in dioceses, as well as their voice and vote, are examples of backlash targeted at women bishops. In the late 1980s anxieties about institutional scarcity triggered concerns about the feminization of the clergy, resulting in growing nostalgia about the male priesthood. In some dioceses women felt pressured to consider the vocational diaconate, or obtained staff and part-time positions, while men ordained to the priesthood were moved into rectorships more quickly than their predecessors.[25] Then as now, women clergy were increasingly visible during a time when resources and membership were diminishing.

Nesbitt's research reveals that backlash against women clergy takes various forms, including direct attacks on women's ordination, devaluation of women's credentials, job segregation by gender, the isolation of token women to limit their ability to enact lasting change, and strategic deployment of traditionalist women to dilute progressive commitments to social change.[26] Nesbitt warns that as more women bishops are elected an "iconization process" could begin to have an impact. Through iconization senior women leaders are set apart and held to a higher standard than male counterparts. When women become visible in senior positions in organizations it can appear on a superficial level that the stained-glass ceiling is shattered, and then it becomes even more difficult to address persistent inequalities at other levels of the organization. For example, it took deliberate intervention within The Episcopal Church for nearly a decade to elect the first woman bishop, even with the support of progressive male leadership.[27] Research in women's leadership indicates that without institutional initiatives focused on monitoring gender equity, individuals alone cannot overcome the structural resistance of the patriarchal status quo.[28]

Nesbitt is currently revisiting her earlier research in relation to the current trends and suggests that while some men may participate in additional backlash now, the tipping point has been achieved, and others are less likely to support overt backlash if "steps are taken to minimize this prospect."[29] Herein lies a challenge for the current House of Bishops during a period of increasing visibility of women bishops.

The Importance of Intersectionality

Gender is *always* an issue, yet it is not always *the only* issue for every bishop who identifies as female in every given context.[30] As Barbara C. Harris stated in a now-legendary speech to the Episcopal Women's Caucus in 2000, the church is a "strange land" where despite so-called progress, people of color, women, and lesbian and gay people continue to struggle to claim a place.[31] Harris's statement addresses not only the ongoing marginalization of people of color, women, and LGBTQI persons but also the intersectional realities of social identities. Gender does not stand alone but is part of the complex and interconnected identities of each individual person. As a framework, intersectionality provides a lens that reveals a deeper understanding of how social power fluctuates between multiple identities and locations, shaping individuals and whole communities.

The term "intersectionality" became prominent thirty years ago through the work of legal scholar Kimberlé Crenshaw as she explained the overlapping identities of Black women (race and gender) within institutions. Crenshaw did not claim to originate the concept, but rather traced the occurrence of overlapping identities within earlier Black feminist thought by writers like Episcopal educator Anna Julia Haywood Cooper (1858–1964). Rather than analyzing the episcopate from a single-axis view, an intersectional perspective recognizes that multiple identities are inextricably linked to religious identities. Intersectionality presumes that each person experiences (consciously or unconsciously) social power differently based on their gender, race, sexual identity, social class, ability, nationality, age, language, immigrations status, and other forms of social difference.[32]

The experience of women bishops is gendered, and for some, race, sexual identity, and other social identity markers are equally or more integral to their perspectives on ministry and the church. On a practical level, intersectional theory means that instead of viewing the episcopacy as an order that transcends the body, or favors white male bodies as the norm, it should instead reflect embodied experience across human communities to create a more hospitable church. "Especially now, as we reckon with the crisis of racial justice in our country and our campus," said Gay Clark Jennings, president of the House of Deputies, at the Women's Lecture at Sewanee, "we must understand that the promise of female leadership in the church will only be realized when we commit completely to dismantling racism, misogyny, homophobia, and all of the interlocking oppressions that are antithetical to gospel work."[33]

Jennings is concerned that as the number of women bishops grows, the church may believe that the struggle for gender equality is finished, while failing to address the injustices that so many women, gender-nonconforming people, and especially people of color face in our congregations and communities. "If we envision our goal to be the equality of ordained women in The Episcopal Church, or if we measure our progress solely by the number of female bishops, we are failing to understand the magnitude of the work to which God calls us."[34]

Jennings points to the systemic racism evident in The Episcopal Church's support of the women's movement. All the Philadelphia Eleven were white, as were all but one of the first twenty-nine women elected to the House of Deputies. However, Jennings states, women of color were essential to the women's movement in The Episcopal Church, though often not recognized or applauded. Sister Margaret Two Bulls Hawk was one of the first women in the House of Deputies in 1970, followed by at least eleven women of color in 1973. "Women of color have long been trailblazers, leaders, and decision-makers in our church's justice work, and we must honor their legacy today by making our work truly anti-racist and intersectional. Otherwise, what we are pursuing is not actually justice, and it is certainly not gospel work."[35]

Theologian Westina Matthews's important new book, *This Band of Sisterhood: Black Women Bishops on Race, Faith and the Church*, is integral to any discussion of women and the episcopacy in The Episcopal Church. It details in depth the stories of discernment and experience in ministry of five African American women bishops: Jennifer Baskerville-Burrows, Carlye J. Hughes, Kimberly Lucas, Shannon MacVean-Brown, and Phoebe A. Roaf. "The process of accepting them and their power will be one of the greatest challenges that each of these dioceses face," writes Matthews. "It continues to be easier for whites to romanticize racial equality than to live into the reality of it. The call to The Episcopal Church in this present moment is to stand taller and to listen more carefully to the call to be what God wants it to be. . . . The Church's most important task is sharing the message that freedom is necessary and the way to find it."[36]

This Band of Sisterhood was woven through conversations between African American women bishops within the context of the devastating challenges of 2020—racial injustice, the COVID-19 pandemic, economic crisis, and political partisanship. One of the noteworthy characteristics of these reflections is the palpable sense of hope despite the horrific challenges that face our communities. Researchers in leadership studies developed the term "positive marginality" to refer to situations where marginalization becomes a space of radical possibility for leaders that subverts structural oppression and transforms the organizations in which they work. "I think there is something special about this time because as Black Women, we've experienced so much," says Shannon MacVean-Brown, bishop of the Diocese of Vermont. "And we still find hope. We're still hopeful people."[37]

All five African American woman bishops resonated with the need for deeper formation across the church. "It seems to me that this crisis has further demonstrated the lack of discipleship, and the need for transformed hearts," said Phoebe Roaf, bishop of the Diocese of West Tennessee. "There are a lot of good, faithful people who have been coming to church for forty years to check a box. . . . Then they begin to think about what they are going to wear to church the next day, rather than to think about the radical nature of Jesus' invitation into new life."[38]

Jennifer Baskerville-Burrows, bishop of the Diocese of Indianapolis, argues that taking discipleship seriously is critical, even if it means that some leave the church. "But I also think the core will be strengthened," she says. "And hopefully, those who are really drawn to Christ and his word and those who want to shape the entirety of their lives around the Good News will grow."[39] Kimberly Lucas, bishop of the Diocese of Colorado, concurs that while we say the Baptismal Covenant, living it is a different matter. "What we've been called to do is to live into this kingdom that we've been given a vision and a foretaste of. . . . And I think that piece is becoming a very visible gaping hole in our ecclesiology and archeology."[40] Carlye J. Hughes, bishop of the Diocese of Newark, believes the challenges of our time are an opportunity for the church to create new ways of being together: "I think converted people who learn how to be fully actualized in their faith can unite with other people to actually do something and change something by their very presence."[41]

In the recent edition of *Race Matters*, philosopher and activist Cornel West writes on the importance of "love warriors" today who have the courage to live with integrity, honesty, dignity, and generosity. Rather than talk about hope, West urges us to *be* hope. "Being a hope means forging moral and spiritual fortitude, putting on intellectual armor, and being willing to live and die for the empowerment of the wretched of the earth."[42] West argues that both behaviors and structures must change if social change is to be effected. This means that we not only need to change church structures to support greater equality, but we must also change the way people think and act. While growth in number and diversity of women in the episcopacy is an opportunity to transform church structures to allow for a more equitable church, deep change will not occur without challenging cultural assumptions that limit human potential and create barriers in relationships.

The Stories of Women Bishops

Integral to research on women bishops in The Episcopal Church are the unique stories of each person. Jewish philosopher Martin Buber believed that telling and hearing stories are sacred action. How does God form women bishops, nurture them, and facilitate change through them? How can these stories inform our future ecclesiology?

The stories of women bishops resonate with what researchers in leadership report—namely, that while women have assumed top leadership positions, they continue to navigate different societal and organizational expectations than their male counterparts. The gender gap widens for women of color. Research also finds that besides women's self-identity as leaders, the organizational context, in this case The Episcopal Church, is a critical factor in either supporting institutional sexism and racism (and other forms of oppression) or disrupting gender bias in leadership roles.[43]

To elicit the stories of both active and retired women bishops in The Episcopal Church, a ten-question questionnaire was distributed to all those listed in the House of Bishops directory in January 2021. An effort was also made to include women elected between January and May 2021. Responses were received until June 2021; about half the respondents chose to return written comments, while the other half opted to participate in Zoom interviews. All respondents were promised confidentiality. Respondents were encouraged to answer those questions about topics where they had the most energy and to pass on those they did not want to answer. Participation included twenty-two women bishops in The Episcopal Church, representing over half of those active and retired as of January 2021. In addition to Episcopal women bishops, data was submitted by an additional eighteen senior women leaders, including women bishops in the Anglican Church of Canada and the Evangelical Lutheran Church in America (ELCA), and others who have ministries closely aligned with women bishops and the House of Bishops. Overall, the experience of the women bishops who responded is marked by the vibrancy of their commitment, authenticity, and passion. The total years of experience in the episcopacy varied from those elected during the first decade of women bishops to self-described "COVID bishops," or those elected and/or ordained during the pandemic.

When asked about their discernment regarding nomination to the episcopacy and sources of support and resistance, the stories suggest consistent trends. There are generational differences between women who belong to the first cohort of women bishops, and those more recently ordained in terms of support structures and experience of resistance. Many of the first generation of women bishops report that they went into the nomination process, sometimes in multiple elections, either to test the process or because they were interested but *certain* they would not be elected! Some nominated themselves. Here there was a concern that to be elected to the episcopacy, candidates needed to have ascended a specific career ladder, including experience as a rector in progressively larger churches, diocesan and/or national leadership, and media exposure. In the first generation it was more difficult for clergy women to translate their credentials in ways that aligned with the expectations of search committees; many of the required credentials were open to women only by limited access. Interestingly, women nominated and elected in more recent years report a more intentional and corporate discernment process. Others saw in them the gifts needed and encouraged or pursued them in the nomination process. Most participated in intentional mentoring, either through an existing program or by seeking out a mentor. The work done by search committees to increase awareness of unconscious bias was commended. As one respondent noted, it is no accident that more Black women are being elected bishop. "It is the calling, encouraging, coaching [of] Black women to enter these discernments that is making the difference."[44]

The responses also suggest that for women bishops the call to the episcopacy is rooted in a particular time and place. While past data shows that clergywomen are more likely to be in congregations with political and theological views different than their own, the discernment process of women bishops shows intentional movement away from this trend and a focus on "fit."[45] The diocesan profile, clarity on what was needed in a bishop, and the availability of personal and professional support systems in the area were integral to the women before they entered the process. Some dioceses were openly seeking a woman, yet the intentional matching of gifts and skills remained of primary importance. Overall, there is a consensus about the need to nurture all sorts of qualified candidates or the church will lose candidates who have a great deal to offer. "We do need to remember that the aim is for mutual flourishing where the discernment for Episcopal leadership is not first a gender question but is first the needs of the diocese and the gifts of the candidates," writes one respondent.[46]

Generational differences are also evident in experiences of resistance and support; women bishops ordained the longest, when women's ordination was an open issue, are more likely to share stories of overt resistance and trauma than the recently ordained. "My experience of the church has been broadly supportive, so much so that when I read *New Wine* I was shocked at how badly early women leaders were treated (if I had been aware of that in my youth, I might have not remained Episcopalian)," writes one respondent.[47] Though the first generation of women bishops survived significant hostility and resistance, generational trauma is systemic, and the impact continues in institutionalized sexism. One respondent noted that her first career was male dominated, and then she entered the church and ended up in the House of Bishops, "Where there were male bishops who wouldn't speak to me either. I have found that there were usually male allies around who were sympathetic, but I don't think I ever saw one confront a bad actor."[48] Most of the first generation of women bishops frankly discussed that they are challenged in ways not experienced by male bishops. "I often say that a white male priest/bishop arrives and is trusted until proven otherwise. When a woman arrives, people question everything and doubt her competency. Women have to earn the trust."[49]

Recently ordained women bishops are to varying degrees aware of the struggles of their predecessors, and report that the resistance they experience is often expressed more indirectly through microaggressions, such as comments on their appearance, "mansplaining" the prayer book or the canons, or expressing disbelief when the answer is "no." As is the case in other organizations, women of color report more direct challenges to their authority than do white women bishops, especially when they need to make someone accountable for their racism. Here it is also noted that while white colleagues are sympathetic, there are not many examples of white confrontation of white racism.

Reports on the degree of support that women bishops experience in the House of Bishops vary. All commented that they believed the intent of the House of Bishops is to be welcoming to all. Those women bishops who have longitudinal experience report that conditions have improved. Some of the factors supportive of the first women bishops included gradual respect for women's ordination and supportive male bishops who offered authentic friendship. Process interventions, such as the use of round tables and the Indaba process, equalized participation to a degree. The election of Katharine Jefferts Schori as presiding bishop in 2006 helped to shift the culture of the House of Bishops, as did the creation of the Church Pension Group's CREDO conferences for bishops.[50]

Women more recently elected report the significance of retreats for women bishops, as well as the efficacy of direct mentoring and leadership programs focused on senior women clergy. Several women bishops commented that the House of Bishops is the whitest and most male environment they have ever experienced. While the intent of the House of Bishops is to be welcoming, all who responded to the survey noted signs of cultural ambivalence toward women bishops below the surface. For example, assumptions that new bishops should not speak publicly until they have attended a certain number of meetings; when men are addressed as "bishop" and women by first names; patterns around recognition for work that is honored; patterns related to whose verbal contributions are heard and the need to restate a point several times; patterns related to who gets the most airtime; priority in committee assignments; episodic competitiveness and one-upmanship—all reveal bias. Some respondents state that they do not fully express themselves in the House of Bishops out of fear that confidentiality will be broken, or that they will become the target of gossip. Several respondents mentioned that with more women in the House of Bishops there is less of a tendency to ask women in table groups to speak for *all* women (over half of humanity). One respondent wondered, if men are ever the numerical minority, will they feel the need to caucus? "A real sign of coming of age is when we all don't have to think alike just because we are women. I think the whole House is getting better but has a way to go. Otherness of thought is still a challenge," writes one respondent.[51] Another respondent voices a related concern, "that we [the House of Bishops] fail to hold each other accountable."[52]

All the women bishops who reported cite the importance of both formal and informal support networks, including family, friends, staff, other bishops, a disciplined spiritual life, spiritual directors, and companion animals. Specific needs that were identified include a greater awareness of the needs of women bishops with school-age children, as well as of single bishops. Church Pension Group data identifies that for female clergy, family dynamics are both a source of constraint and a contribution to wellness. The challenges of balancing work and vocation in two-career households and the often unspoken added expectations on women in families, along with the demands placed on clergy families, particularly when children are in the home, are significant potential stressors for all clergywomen.[53] In addition to support from family and friends, women bishops prioritized the need for ongoing support from the diocese, from the time of nomination through the episcopate. Others voiced a need for access to the Church Center staff. Cognizant of reports that rising numbers of women bishops have diminished the status of the episcopacy, most respondents reported that status was not a primary motivator in their call. Ministry infused with meaning and purpose, along with a sense of call to their diocese, was overwhelmingly the primary motivation.

The stories from Episcopal women bishops suggest that they have a corporate vision of the episcopate; the episcopate goes beyond the ministry of an individual. It is a shared ministry where all are called to offer their gifts and skills to extend care to a diocese. While the office of bishop is a deeply pastoral ministry, it is also a systemic ministry. Women bishops have an awareness that they bring all of who they are to the episcopate. The symbols (images, texts) that guide women bishops in their ministries vary widely. The commonalities and diversities related to images of the episcopacy reflect both ancient roots and the contemporary life experiences of women bishops. Several of the respondents cite the importance of the images evoked in the examination for the ordination of a bishop.[54] Others offer guiding images that are scripture texts, such as the woman with the alabaster jar, 1 Timothy 4, the good shepherd, and the Hebrew midwives in Exodus. Other respondents focus on functional images, such as "bishop as coach" or "bishop as artist." The symbolism of the cross is the guiding image for several women bishops. Several others speak to a sense of the interconnectedness of all creation as their guiding image.

For many of the respondents, it is impossible to reflect on gender without considering their intersectional identities. "Having an increase of bishops of color has brought much needed changes," states one respondent.[55] Respondents report different levels of marginalization due to gender. Some are keenly aware of gender biases and some not strongly focused there, or as one respondent notes, "Some of my character traits—especially the weak ones—were as much a detriment as my gender. Having said that, if I were a man, I'm quite sure that some of these traits would have been seen as positive strengths."[56] Women bishops of color report that it is not possible or even helpful for them to disconnect the complex interactions between race and gender. Two of the white respondents offered the reflection that as white women they utilize their racial privilege to help open doors for people of color. "As white women we can open the way and make some space for diversity that was not there before."[57] In addition to gender, race, and sexual identity, the category of marginalization most referenced by women bishops is age, and the impact of being younger or older in a particular context. The degree of social privilege a person has impacts the level of awareness that women bishops have in terms of experiencing their own marginalization. For example, a few respondents state that gender was not a primary identity for them or struggled with the idea that the episcopacy might be different because of their gender, and yet they detail challenges attributable to institutionalized sexism in their stories.

Most of the women respondents succeeded men, and thus are in some way a "first" for their diocese. Several state that they were a "first" throughout their ministries, and thus the episcopacy was not a new experience in this regard. Some are tired of hearing about firsts at all. Others are cautious about potential tokenism. Still others state that women's leadership was visible in their diocese for a generation, so while they are the first woman bishop, people know enough other women clergy to not make it a big deal. Others state that within their diocese there is not a majority culture that accepts women clergy, so a woman bishop needs to pave the way for others. Overall, the respondents see that their role as a bishop is to enhance the ministry of the whole diocese. Lastly, several of the respondents confirm how much they gained from the mentoring of the "first"—Barbara C. Harris, who died on March 13, 2020. Her passing marks a significant milestone. Her ministry is an example of a "first" who with grace and tenacity, despite years of opposition, demonstrated a significant systemic impact in her ministry.

All the respondents agree that they are called to lead in an era requiring great systemic change. The recent surge of white supremacy and other forms of resistance intended to reset the currents of change need to be confronted, and the church and its leadership need to be realigned to respond. The eradication of patriarchy will take the cooperation of women and men working together toward a new vision rooted in justice and equality. "The acceleration of women's elections has something to do with the diminution of patriarchal power, and also the yearning of many women to claim their own creation in the image of God."[58] The gifts of women bishops can be found within marginalization due to gender, race, sexual identity, and other social identities. "Anything that disrupts patriarchal principles of power opens a window into the liberation movement of the dream of God," writes one respondent.[59] The hope is that a wider and more diverse episcopacy will allow for more diverse approaches, collaboration, and leadership styles. A much broader and deeper pool of gifts is needed in episcopal leadership today to confront the destructive forces at work.

During the historical debates about the viability of women in the episcopacy, Episcopal patristic scholar Rebecca Lyman affirmed that they "represent a retrieval of ancient apostolicity of women as bearers of the gospel," and thus represent continuity with our Christian past into the future.[60] Congruent with this interpretation, Episcopal women bishops have an expansive definition of apostolic authority. A vocation to apostolic service is interrelated with the ministries of all Christians who share in the authority of Baptism.[61] "For me apostolicity is the gift of the deposit of faith entrusted to be shared in our context always in dialogue with the scriptures—the record of the first apostles—and with current experience."[62] Most of the respondents refer to episcopal authority as "a gift to be given away" and a source of blessing and generativity.[63]

> Episcopal authority is ultimately about stewarding the ministry to which one is ordained, on behalf of the Christian community that a bishop inherits, the community that one is called to lead, and the emerging, transforming community that is always emerging. Some bishops lean heavily on particular elements of the received tradition; others attend to emerging needs in community. Both ends of the spectrum are necessary for ongoing life and health yet can become an idol rather than an icon. Something almost always has to die, to be released before new life can emerge.[64]

For many respondents, the metaphor for apostolic authority is the body of Christ. "Do we look like our people? Do we reflect the diversity of God's creation? If the church wants to follow Jesus we need to represent the body of Christ."[65] Here the image of apostolic authority is less about hierarchy than it is about shared empowerment, and a willingness to speak the truth to abusive power. "How can women make a difference? By focusing on the ways that our experiences as women give us insight, perspective, empathy, and strength in new ways to a different kind of future," writes one respondent.[66] Another sees episcopal authority as relational and communal. "To me 'guard the faith' means to create as much safe space for as many people as possible," writes one respondent.[67]

Given the high level of commitment among women bishops, all agree that the ministry is extremely challenging. Half of the respondents reported that their most challenging work is clergy discipline, human resources, congregational dysfunction, or other examples of the abuse of power. Another consistent issue is the dismantling of white supremacy, the impact of which is experienced disproportionately by people of color, and which needs to be at the forefront of the church's mission. Efforts at diminishing the authority of women bishops are both draining and counterproductive. Women bishops of color report how they experience undermining behaviors from both white women and white men. Another common challenge mentioned throughout the data is the spiritual hunger of people in congregations.

Gender and Ecclesiology

Gender is integral to how the Christian church is described, organized, and practiced. Gender in the church and feminist and womanist ecclesiologies are themes related to women and the episcopacy.[68] Within theological discourse, gender in the church is inclusive of those who identify as female, members of the LGBTQI community, and others who are limited by traditional gender roles. Though many theologians are reluctant to limit discussion of gender in the church to issues related to holy orders, over time the debates about women's ordination and same-sex unions have expanded our vision of the church to be more inclusive of all, particularly the marginalized.[69]

The last question for the Episcopal women bishops was related to their vision of the church, or to put it in theological language, their ecclesiology. What is the Holy Spirit revealing to us about the episcopate? About the church? The responses were varied, like Pentecost. "I am aware that the election of so many women bishops, and so many women of color, is perceived by some as a sign of the church's decline. I don't believe it for a moment," writes one respondent. "I see and feel the Holy Spirit swirling and dancing in all her glory as women exercise the fullness of ministry. The church is changing. It is dying in some ways in itself and will be reborn into the fullness that Jesus intended all along."[70]

A common theme among respondents is that the widening embrace of the episcopate is a sign of hope from the Holy Spirit at a time of ecclesiastical, national, global, and ecological crisis. Although women bishops recognize the ongoing threats to institutional survival, they also deeply believe that The Episcopal Church has something unique to offer the world. "We need to resist the 'anesthesia of nostalgia' and realize that our whole life is not about guarding the tradition," says one respondent. "When The Episcopal Church lives out what we are called to do, it can and does change people's lives."[71] Several respondents underscored the importance of a diverse episcopacy to make The Episcopal Church more relevant to younger generations. "We need to broaden young people's perception of who they can be," says another respondent. "Once we do that, we can shift the narrative forever."[72]

Several of the respondents speak to their experience as "COVID bishops" and the challenges and blessings of that experience. "For much of my early ministry here I needed to adapt quickly, work through my discomfort, and explain a virus

I did not understand to people I did not know."[73] Current women bishops affirm the need to take seriously lessons learned during the COVID-19 pandemic. "The pandemic helped us get outside of our four walls," says one woman bishop. "It forced the issue. We are truly out in the world now, and the challenge is to figure out how we can remain there, and not snap back into old patterns."[74] Another respondent affirms this vision: "COVID has shown us we can be the church without a building; and has revealed places in our society and communities in need of healing and prophetic witness for justice and respect for the dignity of every human being and care of the creation."[75] One respondent connects the pandemic with the leadership of the church: "We need a much broader range of gifts in the leaders we call today, particularly as we confront the dismantling of life systems on this planet and as we discern God's dream for creation. Famine and pandemic are, at least in part, the result of human behaviors and destructiveness."[76]

Several of the respondents reflect that during the pandemic it is those churches best equipped to "pivot" that are the most resilient and who use their resources effectively to navigate unforeseen challenges. The ability to pivot is critical when traditional structures are no longer as effective or meaningful as they once were. The grief caused by the loss of security and the imposed isolation during the pandemic must be recognized so healing can begin. Though we are still learning the full impact of the pandemic, it is important to use the disruption to reflect on our model of the church. What is our path toward greater interconnection and mutuality? How can we best practice our vision of the church and the world with intention? Episcopal women bishops—religious leaders on the margins—tell us that we are better served if we pivot and prioritize the quality of our community, rather than focusing on the numbers alone. As one social innovator posits, "It is the impulse of Christian innovation to demonstrate that another world is possible. . . . The world needs us to show up as a hopeful people and to be good news people. And this current crisis gives us the perfect opportunity to turn the world upside down with the gospel."[77]

One Episcopal woman bishop notes that she regrets the "failure of imagination" at times characteristic of the House of Bishops. "So much of what we do is sausage-making. We have a role beyond the General Convention and need to be steadfast in a vision to follow Jesus."[78] As many of the respondents suggest, the growing diversity within the House of Bishops is a signal that the Holy Spirit is calling us to examine our vision of leadership in the context of emergent ecclesiologies. "The episcopate is being reshaped by shifts to more collaborative models of ministry. The stereotype of the authoritarian, hierarchical episcopate is being challenged and rejected (though it has vestiges still at work)," writes one respondent. "The episcopate is rooted spiritually and built on strong healthy relationships with clergy and laity committed to the ministry of the whole body of Christ."[79] "The Holy Spirit is revealing that the episcopate is co-equal with the other orders," states another respondent. "Hierarchy is on its way out."[80]

Comments from women bishops about hierarchy are an intrinsic response to theological concerns raised by other Episcopal leadership about focusing too much on bishops (and clergy) to the extent that we eclipse other orders of ministry, notably the ministry of the laity—the largest order of the church, and the only order where women are currently the numerical majority! The concern here is when bishops are seen primarily in relation to each other, and thus, isolated from connection with the rest of the body of Christ. This isolation is perceived as a split between ecclesiology and ecclesial life. As ecclesiologist Ellen Wondra argues, we need to operationalize an ecclesiology that

> not only shapes but is shaped by the lives and witness of ordinary Christians who are gendered, sexual, postcolonial subjects whose races and ethnicities are integral to who they are and how they live. Only when ecclesiology is explicitly shaped by actual ecclesial life with all its difference can it serve its purpose of informing reflection and stimulating imagination and vision of what it means to be a faith community following Christ.[81]

This is a *kairos* moment, an age of reformation. "I truly believe my episcopate, perhaps all, is about being the bridge to whatever is next. I want to hold the institution lightly and give it just enough support so it can be nimble and flexible to living the gospel as we discern it in this time," writes one woman bishop.[82] The testimonies of women bishops of The Episcopal Church bespeak a vision of the body of Christ in the world. A key characteristic of the vision of women bishops is an ecclesiology that involves dynamic engagement with the margins, affirming healthy traditions yet also seeking to create new spaces, networks, and relationships. It means transformation from self-serving narrow piety to engaged spirituality and social justice. Ironically, this vision of The Episcopal Church is about giving the world more than churches. The church is called to perform as a welcoming table, where members are called to respect the diversity of the other, and to create interconnected relationships between humanity and all creation. "We need to be re-schooled or re-discipled in interconnectedness, communitarian living, and seeking the flourishing of all life."[83] This means holding ourselves accountable when we have strayed from our commitment to seek Christ in all persons and our neighbors as ourselves. The witness of women bishops in the Episcopal Church is about seeking God, giving voice to the voiceless, and evoking creativity, healing, justice, and sacrament. It is a vision of a church where our structures and communities are dedicated to creating spaces for human flourishing, and where bishops, too, flourish in service to a church deeply needed by the world.

CHAPTER 8

The Beginning of Something New

Hector Monterroso

> When we are dreaming alone, it is only a dream. When we are dreaming with others, it is the beginning of reality.
>
> *Dom Hélder Câmara*[1]

Mission, Challenges, and the Episcopate

For thirty-one years, I developed my ministry in Province IX of The Episcopal Church. I was ordained under the canons of The Episcopal Church, in 1986 as a deacon and in 1987 as a priest in the Diocese of Guatemala. In my ministry as a priest, I carried out different ministries, including church planter and priest-in-charge. In addition, for fifteen years, I developed the ministry as secretary-general of Province IX and as provincial secretary of the Anglican Province of the Central American Region (IARCA). I believe that this experience prepared me to assume the call to be a bishop in the Diocese of Costa Rica, where I served from 2003 to 2017. I then accepted the invitation to serve as bishop assistant of the Diocese of Texas, where I currently serve. The ideas that I share in this essay are presented considering personal experiences, analysis of documents, working materials, opinions, and contributions of brother bishops, members of the clergy, and lay leaders from different countries and dioceses in Latin America and the Caribbean.

Context

The church is called to exercise the mandate of Christ, proclaiming the good news, making disciples of all kinds of people. In all reality, the mission of the church is a continuation of the ministry of Jesus on earth, the work that Jesus started and developed around his neighbors, his fellow man, whenever and wherever he was. During this time ordinary people lived in a context of poverty, exploitation, and inequality.

The conditions in which Jesus developed his ministry are not very different from how the church currently develops its ministry in Latin America: extreme poverty, unemployment, discrimination, violence, inequality, poor distribution of wealth, corruption, drug trafficking, lack of application of justice, and power concentrated in a few hands. This entire critical landscape has deteriorated even further during the COVID-19 pandemic.

The sum of all these elements is a sign of the "anti-kingdom"; therefore, they go against the establishment of the kingdom of God. The fundamental task of the church in this context is to announce and promote the values of the kingdom of God—not adapt or surrender to the powers that corrupt this world, or worse, ally with those powers and become an instrument of the anti-kingdom.

In this general context, the preaching of the gospel is a source of hope for society. The values of forgiveness, reconciliation, renewal, and the possibility of a new life are generators of hope and fall on good ground for people and communities who seek with faith and hope a new way of life and the establishment of a more just society.

We know that our work as a church will continue indefinitely until the establishment of the kingdom of God, but while this happens, there is much ahead. From the perspective of the ministry of bishops and the future role of bishops, it is necessary to reflect on some problems that become challenges that limit the exercise of bishops' duties, making it less effective and therefore affecting the mission of the church.

Introduction

When we elect a bishop in The Episcopal Church, all the living forces of the church come together to celebrate the presence and guidance of the Holy Spirit. The Holy Spirit guides the church to continue the mission that Jesus entrusted to his disciples to continue the work of the proclamation of the good news. The consecration of bishops brings new energy to the church, and there is great expectation for change and renewal. The church focuses on the new leadership and expects from its new leader guidance toward new experiences of spiritual growth, the revival of the church to respond to the signs of the times, missionary expansion, prophetic announcement in the face of injustices, dealing with governmental structures, the opening of new churches, new ways of making the gospel present in society, the formation of new leaders, and the call of new disciples. In short, the continuity of the mission.

To a certain extent, Hélder Câmara's words resonate in my mind when I reflect on Episcopal ministry. Being a bishop in The Episcopal Church requires many qualities and skills, but one of the most important is having a clear vision of where you want to lead the church entrusted to you as senior pastor into the future. The bishop is a dreamer who can communicate his dream to the whole church, and by sharing the dream, the bishop invites and encourages all members so that the dream becomes a reality.

Purpose

The Latin American region is extensive, and each country has its geographical, political, and economic peculiarities. Still, there are some points of agreement when it comes to the mission and work of the church. This essay focuses on identifying from the author's perspective some of the challenges that the dioceses in Province IX, Mexico, and Central America face in their missionary work, particularly the bishops' leadership. These challenges should become opportunities for change that strengthen the church and the leadership of the bishops.

The Priority of Establishing a Clear Vision

Part of the bishop's responsibilities and critically important in the performance of his role is the clarity of his mission. To be clear about the mission, each bishop must have clarity regarding the vision of his own life and the life of the church. Having a clear vision will make the bishop's ministry easier and, at the same time, may inspire others to follow it. In the book of Proverbs, we find the following in chapter 29, verse 18: "Where there is no prophecy, the people cast off restraint." Other versions use stronger language, saying, "Where there is no vision, the people die" (KJV).

This need is often manifested; we complain about our leaders, especially in government and other political instances, because they are unclear about where they should lead their governed and their people.

One of the main characteristics of the prophets and other great religious leaders in the Old and New Testaments is precisely the clarity of their mission: their call, their encounter with God, and later the mission that is revealed to them by Him.

An essential characteristic of Jesus is the clarity of his mission. Regardless of the degree of risk or commitment, his priority was always his vision. That vision has different stages: the call, the obedience, the risk, the sacrifice, and finally, the consummation.

To accomplish this goal, Jesus established a process, life discipline, and ministry that began in the desert.

Some disciples of the science of modern management make an interesting analysis of the experience of Jesus in the wilderness. They imagine him in the vision-building stage: planning his ministry, creating objectives, goals, and strategies, carefully selecting his mission partners, and finally, discovering the significance and impact of his ministry. For bishops to develop a fruitful ministry, it is essential to establish a vision.

The important conformation of the bishop's vision must be based on the evaluation and understanding of the social reality in which the church works. Therefore, the bishop's vision requires a clear understanding of social reality in addition to theological, biblical, and pastoral knowledge.

Inspired by the Spirit

When I lived in Costa Rica, I witnessed many foreigners who regularly visit the country. People are attracted to it for different reasons, mainly tourism. There are many possibilities for those looking for adventure and especially extreme sports at different levels. This includes hiking in the mountains in rain forests, zip-lining in the treetops, rafting in the mighty rivers, and rappelling in the waterfalls or rapids. However, the most popular extreme sport is surfing. Many people visit Costa Rica's Pacific Ocean and Caribbean Sea coasts to practice this sport.

Some time ago, I read a book by an evangelical author, Rick Warren, pastor of Saddleback Church in Lake Forest, California. In *The Purpose Driven Church*, he mentions something related to this sport and his relationship with the church.

He says that by taking a class to learn to surf, attendees will be taught everything they need to know about the sport; how to choose the right equipment, how to use it properly, how to recognize a "surfable" wave, and how to catch a wave and ride it for as long as possible and most important of all, how to get out of the wave without falling. But you can never find a course that teaches "How to create a wave."[2]

The essential thing for the practice of this sport is the waves. Without them, it is not possible to practice this sport. For this reason, many are looking for the highest waves with the most pronounced arcs, the most dangerous, highest-risk waves.

Something particular and very similar is happening in the church. The Holy Spirit continually sends us waves so that we, as the church, bishops, and leaders, can take advantage of them properly. The Holy Spirit provides us with different mission possibilities, diverse development opportunities, and many pastoral and calling alternatives.

However, in some cases, we do not realize all the possibilities that we have in front of us, and they reach our doors and we do not take action. Likely, we do not realize all the opportunities that are presented to us because of being absorbed by administrative tasks, poor reading of the context, and the signs of the times. Most evident is that we are suddenly not in tune with the Holy Spirit since laying hands on the day of the episcopal consecration is not enough. Still, the daily tension of living and obedience to the Holy Spirit is cultivated within the framework of prayer and contemplation.

The Holy Spirit guides the church; therefore, it is essential that we bishops and church leaders trust more and more in Holy Spirit provision and not just in our abilities.

An important responsibility that we bishops have is to be attentive to the opportunities that present themselves to inspire others, our priests, the leaders of the congregations, and in general the members of our churches to believe in all these revelations of God and to live inspired by the Holy Spirit. In this sense, the bishop's testimony, compelled by and allowing the Holy Spirit, must be clear, evident, and continuous.

Latin America's Heritage of the Evangelical Preferential Option for the Poor

There is no doubt that the Latin American continent has inherited a perspective and approach that cannot be hidden or not taken into account: the evangelical focus of the preferential option for the poor. Therefore, we bishops must discover for ourselves, and generate for others, a sensitive Latin American ecclesial leadership. This leadership must direct its action from the preferential option for the majority to an increasingly growing impoverished and marginalized context, which has a nonexclusive perspective.

The Identity of The Episcopal Church

In developing its mission in Latin America, The Episcopal Church has faced and continues to face a critical situation regarding its identity. For many people in Latin America, The Episcopal Church, at first glance, looks like a Roman Catholic church that differs somewhat because its priests can marry. This unfamiliarity with The Episcopal Church is a sad note of introduction. Bishops have had to develop the ability to educate individuals, institutions, and the media about our church's identity. Looking like the Roman Catholic Church in Latin American countries is not necessarily an evangelistic or missionary advantage.

One of the strengths that bishops require in their role is the strength of communication and the courage to speak fearlessly about the identity of The Episcopal Church. It is imperative to develop a clear communication and information strategy about The Episcopal Church so that more people can appreciate the positive elements in which the church is involved in each country. This will require taking advantage of the boom in communication through social networks.

The Pandemic, Some Effects, and Opportunities

The decline in people's participation in liturgies and ecclesial actions has been a constant factor in recent decades, of which the pandemic has been a simple catalyst. As the world slowly recovers from the pandemic, with frequent setbacks, the church has a long way to go in this adaptation process that some call the new normal.

Churches have spent months changing on the fly, restructuring services, updating and learning new technologies, and expending extra energy at a rate that could not have been imagined in the past. Some changes are likely to fade and be forgotten, while others, such as the increased use of social media and virtual celebrations, will likely remain a new way of pursuing our mission.

Episcopal and Anglican churches in the Latin American region face many challenges with Sunday attendance, as most churches in North America have been grappling with. Added to this is the uncertain outlook with intermittent government restrictions as new waves of the virus continue to appear, the critical economic situation that has not yet been fully realized, and the need for creative ways to participate in and cultivate people's spiritual character.

Many of these churches have long suffered a series of neglected challenges. The COVID crisis has imparted an urgency to this problem, and this is perhaps the opportunity they need to be shaken; as we learn from the apostle Paul, "Fool! What you sow does not come to life unless it dies" (1 Cor. 15:36).

This opportunity to be shaken presents us with unique gifts that the Lord has blessed the church with, which can be harnessed should bishops and their people decide to reimagine their new purpose and maximize their potential. Some of these gifts include:

- A small but highly committed and motivated membership
- Government and institutional recognition
- Reputation associated with historical heritage
- Recognized community contribution
- International relations (companion dioceses, Episcopal agencies, The Episcopal Church, the Anglican Communion, Episcopal Relief and Development, etc.)
- Healthy ecumenical relationships

- Assets (real estate and financial endowments)
- Balanced theology—via media

Episcopal, clergy, and lay leadership driven by decision-making focused with a clear vision, guided and driven by the Holy Spirit, will find in this set of gifts all the necessary elements to respond to the needs of people in the Latin American context. These elements will contribute to The Episcopal Church becoming a relevant movement and community to fulfill its mission.

But for every advantage, there seems to be at least one disadvantage; some of the challenges include: lack of planning for leadership succession, massive losses of youth, limited ministries with a disproportionate emphasis primarily on the sacramental, shortage of continuing education programs, outdated infrastructure, and an economic crisis partly due to poor administrative decisions and a particular incapacity for renovation, innovation, and new interpretation of what a church beyond the four walls should be in the twenty-first century. Perhaps some of these current problems have roots in their chaplaincy origins, shared by many of the dioceses. Unlike missional communities, these churches have watched time pass from a somewhat passive place.

One challenge is coping with the distancing that many members of our churches have experienced from lockdown and isolation. A form of spirituality and individualized participation has emerged—each one at home, following the church life while socially distanced. This effect has a direct impact on a sense of community, which is strengthened with face-to-face interaction, shared experiences, and face-to-face activities. The challenge is to return to community participation that links people.

Another great opportunity lies in the inherited governance structure that must flourish and transform into communities of truly empowered leaders. It is imperative to ask questions, to demand transparency and ethical-evangelical coherence. Otherwise, dioceses risk following in the footsteps of those who have sadly fallen into financial and administrative scandals.

Diocesan conventions, councils, and committees must be strengthened; members must be educated to serve the church effectively. Lay leaders and clergy must meet the criteria necessary to elect, support, and pray for their pastors; they must genuinely occupy their place in the life, worship, and government of the church.

We can remember the words of Ecclesiastes 7:5: "It is better to hear the rebuke of the wise than to hear the song of fools."

Leaders—in this case, bishops and staff in critical positions—must embrace more open and transparent reporting mechanisms, which foster a clear and established culture of constant accountability. It makes sense to start focusing more on results and adopt some metrics to measure performance, identify learning opportunities, and invest more time and energy in the core elements of ministry.

Time spent participating in forums, meeting with certain organizations, or holding representative positions in areas where there really is not much experience or moral authority to speak properly and be a true role model should be subject to a thorough evaluation in terms of how much dioceses, congregations, and ministries are growing or benefiting tangibly.

Many of these activities, which occupy a large part of the bishops' time and energy, distracting them from their pastoral vocation, also involve a great deal of travel and associated onerous costs.

Some dioceses have not persisted in improving the transparency of reporting to their diocesan councils or conventions. Audit reports and the status of diocesan assets and properties are not available to their delegates. This is likely to be due to internal situations in some cases, but in dioceses where this information is not available, there is general dissatisfaction among the membership.

A vital sign of the leadership crisis in succession is the lack of generational change on the horizon. On the other hand, most of the newly ordained clergy are not emerging as leaders within congregations. Still, they come from different Christian denominations, mostly mature adults who have not found in these other denominations a door of welcome to meet their expectations of holy orders for various reasons.

The great challenge here is to empower those who can find in the Episcopal faith a friendly and nonjudgmental way of setting forth before God their aspirations for ordained ministry and submitting to God's will, trusting that the Holy Spirit will guide them through a journey aligned with perseverance, creativity, audacity, and above all, commitment to breaking paradigms about what it is to be a church.

Episcopal leadership, specifically, will face breaking paradigms not only in the twenty-first century but in a postpandemic world, with all the transformations that are emerging and will continue to arrive. Then some might see in ordained ministry an end in itself, a goal that typically focuses on the altar and not on a fruitful path of community service and congregational development; they do not perceive themselves as individuals thirsty to reach more souls for Christ.

Episcopal leaders will be challenged to guide their communities and increase their ability to reach people from more spheres of society. The church must pray that God provides us with sensitive hearts; it must practice God's mandate to attend in loving service to the needs of others. Sometimes these needs have economic connotations, and some are basic, but there are also spiritual ones. The church hears the call of Christ best when there are heterogeneous Christians blessed with different gifts and abilities. It is essential that churches also reach out to economically stable sectors of the population. By experiencing a living relationship with God, they are motivated to serve in his church.

Another essential factor to consider is the leadership training resources and initiatives that are available. In recent years, dioceses have been sharing experiences and accessing resources from their partner dioceses in The Episcopal Church. Still, they also participate and have access in some way to help from the Anglican Communion. However, despite having participated in countless meetings and forums, there are few or no apparent results. The lack of results probably is related to the continuity of a learned and rooted model that allows little or no significant change.

Imagine an individual who, after a medical diagnosis, decides to initiate a change in lifestyle. So he visits a store where they display fitness equipment and buys one of those machines. He also goes to a store where they sell nutritional supplements and purchases a line of products for consumption. Likewise, he randomly adopts elements of different diets—keto, Atkins, and so forth—without any rigorous and controlled process. That person likely ends up altering his state of health more. His glucose levels, cholesterol, and triglycerides could be compromised. He could end up with muscle atrophy or muscular contractures if he does not have the proper technique to perform exercise routines.

When experts analyze different diets or physical training programs, you can almost always see positive results in most of them. Still, regardless of the program, there is a common factor. It is the relativity of the individual and their particular condition. There are no universal methods but personalized plans for each person. The ideal program for each individual is relative to their situation. Once one is adopted, success depends on the discipline, rigor, and perseverance with which it is followed and close and intentional guidance from a professional.

Some Episcopal and Anglican churches in the region face a critical situation in many aspects, but far from making deep analyses and taking rigorous measures, the bishops are pointing everywhere. Some believe that by participating or randomly sending members of the clergy or laity to different forums or programs, they are helping to solve their problems, when in reality they are not. On the other hand, lay leaders who are commonly burdened with responsibilities in their diocese end up overwhelmed and sometimes disappointed. The disappointment about not getting results ends up demotivating the clergy more.

Here is an opportunity for the bishops to chart a different direction. This includes assessing all human and material resources and rebuilding the diocese. They must have courage to set mission priorities and focus the wider leadership in order to meet mission goals. Bishops must model consistency as they act with humility, vision, commitment, and hard work.

Stewardship and Self-Sufficiency

One of the projects in which the church, and particularly the bishops, fails in Latin American churches is in the processes of stewardship and self-sufficiency. We are always talking about stewardship and self-reliance, but we never get serious about it. The parish model that is typical in the United States has not worked in Latin America. Churches are not self-sufficient, nor do bishops work for churches to achieve self-sufficiency. An example is that most priests receive their salary from the diocesan budget and not from their respective parishes or missions.

Most dioceses pay clergy's salaries from their diocesan budget. This administrative practice has had a very negative effect on the development of stewardship and economic self-sufficiency. Many churches do not understand or make stewardship a method to support their regular expenses. Furthermore, the relationship between the bishop and the priests has a more administrative than pastoral dimension.

The role of bishop in the coming years faces a critical challenge due to the scarcity of economic resources. The bishop's responsibility will be to focus on the self-support of his diocese.

This self-supporting effort must begin with a good organization of diocesan finances, with adequate education at all levels of the church about the responsibility and commitment that each member has for the support of their church. In addition, the bishop must offer meaningful proposals for the mission and not just focus on spending money on administration and maintenance of the office. As the saying goes, "money follows mission." This is a popular and authentic expression; members of the church contribute as they witness concrete transformative action. The bishop must become a generator of ideas and strategies that connect his vision with the mission and ministry of the church.

Most of the dioceses in the region have sufficient conditions to emerge stronger from this crisis if the bishops decide to change the direction that the church has followed. Dioceses have resources and investments; some have significant funds. But dividends and resources from appropriations and donations are invested in sustaining a costly and inefficient structure. The clergy depend on the diocesan budget to receive their salary and have not been trained and challenged to build the parish model that implies self-support.

The clergy, for the most part, receive uncompetitive salaries. Some salaries are barely enough to cover the minimum amount established by different governments. What would happen if the church offered living wages above the minimum that were competitive?

Another resource available to dioceses is properties. Some are for rent, others are idle, and others are in a disgraceful condition. Some of them functioned as congregations in communities that, over time, have undergone solid social transformations. Indeed, if a professional analysis of the environment were made, it would perhaps conclude that many of them do not have any potential to be reactivated, even if there were the resources to invest in them. A significant challenge for the bishop and his leadership is to make intelligent decisions regarding properties and pastoral support for communities whose functioning and sustainability have been unfeasible for decades.

The bishop and his leadership can identify a large swath of the population that is not served by any community of Christian faith or where the options for these populations include only the two ends of the spectrum, recalcitrant evangelical offerings or Catholic churches, traditional and passive.

What if the dioceses had some properties to reinvest resources in planting new churches in strategic areas for evangelization and mission? They could reach people who, if spiritually motivated and accompanied, would have the potential to develop excellent service ministries.

Missionary Action

The presence of The Episcopal Church in the IX Province, IARCA, and Mexico is characterized by being a minority. The church, which was born as a missionary effort with great expectations for growth and expansion, has experienced stagnation in recent years and is worryingly seeing its membership decline rapidly. Missionary work and development of the church presence have halted and are undergoing considerable reduction. In some dioceses, the funds available and the attendance numbers are truly alarming.

The presence of The Episcopal Church is distributed mainly in rural areas and moderately in large urban areas. This geographical distribution has not followed any intentional missionary plan but instead has been dictated by divine providence. In many cases, Episcopalians who migrate to other cities become missionary guests to new mission fields. Although this situation has not responded to a planned missionary strategy, it is unmistakable that the Holy Spirit leads the church. Bishops, guided by the Holy Spirit, must make an effort to interpret these opportunities and develop a combined strategy, empowering each layperson as a potential missionary.

The other way the church expands its presence is through the service and assistance it provides after natural disasters. Some dioceses have seen their communities grow or a new presence established in places where the first outreach was through relief immediately after a natural disaster. These approaches include rebuilding houses, offering emergency aid with food and clothing, holding medical days, and other activities that allow affected communities to start a new life. The bishops have played an important role in partnering with national and international emergency government organizations, including Episcopal Relief and Development.

Although throughout Latin America there are significant pockets of poverty, there is also wealth, and in some countries, there is still a thriving middle class. Other denominations reach more diverse sectors of the population with much greater success than our churches. A healthy congregation is one where the people aware of God's grace act in response to his divine mandate to love their neighbor. A healthy community with active ministries represents the heterogeneity of society. Amid that diversity, Christ is manifested when the people decide to lovingly serve others.

Many dioceses function as bridges, attracting resources from the state and international episcopal programs to serve local social programs. These local programs are run by diocesan personnel, which is very positive. However, it is time for church members, motivated by Christ's transformation in their lives, to develop active ministries of service in their local communities.

One of the areas in which the church has created an essential impact in Latin American countries has been education. Some dioceses have invested significantly in private education, particularly in places where educational deficiencies are evident. The creation of primary and secondary schools, in many cases, has been a well-directed missionary tool. In addition, it has been a vital resource for economic sustainability. At the same time, it has benefited many people who would not have an educational opportunity were it not for the participation of The Episcopal Church.

Bishops will have a good perspective on their future work if they focus on these three areas, investing time in the formation of each layperson to be a potential missionary, multiplying the effort, and giving the church the capacity to develop active discipleship. This effort could be focused primarily on the areas of service and education.

Bishops and churches have the challenge of fostering a presence in the social context, not only an intra-ecclesial voice but also, in other social spheres, using evangelical, ecclesial, and humanistic arguments, a model of life and fair, fraternal, peaceful, inclusive, and respectful interaction.

Expectations

From recent episcopal elections in The Episcopal Church in the United States, Latin America, and Anglican Communion, the following expectations emerge for exercising the episcopate in the next decade.

The bishop is expected to develop a ministry that includes:

1. Leading the church to become a relevant community of faith that encourages people to connect all daily activities, needs, problems, successes, and failures. The gospel and the faith guide their solution.

2. Helping, through their spiritual growth, the members of the church to face daily life and live a life directed by and centered on the word of God.

3. Guiding the church in the face of social problems, clearly acting in defense of minorities and the most vulnerable, as well as the impoverished majorities. It should be a prophetic voice that the church hears and follows to confront constant injustices.

4. Motivating a missionary spirit in the church membership; leaving the sacred precinct and exploring new ways of doing mission; learning to pray and celebrate in public places where people meet in their daily lives.

5. Being a leader against racial discrimination and a banner for racial reconciliation and social justice. This search for equality of gender, ethnicity, and race should be easy to identify in all the churches of the diocese.

6. Exploring new forms of worship, music, and the use of new technologies to include and add more people to Christian discipleship.

7. Promoting cultural diversity and the learning of at least one other language for the clergy of the diocese as a multicultural missionary strategy.

8. Insisting on theological education and the promotion of ministerial vocations.

9. Empowering lay leadership to become missionaries and disciples.

10. Continuing to develop a ministry of service focused on education and human development.

11. Focusing their ministry 90 percent on diocesan work and the rest on episcopal work, ecumenical activities, or work related to the representation of the church in other provincial or Anglican Communion events.

12. Being evaluated at least every four years. The evaluation should be conducted according to the vision and the diocesan goals.

13. Giving direct, exceptional attention to children and youth, ensuring that each congregation focuses on this responsibility.

14. Strictly controlling the processes of continuing education of the clergy to promote new ministerial vocations.

15. Promoting new vocations and pastoring their ministers.

This is a list of priority issues and tasks that lay leaders and clergy have identified in hopes of reviving and resuming the missionary spirit that has characterized The Episcopal Church in many parts of the world. Bishops are a vital component of the mission, and their missionary role must support the future of their ministry. This missionary role can be interpreted almost literally. It should not be focused on serving an established and functioning church. It should show a vision for the diocese that can be easily understood and can lead and inspire its faithful to join it.

The primary function of the bishop as missionary leader should be focused on opening a path, venturing into places where the church has not had a presence, planting the new seeds of the Episcopal presence, building a new form of church that adapts to the Latin American reality, and adapting worship and new liturgical practices in accordance with the local spiritual elements. The bishop's missionary vocation must be based on the study, reflection, and application of the Word of God contained in the Old and New Testaments and prayer as the pillars of his discipline of life. His ministry must also include ending inherited administrative and organizational models that are not compatible with local culture. The bishop should make intelligent decisions to invest available resources and allocate them to form new generations of priests who share the missionary vision. He should adopt modern management principles that include planning, directing, and periodically evaluating their performance.

When we face challenges of such magnitude, we have two options: to meet them or not to face them. Meeting them involves a lot of work and giving up the comfort of continuing to do the same. However, the bishops are called not to conform and not to sit still. When there is too much comfort at work, it is time to do something different.

As Dom Hélder Câmara said,

Pilgrim, when your ship long moored in harbor gives you the illusion of being a house; when your ship begins to put down roots in the stagnant water by the quay: put out to sea! Save your boat's journeying soul and your own pilgrim soul, cost what it may.[3]

CHAPTER 9

The Bishop amid a Multiethnic Context

Robert Fitzpatrick

Introduction

At ordination, a bishop in The Episcopal Church promises to "encourage and support all baptized people in their gifts and ministries, nourish them from the riches of God's grace, pray for them without ceasing, and celebrate with them the sacraments of our redemption."[1] At one time, too often and for too long in our history, our interpretation of these promises and vision for the church led to helping or cajoling all of God's people toward an ideal of being an upper-middle-class, university-educated, white, Western European (ideally English) American (i.e., a citizen of the United States). It was an imperialist enterprise for the church within the broader American culture.

This enterprise had positive results with the building of schools and hospitals. It provided the means for social mobility and literacy. It was also stifling and degrading. It devalued languages and cultures in a way inconsistent with the gospel of Jesus Christ. It therefore hurt and divided God's people. Bishops participated in this enterprise as leaders of the church and as products of their time.

Bishops of The Episcopal Church can no longer minister and lead with such an imperialist mindset—even subconsciously. We are called upon to meet God's people where they are, to honor our cultural and linguistic differences, and to be culturally competent in a diverse community while holding onto our identity as followers of Christ Jesus in The Episcopal Church. How can we possibly do that?

I have been the diocesan bishop of Hawai'i since 2007 and the bishop-in-charge of The Episcopal Church in Micronesia since 2009. I also served as a parish priest and as the canon to the ordinary in the years before being ordained as a bishop on the island of Oʻahu. My episcopal ministry has, therefore, been in a context that is both multicultural and geographically separated from The Episcopal Church on the North American continent. I think Hawaiʻi provides some insights into the future ministry of bishops in a truly multicultural and multilingual church. According to the World Population Review, Hawaiʻi is the "most racially and ethnically diverse state in the U.S., with about 38.6% of the population being Asian, 24.7% white, 10% Native Hawaiian or other Pacific Islander, 1.6% Black, 0.3% American Indian and Alaska Native, and 23.6% being multi-ethnic."[2]

My own growth has come from two sources. First, there has been formal study, conferences, and books. When I first arrived in the Islands, I was helped by a conference and resources from the Rev. Eric H. F. Law.[3] More recently, Ms. Rosa Say's insights from management in the visitor industry have been practically helpful.[4] There have also been many books and papers from the University of Hawaiʻi and other sources on culture and society.

The second source has been more important: people. I have been mentored and corrected by God's people. Some, of course, stand out to me every day. The late Right Reverend Richard S. O. Chang was my boss, my teacher, and my friend. The untimely death of the Rev. Canon Malcolm Nāea Chun also took from my side an insightful cultural mentor. The Rev. Charles Kamohaliʻi Hopkins, Professor Alberta Pualani "Pua" Pung Hopkins, the Rev. Canon Darrow Kanakanui Aiona, and Ms. Lucille Setsuko Caldwell were also valued guides—although, I must admit, I did not always understand it at the time. There are many others in Hawaiʻi, the Philippines, Micronesia, and Aotearoa who have guided my way. As we become increasingly interconnected through the church throughout the world and in the Islands, the list of those I consider mentors continues to grow.

I have further come to understand that we live in more than one culture at a time. Our culture defines our norms of behavior, our family systems, our values, our customs, our arts, and our beliefs. We operate in the larger culture of ethnicity, race, or national origin, but also in subcultures. Being culturally competent requires navigating between cultures in a healthy and respectful way. As a bishop of The Episcopal Church, for example, engagement with a congregation made up of military members and family presents a community with a unique language, sense of time based on postings, and understanding of authority that demand a special response. Members of such a community function with their own set of norms and values, and yet operate within the larger culture.

Finally, there is the ecclesial culture of The Episcopal Church. A bishop promises to "solemnly engage to conform to the doctrine, discipline, and worship of The Episcopal Church."[5] The Constitution, canons, and authorized liturgical materials are the bounds in which we have mutually agreed to function in our corner of Christ's church. While we must be careful to engage them with generosity and openness to allow different cultural expressions, we also must give care to the limits. These too will be different from community to community. The *Kānaka ʻōiwi* ("people of the native bones" or Native Hawaiians) have taught me to respect the protocols, social norms, and values of the host indigenous people of the Hawaiian Islands. I have also gained a renewed appreciation of understanding the limits and protocols of my culture as an Episcopalian. Such limits and protocols provide for communal self-differentiation and identification. While we must be careful that they are not oppressive, they can be of deep meaning.

A bishop must follow the example of Peter and the Jerusalem Church in Acts of the Apostles, chapters 10 and 11, in the encounter with Cornelius and the opening to Gentile "God-worshippers." The bishop is constantly balancing things essential with things indifferent. So, a bishop must be a learner from those around them.

Haʻahaʻa: Humility

Being a bishop in a truly multicultural church begins with humility. This is basic. The term in *ʻŌlelo Hawaiʻi* (the Hawaiian language) is *haʻahaʻa*. In the language, a term is doubled to give it added emphasis. This is particularly important for those of us given pride of place by our office. In most settings, I think it must mean not to speak first, but to listen. It requires offering a word of invitation to others. Being clear with yourself when you do not have an answer to a presenting question begins with listening. There is no need to fake your way. Much of the time it means just being quiet. As bishop, if you have nothing to say, then listen. If one is unsure of the language and values of the community, it is best to say nothing.

I have found this particularly true with language. It is important to be aware that language carries culture. So, for example, *ha'aha'a* is a primary value because a person learns by example. No book can transmit true knowledge. One must be quiet and listen. Through the years, I have worked hard on my liturgical *'Ōlelo Hawai'i*. I did not publicly say anything out loud in the liturgy until an elder at the cathedral told me that I was ready. I could sing the hymns and participate in the responses, but until "Auntie Paulette" gave me permission, it was not appropriate for me to try to speak the language of the land. I could pronounce the words, but they had to both mean something to me and be clear for the hearers. Respect is more than just "trying" to speak the language of another community.

Humility also recognizes humility in others. For some, it is a central cultural value to respect authority. That might mean when there is a disagreement that "yes" may mean "yes," or it might mean "maybe," or really "no." It is important not to disagree with the bishop. This is particularly true in situations that bring shame. For example, when a congregation needs financial help, it is not uncommon for a congregation with a largely white, North American lay leadership team to directly ask for a grant or for other help. For others, the process itself is difficult, but more, it can be a sign of failure and shame. This is especially true if the congregation was once receiving a subsidy and now again needs help. Further, for some, it is not appropriate to ask for help. The leader—the bishop—is supposed to know. Such knowing only comes with careful listening.

The same struggle can impact when a postulant from a nondominant culture attends a North American seminary in a traditional Anglo-European dominant culture. The issue of how and what help to ask for impacts the seminarian. The bishop has to be aware of the general strain of being outside the home culture for a seminarian, but this is in addition to the strain of ordinary seminary life. Those attending seminary often want to help—they are just at a loss about how or what to ask for.

Humility for the bishop is grounded in silence and listening. It is grounded in the admonition of the Letter of James: "Know this, my dear brothers and sisters: everyone should be quick to listen, slow to speak, and slow to grow angry."[6] A bishop cannot support the multicultural church by talking first or loudest. For me, the image is that the bishop should be the first to help put away chairs and do the dishes. It is at such times that the bishop can learn the most.

Humility ensures that the bishop does not engage in cultural appropriation. I am never going to be *Kānaka ʻōiwi* (Native Hawaiian), but always a "settler" on and a "guest" in these islands. I hope and keenly desire to be a welcome guest. I can do my best to understand and learn from the language, culture, and values, but I must not claim them. They can and will influence me, but they are always a gift and not a possession. The same is true as I serve other communities in God's church.

Mālama: To care for

In the consecration of a new bishop, the prayer asks "that *he* may feed and tend the flock of Christ, and exercise without reproach the high priesthood to which you have called *him*, serving before you day and night in the ministry of reconciliation, declaring pardon in your Name, offering the holy gifts, and wisely overseeing the life and work of the Church."[7] This prayer is summed up in the Hawaiian word "*mālama.*" The term can be used to reflect caring, serving, supporting, preserving, and protecting. It is the very ministry of a bishop.

Humility gives the bishop an openness to truly care. It begins with coming to understand what is heard. This is where the study of culture and history is important. More important, however, it is taking the time to talk. The local colloquial term for it in Hawaiʻi is "talk story." This indirect form of communication is based on relationships, experiences, and narratives.

The church's practices sometimes make this difficult. Interestingly here, I do not mean the basic structures outlined in the canons, but our actual practices and policies. For example, the Commission on Ministry in Hawaiʻi was once interviewing a nominee for ordination from Polynesia. When he arrived, he was joined by over a dozen people from his congregation. In keeping with the cultural traditions of his island home, others were there to speak for him. It would not be considered proper for him to speak for himself, and to especially share his good qualities or place of leadership in the congregation. There had to be someone else to speak on behalf of the nominee and the community. We had to work through an understanding of calling. It is the bishop's role to act as an intermediary and to help make things right.

An important element of caring is apologizing. There are times that we say the wrong thing or we are misunderstood. Caring for God's people includes the ability to say "I'm sorry." I think this is important when dealing with a congregation or group from a culture not one's own. It is particularly important for bishops from the dominant culture. As a person of honor, a word or gesture can be taken with utmost seriousness and unintended authority. Frankly, a misspoken statement can be based on bias and cultural superiority, even if unintentional or unconscious. When brought to one's attention, an immediate apology is all one can do, and then learn from the mistake with the intention of doing better the next time.

"Talk Story"

Those in the dominant western culture sometimes call an encounter "triangulation" when it is about something deeper. A senior or a friend might be asked to speak to the bishop or priest about a problem. This happens particularly in the case of conflict within the local congregation and especially with the priest. The unspoken "rules" of authority and a sense of inferiority because of language, social status, or education may make the delivery of a message the beginning of a much longer conversation about control and shame. While permission can be given and conversation encouraged, it often happens in less formal settings.

As I noted, the local term in Hawai'i for the process of talking and listening for wisdom is " talk story." With the merging of cultures from many places into the Islands, there is a premium placed on relationship. Those who grow up in Hawai'i are conditioned to understand and respect relations of family (near and distant) and of generations. For a younger person to refer to an elder as "Auntie" or "Uncle" is a mark of respect and an acknowledgment of relationship beyond biological family. Relationships can be built only by passing on stories from generation to generation. This takes time. In such communities, I have learned more by painting a parish hall or helping in the kitchen than I have in a vestry meeting. While that is certainly true in all congregations, it is essential in high-context relational cultures.

Frankly, the single biggest pressure I have found in being a bishop is not having the time to "talk story." Patience and time are required. That too often does not fit into a schedule of demanding board and committee meetings. It also runs counter to the corporate culture that is so much a part of North American business life and therefore has infected The Episcopal Church. While diocesan staff members can help, there is the reasonable expectation that the bishop will be present as well. The only answer I have found is working it into the schedule and ensuring my door is open to everyone—at least I try.

Hoʻohanohano: Dignity

The words of the promise to "respect the dignity of every human being" in the Baptismal Covenant have become habitual in The Episcopal Church.[8] My Hawaiian mentors have taught me that *hoʻohanohano* is something more. The prefix *hoʻo* informs the hearer that there is action or causation. *Hano* is "honor" or "authority." *Hoʻohanohano* is "to give" or "to bestow" upon another "dignity" or "honor." It is active. There is implied in this something more than respect. It is the active engagement of bringing folk from other cultural groups into the circle of conversation and leadership.

Systemically, I have found this easiest to do through the bishop's power of appointment. As the bishop, I have had some control of who will serve on commissions, committees, and task groups. Likewise, I have a direct say in who can be appointed as a vicar or a priest-in-charge. I can also call on folk for advice.

I have been somewhat frustrated by election processes in the church. This includes at the diocesan level and when vestries call rectors. I do think things have changed. Even in Hawaiʻi, however, we still—systematically—default to the safe, college-educated Euro-American fresh from North America when electing at convention or for a rector. Why? Deep down, I think we Episcopalians still have an ecclesial cultural bias about what it means to be a good "Episcopalian." This can be true for those who are not themselves from the historic stereotypical cultural group understood to be Episcopalian. It is true even in Hawaiʻi. We are changing. As we come to the realization that The Episcopal Church is no longer part of the cultural or economic elite, we are refining and, I pray, open to new possibilities. We have not yet learned to listen to or respect the intelligence of everyone. This is especially the case for individuals who do not speak "standard" English. The bishop must be a continual advocate for that change.

As a bishop, there is an added responsibility of trying to encourage and to challenge. It includes welcoming those who will challenge the bishop. There is no reason for the bishop to be defensive. I can see in new ways only if another person points out the blind spots in my perspective and challenges me to see in a new way.

Pono: Harmony, Righteousness, and Justice

The concept of living "*pono*" is often used in Hawai'i. In fact, it is in the state's motto: *Ua Mau ke Ea o ka 'Āina i ka Pono*, officially translated as "The life of the land is perpetuated in righteousness" (it should be noted, however, that "*Ea*" is better translated as "sovereignty" and not "land"). In my many conversations with the elders about the meaning of living *pono*, I have learned that it is essential to the host people of the Islands, but it is also somewhat elusive. The late canon Malcolm Nāea Chun told me a story recounted by the historian John Papa 'Ī'ī to help understand *pono*.[9] When King Kamehameha I (c. 1758–1819) was visiting the island of O'ahu, the local chief, the king's nephew, ordered fish to be gathered from fishponds. A great mound of fish was piled high as an offering to the king. There were so many fish that they were left spoiling on the shore. The king was not pleased. He bowed his head and cast his eyes away at the waste and in shame. The situation was not *pono* and had to be rectified.

To live *pono* is to live with true harmony, righteousness, and justice with creation and with one another. It has become my watchword for the essence of the Christian life.

Now, as the bishop encounters God's people with different cultural values and understandings there are bound to be conflicts. This was particularly the case when the diocese was involved as the state of Hawai'i moved to legalize same-sex marriage. As a diocese, we had for decades welcomed gay and lesbian clergy. The diocesan convention and I were actively supportive of the changes in the laws. In fact, the conversations about full inclusion had been going since the episcopacy of Edmund Browning (bishop of Hawai'i from 1976 to 1985). In the midst of this, the culture of The Episcopal Church was changing. While the diocese as a whole had come to a consensus, some continued to struggle with identifying primary cultural values even over theological ones. We have to keep talking, listening, and talking story.

There are also surprises. Once while helping a small rural mission congregation as they were seeking a vicar, we had to have a conversation about the characteristics of their next priest. There was a sizable Filipino group in the congregation. This included seniors who had emigrated to work on the plantations and their children. It was soon clear that one senior woman spoke for that part of the community—or at least no one would contradict her. In the midst of our conversation, I pointed out that there might be a woman candidate, or even a priest who was homosexual who would want to come with a "partner" (as we still said at the time). The matriarch said little except "No woman priest." Quiet settled over the room. I explained that we could not promise that and asked her to be open to possibilities. I also promised to listen to her when it was time to make a decision. She looked at me and said, "Alright, but no woman priest."

Outside there was time to "talk story." Her son wanted me to know that his mother had been raised in the Iglesia Filipina Independiente (IFI) and just did not like the idea of a woman priest. I did not try to explain that the IFI now had women clergy. I did ask why she did not react to having a homosexual priest. He laughed and said we have always had "gay priests," and then with a smile said, "We just didn't talk about it in the village back home." He said that the "ladies" (the senior Filipinas) just could not imagine a woman priest.

After visits by two candidates, I returned to meet with the congregation. The matriarch immediately wanted me to know that she wanted the "woman" to be her priest. After a short conversation and a good meal, I went up to her son. He smiled and said, "Mom and ladies decided that the haole[10] woman priest was really nice, and asked questions about their children and grandchildren. Even though she is from the mainland, that lady knows how to 'talk story.'" Thus began several years of a fruitful ministry. Sometimes living *pono* shines through and overcomes cultural barriers and historic understandings.

Kuleana: Responsibility and Authority

The oversight responsibilities are part of the bishop's *kuleana*. This is the specific responsibilities and role of bishop. At ordination, the episcopal ordinand promises to "encourage and support all baptized people in their gifts and ministries, nourish them from the riches of God's grace, pray for them without ceasing, and celebrate with them the sacraments of our redemption" and to "guard the faith, unity, and discipline of the Church."[11]

I am a haole male bishop serving in a diocese and in islands with no group or cultural constituency with an absolute majority. Further, the Hawaiian Islands are now part of the United States and, therefore, The Episcopal Church because of an imperialist—political and cultural—history. Although I have spent many years in the islands, I am from North America and will always be a "settler" in the islands and a "guest" of the indigenous host people. I am still the bishop and have a *kuleana*. I share this to note that all bishops live in social and historic contexts in which they must engage other cultures and worldviews within the church. How we both own our authority and engage others defines our ministry. While we can certainly define our personal preferences as bishop, and honor ecclesial and canonical boundaries, we must also adapt.

Sometimes it can be in the small things that one can honor culture. For example, in congregations with members originally from the Philippines and the Iglesia Filipina Independiente, I have come to expect having my hand taken to individuals' foreheads for a blessing. One congregation with a core membership from the Philippines as well took a collection to buy me a new pectoral cross. To my mind, the congregation members could not afford such an extravagance. I soon understood that the issue was that the cross I wore was too simple and they wanted their bishop to have the appropriate bling. It was a matter of honor and respect. So, I now have and wear a fine cross of gold with an amethyst in the middle. My episcopal authority is embodied in that cross.

There are also difficulties. The struggle comes when congregations are in conflict or there is an endangered pastoral relationship. What happens when the bishop is told, "Bishop, you don't understand us" or even "Bishop, you're being racist"? This is not a concern for a haole bishop alone. I have personally heard this said to (and heard stories from) bishops of other cultural and racial backgrounds when encountering nondominant groups in the church. The very culture of The Episcopal Church has a bias toward particular forms of accountability, organizational models, authority, and forms of communication. It is never easy to be called a "racist" or even to hear that you just do not understand the situation because you're haole.

What can the individual bishop do? First, I have found that I have to engage in some self-examination at that moment. The daily spirit practice of the Examen certainly helps with that. Such a reflective act also includes engaging and questioning the very practices and policies of the church. I also think it important, when possible, to engage in such pastoral situations with others with the same cultural understanding. Ask for help. The bishop must be clear on the limits of the canons and policies providing the basis for the engagement. Is it a personal conflict of individuals? Is it that someone is being autocratic? Is there a failure in administration? Is this an issue of leadership (lay or ordained)?

Such times are always difficult, but when the bishop is coming from another culture or historic perspective, the situation is exacerbated. Perhaps the bishop doesn't understand. The written canons and the policies articulate our common culture—The Episcopal Church. This is not to insist on legalism, but a call to understand the "container" of our shared church life. I think that the canons of The Episcopal Church (and rubrics in the Book of Common Prayer) are very broad and adaptable. The same is true of most diocesan canons. Policies were usually written to address a presenting problem. The stumbling block is often in application. In situations of congregational or pastoral conflict, the bishop has a responsibility of oversight and reconciliation. This requires special care when the bishop is caring for clergy and congregations from cultures other than their own.

Ho‘omana Pīhopa: The Bishop's Spiritual Authority

The often-unspoken authority of a bishop is spiritual. At the prayer of consecration, God is asked to empower the new bishop "serving before you day and night in the ministry of reconciliation, declaring pardon in your Name, offering the holy gifts, and wisely overseeing the life and work of the Church."[12] As I noted, ho‘o shows action. "Mana" is a word that connotes spiritual power. The bishop (pīhopa) is expected to have spiritual authority. God's people should expect their bishop to pray and to teach the Good News with authority.

This means that a bishop might be called on for ministrations that require a special role. For example, I have more than once been asked to offer prayers of exorcism because members of a "community" (office workers in a state government building and staff in a school) had come to believe a space was in spiritual conflict (I might have used the word "haunted," but that does not quite capture what was being experienced). The mana of the bishop was needed because of the importance of the spaces in the histories of the islands. Further, there were historic connections to the Hawaiian monarchy and therefore former bishops. I was being called on to fulfill a responsibility because bishops in the past had served as chaplains to some of the monarchs. I consulted with *Kānaka ʻōiwi* elders (especially clergy) and blessed the spaces with prayers (in English and Hawaiian), sea salt, and water as appropriate (with the assistance of a *Kānaka ʻōiwi* clergyperson). It was both culturally and theologically in keeping with the teaching of the church and Hawaiian cultural practices that all can understand, Hawaiian and non-Hawaiian.

Spiritual authority is grounded in the bishop's call to "be faithful in prayer, and in the study of Holy Scripture," and to be the "chief priest and pastor."[13] Just as God's people must expect their bishop to pray, so they can expect the bishop to care and to instruct them in the faith. Each bishop will have their own gifts and foci. The bishop's pastoral care is by nature of the ministry for the diocese and church as a whole. It is a ministry of oversight. I think it especially important when engaging with clergy and God's people from other cultures to be aware of how best to teach to be heard and offer support in a meaningful way. The bishop should be expected as best as possible to adapt to the needs of God's people rather than expect the people to adapt to the bishop. Spiritual authority is from God and not the bishop.

ʻOhana a me Aloha: Family and Love

The bishop is in constant relationship with the "family of God." The modern American notion of the nuclear family fails to adequately reflect the nature of the church. In many cultures "family" means something far more extended and interconnected. The Hawaiian term "*ʻohana*" includes those who are related by blood, by adoption (either formally or informally, *hānai*), and by intention. The attitude of the bishop is important when encountering communities of another culture and language. Is this people truly part of my *ʻohana*? To be in my family, I have to love the other even when I'm confused, frustrated, or dumbfounded. *Aloha* is more than "love." It is ground of life in God. *Ha* means "breath" and, therefore, to share *aloha* is to share breath—to share life. As a bishop, I have experienced the *aloha* of God's people. I have been allowed to be part of the many extended branches of God's *ʻohana* throughout the Pacific. I am still learning that *ʻohana*, family, can include everyone and all of creation. That for me is the key: keeping learning and growing.

I look again to the story of Peter and Cornelius in the Acts of the Apostles (10:46–48 NIV): "Peter said, 'Surely no one can stand in the way of their being baptized with water. They have received the Holy Spirit just as we have.' So he ordered that they be baptized in the name of Jesus Christ. Then they asked Peter to stay with them for a few days." Bishops must be careful to include those of all languages and cultures. We are the ones who must adapt and change. Bishops are often called to "show compassion to the poor and strangers, and defend those who have no helper."[14]

CHAPTER 10

The Ministry of Bishop as Leadership

Robert Wright

Serving as a bishop is a profound privilege. It's also a puzzlement. It's both a strange and a great way to follow Jesus! It's a *both/and* kind of job. A bishop finds him- or herself occupying seemingly contradictory spaces simultaneously. Routinely a bishop will be at the center and the edges of things, occupying the metaphorical balcony for oversight and the bustling dance floor of activity concurrently.

The bishop is a peer to all the baptized and yet conferred with a unique role and authority among the baptized: concomitantly, a guardian and creator; a conservator with a risk-taking streak—or a risk-taker with a heart for conservation. A planter and plucker-*up* of things. A compelling speaker and a more compelling question maker. A see-er of tomorrow, today. An embodiment of God's grace and mercy, particularly to the errant and weak while establishing and maintaining boundaries and discipline. A steward of "why" in a "what" and "how much" world. Given to many words but thriving in silence. A solitary soul adventurer situated in community, making a living as a public theologian.

Despite the Risk

I write to speak of the ministry of bishop as leadership. This offering comes in the tenth year of my episcopate as a bishop diocesan in a particular place among particular people. I am aware that it is a precarious thing to hold forth from one's specific context about leadership and the episcopate in general. Contexts differ wildly. Resources for ministry and uniqueness of institutional history may vary tremendously. What works in Oregon doesn't guarantee anything in Oahu. What is pitch-perfect in Mississippi may be tone-deaf in Minnesota. Still, this discussion is worth the risk, because there are practices and paradigms that transcend particularity for the effective exercise of *episkopoi*.

The big idea of this offering is the exercise of leadership as a spiritual discipline comprised of ethical practices that are adaptive in nature. The faithful application of these practices will deftly account for diversity of contexts, individual giftedness, financial resources, and the specificity of challenges.

The goal of the practice of leadership is to identify, embody, and develop capacities that mobilize individuals and groups to make progress on significant problems, which is precisely what Jesus taught and modeled.

Applied Soul Force

I have been fortunate to have studied the theory and practice of leadership, over the last two decades, in places like the Harvard Kennedy School, the Kansas Leadership Center, and MIT. In these places, labeled "secular settings" by some, I've found a new prism through which to better understand the genius of God, God's coming among us.

I have picked up a more expansive and nuanced lexicon to understand Jesus, Peter, Paul, and their work, not only as faithfulness but also as experiments in community mobilization to close the gap between earth and heaven. From this perspective, now I see the Samaritan woman as empowered by an encounter to engage in heart talk that creates new possibility for her community. And the Gerasene demoniac as being invited to leverage his wounds and healing for community healing. The point being, at the intersection of biblical exegesis and leadership studies is an incredible insight and energy source to create and sustain ministry, especially for the complex ministry of the bishop.

Theologically speaking, this approach to ministry and leadership provides new understanding and appreciation for the reality of *imago Dei* and the capacity gifted to the human family by a good God. And it rescues the ideal and practice of Christian love from sentimentalism and rightly identifies, appreciates, and applies it as the soul force it is.

Examples of applied soul force as leadership practices would be the diagnosis of a leadership challenge, which is usually the first task in the exercise of leadership and is really about refusing or being healed from blindness. The self-management necessary to exert leadership can be understood as an invitation to Christian maturity required to do difficult work. Energizing and mobilizing others to take up leadership are actually about love poured out. And intervening skillfully in a challenge is about commissioning and sending people to make a difference. So, then, the practice of leadership is a spiritual discipline guided and supported by a transformational biblical hermeneutic to increase human capacity to bring the love of God into the real world.

It All Belongs to God

Still, some choose to limit themselves and others by sticking to and commending a narrow slate of options for parish Christian education, seminary formation, and even bishop orientation and continuing education. This is an impractical and hazardous approach. In the face of real church and world problems it is like sending "sheep to be slaughtered," but not how Paul meant that phrase (Rom. 8:36, quoting Isa. 53:7).

Worship of God means God deserves our best, and equipping the people of God means positioning them to offer their best to God and the world God loves. High-quality learning exists beyond the church and it will benefit the church. But some worry by studying leadership in nontraditional places for the church that we are somehow attempting to "baptize secular ideas." My worry is different. I worry about the church and her ministers, underserving God, the gospel, the baptized, and the world by not taking full advantage of all the learning around us. And incidentally, aren't we supposed to be baptizing anyway?!

"The earth is the Lord's, and the fulness thereof; the world, and they that dwell therein," proclaims the author of Psalm 24 in his opening line (KJV). If it all belongs to God and God is revealed in all things anyway, perhaps our rationale for sticking exclusively to ecclesiastical educational offerings needs to be reviewed.

Not only that, but the examination for the ordination of a priest seems to support my point: "Will you be diligent in the readings and study of Holy Scriptures, and in seeking the knowledge of such things that make you a stronger and more able minister of Christ?"[1] New focus on leadership practices as spiritual discipline throughout the church will make us more able ministers of Christ for the church and the world today.

Beyond the Title and Role

I'm pretty sure my obsession with the theory and practice of leadership began when I enlisted in the US Navy seven days after graduating high school. Boot camp, to be specific—Great Lakes, Illinois. We called it Great Mistakes! Early on, I was given a small bit of authority over other new recruits. I was given a role and a title. Not exactly sure why. But there I was.

Back then I thought title and role were synonymous with leadership. Most people do, especially in the church—how about you? Now I know that the exercise of authority with title and role isn't synonymous with the practice of leadership. The more precise nomenclature would be formal authority. Formal authority is a good, necessary, and respectable thing. It makes the trains run on time. That's what they were asking me to do in boot camp, to help make the trains run on time, help solve some day-to-day concerns. Maintain order.

Formal authority is an essential resource for everything from parenting to running a business and running a country. A bishop has formal authority conferred by their electing diocese, and the entire House of Bishops is asked to lend its authority to give consent to that election. With the laying on of hands, the garb, and the receiving of the crozier, the conferral is complete. Power is conferred by a group, for specific service.

A bishop is endowed with the authority to: confirm, reaffirm, receive, and ordain; to teach, discipline, convene, establish, and decree. Read the examination for the ordination of a bishop in the Book of Common Prayer and you will see the job description is clear: protect, direct, and order. All these are essential actions necessary to guide and govern the church. And I'll just bet that if you were to keep a bishop's journal day-to-day, you would see that the work regularly falls neatly into those three categories: protection, direction, and order.

That said, let's pause a moment here to thank God for those who exercise the privilege of authority thoughtfully, prayerfully, and skillfully! I don't know where the world or the church would be without people dutifully living into their conferred formal authority. Still, as normative and essential as formal authority is to regular operation, it's distinct from the exercise of leadership.

Think of it this way: the work that formal authority does today once required the resource of leadership in the past. Consider the women's suffrage movement in the United States. The right to vote for women in our country is a settled matter now, thank God. But there was a time when women, with the aid of allies, had to exercise leadership to confront formal authority—that is, those who protected, directed, and ordered the status quo to deny them that right.

There's a creative tension between formal authority and the practice of leadership in any institution and system. And as bishop one piece of our work should more routinely be increasing the likelihood of leadership behavior in our systems while maintaining the formal authority bestowed. I said at the beginning it was a "both/and" job!

What if in your bishop's journal you tracked not only the times and ways you exerted formal authority but also when and how you exerted leadership? Here's a question: What leadership work might you and I be called to do now so that a problem will move to the work of formal authority in the years to come?

While formal authority and leadership should not be understood as perpetually opposed forces, there is a perpetual tension between the two. We could show this in a Venn diagram illustrating the difference between the two ideas as well as the potential overlap. Or it could more imaginatively be understood by thinking of two people dancing the tango! The dancers—two distinct entities—in close quarters, guiding and directing each other from point to point on a dance floor as many watch.

But formal authority rarely wants to dance with leadership, and who would take the lead in the dance anyway? It is the rigid maintenance of formal authority that so often is to blame for leadership being refused a dance. Why? Because formal authority is conferred by others and therefore can be taken away when it's perceived that the authority figure, the bishop, has crossed the line. Leadership has at its core the inevitability of redrawing formerly established and acceptable lines.

Don't we get a peek at this dance as we watch Jesus take up his wandering work of mobilizing folks all around Galilee? As he journeys, he is pelted by questions about the nature of his authority by the Pharisees and scribes and eventually Pontius Pilate. The questions intend to reveal the origins of his authority, where he was trained, his agenda, and his pedigree.

The questions reveal little tolerance for individual agency or disequilibrium in the system—two ingredients absolutely necessary to accomplish leadership. Their questions suggest that they imagine that part of being a formal authority is to disempower any expressions of leadership beyond their ranks.

Jesus, on the other hand, seems to understand that what we are calling leadership here can be taken up by anyone, anywhere, anytime without the benefit of title and role. Either Jesus democratizes leadership by his example and teaching or simply points to its preexistent, ubiquitous, distributive nature! Incidentally, neither Jesus, John the Baptist, Mary (Jesus's mother), or Peter was ordained or possessed formal authority, and yet each exerted leadership that the church argues changed the world!

To read the entire Bible through this lens reveals that it is a wonderful testament to men and women, overwhelmingly laypeople, who without the benefit of formal authority made a difference in the real world. The converse is also true. The Bible tells us of men and women who possessed formal authority, title, and role, but who found themselves in opposition to God's mission being brought about by leadership activity from the edges of an institution or society.

Time for a Definition

I've argued so far that leadership is a spiritual discipline and is distinct from formal authority. Now, it's time that I offered a working definition of the word "leadership." Here are two. The first definition comes from Ron Heifetz of the Harvard Kennedy School and his important work in adaptive leadership. From him we learn that "leadership is the capacity to mobilize people to address tough problems—especially problems they would rather avoid."[2]

I find everything I need in this definition to inspire, locate, and instruct me as I attempt to follow Jesus alongside others and exercise leadership as a bishop. Still, there are others who may prefer a definition that uses the more familiar vocabulary of the church. That definition might be: "Leadership is the God-given capacity residing in an individual and community, which is aided by the Holy Spirit, to effect progress consistent with the teachings and example of Jesus of Nazareth."

With those definitions in mind, I hope your mind is searching for flesh and blood examples of those definitions. What names come to your mind? For me it is C. T. Vivian, Bayard Rustin, Diane Nash, Ella Baker, and Marian Wright Edelman, just to name a very few.

The truth is men and women over the millennia, names we know and names we will never know, some of them bishops of the church, attempted to exert leadership because they deeply held it to be consistent with having a life with Christ. They seem to evidence with their lives the idea that life as a member of Christ's church wasn't confined to a place to personally belong and be fortified but rather a cosmic and terrestrial community with which to believe, belong, and become. Their following of Jesus viewed through the lens of the definitions of leadership provides myriad examples of the competencies the academy calls leadership behavior today.

Leadership understands that there is a capacity within each of us that allows us to identify the gaps between what we say and how we actually live and to find common purpose relative to that acknowledgment and make progress across that gap. The enabling and normalizing of that kind of work are what we should call leadership. And that kind of work, in a word, is consequential.

Of the many things a bishop should be, he/she should be consequential. It should go without saying that a consequential bishop is more than an affable, eloquent, and overbusy bishop, though a consequential bishop may be those things as well. In Matthew's gospel, we hear Jesus convey his notion of being consequential. He said we should be "salt" and "light" (Matt. 5:13–16). No surprise he chose two generative substances understood primarily by their effect.

You and I are not leaders by virtue of our ordination to the episcopate. Not even a little. Not according to the definitions provided. Rather, beginning at previous ordinations and now our ordination to the episcopate, a dynamic and generative question hangs in the air and remains for the duration of our episcopate: Will you use the authority conferred by the Spirit and the people to exert leadership? I have thought of that question in some form nearly every day of my ten years of being a bishop.

Leadership Is Rare

The exercise of leadership is rare. Relative to leadership the exercise of formal authority is more common, more acceptable, and easier and regularly provides more satisfaction to the most people. Formal authority is less messy and less dangerous. Formal authority gets the most thank-you correspondence!

It feels good to run a meeting competently and complete an agenda, even if that meeting or agenda tends toward technical things and avoids acknowledging the gap between who institutions say they are and how they actually live. It feels better to raise money, build a building, and cut a ribbon than it does to wade through multiple interpretations of institutional reality, land on a clear sense of purpose, and then run data-driven faith experiments led by that purpose. Making progress on a problem that people are reluctant to even acknowledge can't be achieved in a set amount of time, like constructing a building. A process like that will demand that each member of the organization and especially the one leading the intervention grow and develop new capacities.

Leadership is about growing and the facilitation of growth. No wonder when the apostle Paul speaks of leadership, he says it is reserved for the "diligent" (Rom. 12:8)—that is, rigorous, assiduous, tenacious, and sedulous. Leadership is rare because its exercise is routinely thankless, laborious, slow moving, slow to reward, costly, disequilibrium creating, dangerous, demanding and causing loss, regularly and vehemently opposed, and regularly and often dramatically defeated by the status quo phenomenon.

Leadership is intended more than it is attempted and attempted more than it is sustained. Remember, many of the people we now call martyrs exerted leadership by tending to problems and gaps and, as a result, were publicly maligned before paying a financial price or the ultimate price.

Each January we celebrate Dr. Martin Luther King's birthday, but we might keep before us that, in the year before Dr. King was assassinated, a national poll reported that 75 percent of Americans disapproved of him, while another poll showed that he was voted the "most hated man in America."[3] What must it have felt like to be him every morning? How did he sustain himself in his work? There's a good reason why Ron Heifetz and his friend Marty Linsky authored a book titled *Leadership on the Line: Staying Alive through the Dangers of Leading.* The cost of exerting leadership is high and therefore leadership is rare.

I'm convinced that many among our ranks began as people called to be lifesavers and world changers but now find themselves consciously or unconsciously colluding with an institution that elegantly fends off practices of leadership, adaptation, and progress. The truth is, most of us are in no danger of being martyred. The danger we face is the slow hemorrhages caused by a thousand paper cuts and the personal structural damage by corrosion of vocation. By the way, corrosion in Latin means to be "gnawed through"! Which brings me to burnout.

Among our ranks, we speak of burnout of clergy, including bishops, and we point to poor boundary keeping and overwork as the chief reasons. I agree. But perhaps more thought should be given to the idea of burnout as psychological and spiritual fatigue due to the frustration of failing to reach the true scope or scale of vocation. The world and the church have real problems and fatal flaws. This is the reality. And in response to a plethora of existential threats, we deflect, underestimate, avoid, resist, and oppose to our own peril institutionally and personally.

Leadership is about identifying existential threats and making progress on their defeat. But what stymies the exercise of leadership is what I call the unholy trinity of responses to reality. Walter Brueggemann has written that, rather than face reality, what we default to individually and collectively is "despair, cynicism, or denial."[4] One of the primary tasks of leadership is to creatively, with political savvy, even good cheer, refuse to participate in a cover-up or even sentimental distraction from reality.

What got Dr. King his aforementioned poll numbers was his refusal to allow an uncritical sense of patriotism and even the concern for his own life to cause him blindness or laryngitis about racial injustice, economic disparity, or an unnecessary war. Said another way, leadership refuses the practice of work avoidance even in the face of risk.

People swoon when they hear Dr. King's "I Have a Dream" speech, and understandably so. But it's his speech given at Riverside Church in New York City in 1967 that I often commend as a resource for understanding what it means to get reality in the room. What he accomplishes in this, his longest speech, is "to address problems, especially problems people would rather avoid." He articulates the gap between heaven and the United States. There are numerous examples of this bravery in our biblical heritage also.

The Hebrew midwives Shiphrah and Puah, Esther, Jeremiah, and Jesus, to name a few, all refused to participate in the cover-up. They refused systemic seduction! Each exercised self-management, which is critical to the practice of leadership and is a spiritual discipline. Each models being a differentiated personality, rightly subordinating their ego needs for an overarching purpose. This is a critical piece for leadership because what systems don't want and therefore the church doesn't want is too much reality. So, to keep the full measure of reality at a distance, we collude consciously or unconsciously to mitigate truth. We prefer flattery over facts, myth over truth, and euphemism over reflection. Listen to what Isaiah felt compelled to say to his community: "Woe unto them that call evil good, and good evil; that put darkness for light, and light for darkness; that put bitter for sweet, and sweet for bitter" (Isa. 5:20 KJV).

Isaiah is refusing to participate in the cover-up, refusing it as a norm for his community, and refusing to speak and behave as if God endorses the cover-up. The practice of leadership remains hypersensitive to being seduced into a cover-up. The bishop mustn't be seduced to aid and abet the cover-up. What is crucial to remember about Isaiah's words is that "woe" is not condemnation for taking up a particular behavior necessarily; rather "woe" is a funeral word, meaning that a particular path will lead to death and dying.

If that is true, then, systematically and normatively getting the truth in the room and attending to reality in the church are not only spiritual formation but essential for life abundant and even resurrection. I can't think of a better competency for us as bishops to be developing in ourselves and our dioceses. Developing this competency will begin to transform each meeting the bishop convenes from an exercise in simple authority to an exercise of leadership.

Love and Not Love

But the exercise of leadership isn't simply new techniques, an improved lexicon, or hypervigilance. Those are all important features but nevertheless technical matters. What truly drives the adaptive work of leadership is something very old and very real.

Early into my time as bishop, I invited Ron Heifetz to address the clergy and some key lay leaders in the diocese. I did this because I'd been convening a conversation about leadership as discipleship diocese-wide. Ron was to be the cherry on the top of that milkshake.

Prior to his visit, I, with colleagues, designed a learning module around leadership and made it mandatory for all newly ordained clergy as well as any new clergy to the diocese. We call it "Learning to Lead." There is also "Called to Lead" for lay leaders and "Steps to Lead" for teenagers. The purpose of each offering was and still is to better equip people for the application of faith in the real world and changing church. My hope was that Ron, with his considerable credentials and his winsome way, would amplify and fortify my reason for focusing on leadership and leadership development. He did just that. In story and paradigm that day he showed us why he gets the big bucks. He charmed and taught us. He challenged us to see again how God was alive in our work.

But it was the day before the seminar that provided a mountaintop moment for me. In one of Atlanta, Georgia's, fanciest restaurants we met Ron for lunch. From the window of this penthouse restaurant, we could see Stone Mountain, a piece of granite five miles in circumference etched with the images of Confederate generals: Stonewall Jackson, Robert E. Lee, and President Jefferson Davis. Just after the iced tea was poured, I pounced. I had read all of his stuff. Viewed all the videos. Even taken the courses at the Kennedy School. And now, the oracle was in front of me. I couldn't help myself. I gushed, "How cool is this—I'm talking to the guy!" Lots was said. And upon reflection he asked more questions than he offered answers.

As the lunch continued and I blathered on about all the techniques of leadership, Ron interrupted me. It seemed like the room fell silent. It felt like he and I were alone together. That's when he said it: "If you're going to engage in leadership, leadership that changes things, you're going to have to love." Oh, the irony! The poetry. Here I am the follower of a Jew of long ago who taught at table, sitting with a Jew at a table right now, and he's telling me it's all about love! All this while, looking at a mountain that Dr. King referred to in his "I Have a Dream" sermon. Never thought my mountaintop would be Stone Mountain!

The rest of the lunch was a blur. We talked about the logistics of his visit the next day, but I'd been struck by lightning. I knew it was all about love but somehow, I didn't. I have come to know that being a bishop is the practice of focusing love through the exercise of leadership to the glory of God and the benefit of neighbor.

I have come to understand that the capacity that resides and can be developed in the individual and community is love. Not the sentiment but the soul force! Love is who God is and therefore is the most eternal and durable force in the universe, which is actively overcoming everything that is not love. So, then, leadership is a particular way to make love real, delivered through distinct practices that will mobilize people to effect progress consistent with Jesus's example and teaching.

What we face regularly that is not of love is fear and anxiety. We are anxious creatures, God's "peculiar treasure" (Psalms 135.4 KJV). And our anxieties have, do, and will form our institutions. Some argue that part of what a bishop is called to do is hold anxieties for the diocese. Formal authority might take up that calling, but leadership wouldn't. Leadership will love enough to share the responsibility for the future of the group with the group and name and work through the anxiety.

I wonder how anxiety has shaped you. I wonder how anxiety has shaped your diocese. I wonder, how will it shape your episcopate? Our anxieties drive our relationships with the truth and with one another. They keep us meek rather than bold. They keep us coy rather than candid. They keep us fearful when faith is needed.

The practice of leadership invites us to increase our capacity for holding steady in the face of personal and institutional anxiety. Holding steady is not inaction or indifference and it's not just "keep calm," as the T-shirts advise. Holding steady is a proactive stance. The chess player waiting for his turn to move is not inactive. The scientist waiting for the results from her latest experiment isn't being passively inactive.

Holding steady is not to be confused with rigidity. Rigidity suggests an inability to bend, while holding steady is an embodied spiritual stance on the way to adaptation. But the Harvard Kennedy School wasn't the first to come up with this notion. Holding steady is what the apostle Paul is referring to when he says, "Having done [everything] to stand. Stand therefore" (Eph. 6:13–14 KJV). That is, having executed the plan according to the purpose, now we actively wait and watch the effect iterating based on a constant feedback loop. Holding steady is what Jesus does before the devil, the Pharisees, and Pontius Pilate. It's what he was doing as he wrote in the dirt at the stoning of a woman while he waited to see if there was any honesty in her almost-executioners.

In each example, Jesus holds steady because of his radical clarity of purpose. Requisite for holding steady effectively and graciously is clarity of purpose. Rigidity immobilizes us because of ego. Purpose allows us to hold steady until we learn what the next refinement is to be that is consistent with our purpose. So many biblical images come to mind. There is the tree planted by the water in Psalm 1, not rigid but active under the surface by sending roots and iterating to sustain itself. And Paul, in Ephesians 4, on the way to gaining the stature of Christ, says, "be no more children, tossed to and fro, and carried about" (Eph. 4:14 KJV).

When to hold steady and for what purpose seems to be a measurement of Christian maturity for Paul. This is a critical leadership competency because much of the opposition to change lives in a place often beyond the reach of logic. The average person doesn't oppose change for change's sake; rather they resist and oppose it because it represents loss. So, then, leadership must artfully acknowledge loss as a step of transformation. This is a capacity we must increase among those who live out the strange vocation of bishop.

I do believe our eucharistic liturgy prepares us for the work of getting the loss in the room and holding steady as it is processed on the way to authentic hope. Sunday after Sunday we say, "Christ has died, Christ has risen, Christ will come again." These words, this theology, this understanding, this gift is what, at least on paper, should put the church out front in leading individual and institutional adaptation. For us, through the eyes of faith we rehearse and believe that grief and loss become transformational and provide meaning and reliable coordinates for how we live in the real world.

My honest desire in making this offering isn't just to convey the magnitude of the problems that face Christ's church or her ministers. Neither is it to suggest we are just a few continuing education modules away from Episcopal Church nirvana. Rather, the world has changed, and the church has changed. But we have not been left "orphaned" (John 14:18). God is still trustworthy! There are resources to harness an immense capacity within us. "Life is changed, not ended," and so must we. Christ's next iteration of his church is pushing up through the cracks in the concrete all around us.[5] What is required of us as bishops at this critical juncture? I am convinced the answer to that question is leadership.

CHAPTER 11

Rejecting the Bishop as Sole Visionary

Kym Lucas

O, de blin' man stood on de road and cried
Cryin' O, my Lord, save-a me
De blin' man stood on de road and cried
Cryin' what kind o' shoes am dose you wear
Cryin' what kind o' shoes am dose you wear
Cryin' O, my Lord
Save-a me
De blin' man stood on de road an' cried
    Cryin' dat he might receib his sight
Cryin' dat he might receib his sight
Cryin' O, my Lord, save-a me
De blin' man stood on de road an' cried
Cryin' dese shoes I wear am de Gospel shoes
Cryin' dese shoes I wear am de Gospel shoes
Cryin' O, my Lord
Save-a me
De blin' man stood on de road an' cried

Traditional spiritual

Having been an ordained church leader for most of my adult life, I must confess growing increasingly agitated when people quote Proverbs 29:18 to me regarding congregational life. My agitation chiefly centers around the supposition that "vision" comes from the professional Christian (the clergy) and is visited upon the people.

At every job interview, I have been asked, "What is your vision for our church?" And as bishop, in most every meeting with clergy and lay leaders I am asked, "What is your vision for the diocese?" Those questions assume that I have been given some secret *gnosis* about the community or been infused with divinely imparted ideas about who they should be and what they should do. Surely, as a bishop, I would have "The Vision" for the diocese. And while I was not surprised, I confess some disappointment that the pointy hat did not improve my powers of prognostication or open a 5G line to the divine. On the contrary, these days, I find myself even more annoyed by the expectation.

My typical rejoinder is quoting the prophet Micah: "And what does the Lord require of you, but to do justice, love mercy, and walk humbly with your God?"; or reciting 2 Chronicles 7:14: "If my people who are called by my name humble themselves, pray, seek my face, and turn from their sinful ways, then I will hear from heaven, and will forgive their sin and heal their land."

For the church, vision cannot be about an individual's great idea or new and improved marketing strategy. The church's vision must be centered on faithful living and leaning into our call to reconcile and heal our broken world. Vision is about recognizing how blind we are, striving to see what God is doing in our context, and aligning ourselves with God's purposes. "Thy Kingdom come, thy will be done, on earth as it is in heaven."

When it comes to seeing clearly, the story of Saul on the road to Damascus serves as a powerful example. In that story, Saul has received credentials and direction from religious authorities and is heading out to arrest followers of Jesus and bring them to Jerusalem in chains. On the way, Saul sees a bright light; he falls to the ground and a voice, identifying as Jesus, speaks to him. When Saul gets up, he can "see nothing." For three days he waits, until fearful but faithful Ananias comes, lays hands on him, and prays for him: that he might once again see and be filled with the Holy Spirit.

In many contexts, the assumption is that the bright light blinded Saul, but that is not what the text says. The text says Saul sees the light, falls on the ground, and gets up seeing nothing. The underlying reality is that Saul was already blind to so much. He was blind to his own self-righteousness and blind to the suffering of those around him. He was convinced that by defending his religious institution and violently enforcing his beliefs, he was serving God. Saul was even blind to his own self-destructive tendencies; Jesus says (in a verse sometimes omitted in translations) that "it is hard for thee to kick against the goads," intimating that Saul was damaging himself with his persecution crusade (Acts 26:14 KJV after Eccles. 12:11—"goads" meaning a sharp stick used for herding).

For the church to faithfully participate in God's vision, we must recognize our blindness. There is much in our communities, and in our world, we have turned a blind eye to: children in cages at our border, the continued legacy of white supremacy, unjust economic structures and growing economic disparity, the rise in homelessness and rates of suicide, just to name a few. We church folks have been much more concerned with sheltering in our buildings, debating about who "deserves" to be at God's table, and wringing our hands at our decreases in attendance and in political power. At our Baptism, we Episcopalians vow to renounce the "evil powers of this world that corrupt and destroy the creatures of God," but we have spent precious little time examining the ways in which we participate and reinforce the systems that continue corrupting our lives and destroying our planet. We cut ourselves off from God if we are searching for a "vision" without rigorous examination of our hearts and the condition of our community. Ironically, vision often becomes the trope we hide behind to try to prevent the light of the Christ from exposing our blindness.

The Johari Window Model

Another critical piece in understanding the role of vision in the church requires acknowledgment of an individual's inability to see everything. The model of the Johari window can be helpful in understanding the limits of our field of vision. In this model there are four spaces: (1) the open space, where things are obvious to everyone; (2) the hidden space, where we know things that others don't know, (3) the blind space, where others know things that we don't know, and (4) the unknown space, which for me is the space only God knows. The church cannot have any faithful vision until we are willing to address our blind space and strive to see from the perspective of the other.

In the Road to Damascus story, Ananias sees Saul as a murderous persecutor of the faithful, which is so far from Saul's view of himself, but Ananias's view matures (with a little divine persuasion) to where he sees Saul as a child of God, beloved by Jesus. He lays hands on Saul, without a word of reproof or derision, and "something like scales" falls from Saul's eyes. Saul is healed, restored, and made whole because a man beneath his notice, a man for whom he had nothing but disdain, enabled him to see differently.

Being a near lifelong Episcopalian, I have often fallen into the trap of believing that this "branch of the Jesus Movement" is the best. We have the best words and the best music. We have the prettiest buildings and the most progressive theology. And we are a church built with blood money: from the slave trade and "captains of industry." We are steeped in the false belief that our Anglocentric culture is intrinsically more valuable and more faithful than other cultures.

Talking to others about The Episcopal Church, I've heard our faith described as anemic, our worship called boring, our culture designated exclusive, elitist, and snobbish. It is difficult to hear yourself described in ways that you don't recognize, but God reveals deep truths to us embedded in the vision of others.

In his book *Canoeing the Mountains*, author Tod Bolsinger points out how when Lewis and Clark found themselves way "off the map," they began seeking counsel from those who were ordinarily beneath their notice: an indigenous nursing mother and a slave descended from Africans. These voices contributed to the success of the mission in ways that neither Meriwether Lewis nor William Clark could have anticipated when they set out to find a route to the Pacific Ocean.

No vision will be faithful if we refuse to listen to the most marginalized voices in our context. The church must be willing to see the truth of its failures, its faithlessness, and all it has ignored before we can see the alternate path to which we are called.

In so many cases, what church folk call "vision" is rooted in self-absorption. A church has a "vision" to grow their attendance; a church has a "vision" to build an addition on their current edifice. "Vision" in this context is simply a strategy for perpetuating and sustaining our institutions. If the "vision" is only about self-aggrandizement and filling our coffers, if the "vision" is not chiefly about love of God and neighbor, it is just another sort of blindness.

Vision must be rooted in the first and greatest commandment, "Love the Lord your God with all your heart, with all your soul, and with all your mind." And a second is like it: "You shall love your neighbor as yourself" (Matt. 22:37, 39). The church has often behaved as if this is an either/or proposition: you can love God (through prayer and praise) *or* you can love your neighbor (through service and advocacy), all the while placing your own needs first. This false dichotomy skews our vision, because it denies reality. As Saul learned, we cannot love God without loving our neighbor, nor can we love our neighbor or ourselves rightly without encountering the one who is love and relationship.

A vision rooted in love will be characterized by justice, mercy, and humility. Our understanding of justice comes from the Hebrew *mishpat*, which means to act with fairness, equity, and impartiality in any situation. *Mishpat* is connected to *hesed* (loving-kindness) and *tsadek* (righteousness) because justice is the result of right relationship: "Justice is love in street clothes," as the Rt. Rev. Robert Wright of Atlanta is fond of saying.

The church has too often been on the side of injustice in our world. From the Crusades to the enslavement of Africans for profit, from the oppression of women to the abuse of children, the church has chosen the world over the gospel again and again. We cannot live faithfully unless we reject the systems that corrupt, oppress, and exploit.

Clear vision can never be severed from truth—that is, the being of the triune God. Vision disconnected from truth is illusion. Again, listening to disenfranchised people speak their truth challenges our view; truth from the margins shows how far the truths that we live by vary from the divine truth to which we are called. Tough discussions and vulnerable conversations help create awareness of our blindness. Sometimes we can hear what we cannot see. Creating space and being committed to hard conversations provide the groundwork for a clearer, more faithful view.

A faithful vision must also reflect mercy (loving-kindness) and humility. We only know of God what God reveals to us. And our vision will never be perfect in this life: "now we see through a glass, darkly" (1 Cor. 13:12 KJV). Still, we must commit to following where our Lord leads, proclaiming and demonstrating that the kingdom of God has come near to us.

The church has spent an inordinate amount of time maintaining our institutional structures as if we were in the "survival" business and not the business of "abundant life." And while the institution offers stability and structures of accountability, it cannot be the rock on which we stand. We must stand on our confession and witness of a life transformed by our encounter with God through Christ. "On Christ the solid rock I stand. All other ground is sinking sand."[1]

As bishop, I represent the institution and not necessarily the most faithful parts. I serve as administrator, theologian, pastor, and prophet. Those roles are difficult to tease apart, and my husband often reminds me that a theologian's primary job is pointing out that which is not God. This is not an easy task in a culture that expects clergy not only to have all the answers but also to make everyone feel good about themselves.

In this context, it is incredibly hard to say, "Your building is not God," "Your liturgy is not God," "Your political ideology is not God," "That Bible you're wielding as weapon? Not God," "Your bank account? Also, not God." While these may be useful tools to help us seek, find, and serve God, they are not, in fact, the God we have come to know in Christ, through the Spirit. The triune God is so much more and calls us to a life and a love that are so much more than we can possibly imagine.

And in the time of pandemic our imaginations have been particularly challenged. The advent of COVID-19 exposed us: our vulnerability and our brokenness. Congregations found themselves exiled from their buildings, and as a nation we found ourselves watching Derek Chauvin's dispassionate expression as he squeezed the life out of George Floyd. Communities of faith were forced to ask themselves what they actually believed about God, about grace, about redemption. Many in leadership looked to me, their bishop, to tell them what to do, to offer them a vision. But I suspect that most of the discussion around "vision" was primarily a request for certainty. It was a desire for someone to foretell the future, to assure them that a life in faith provided exemption from pain and sacrifice. But discipleship is neither pain- nor sacrifice-free. Following Jesus is costly, because real relationship is costly. Faithful vision includes this hard truth: if we are following Jesus, the cross we are called to pick up and carry soon comes into view.

The vision of church hasn't really changed in two thousand years. We build communities that form each other in faith. We worship together and empower each other to strive for justice; we form communities centered on Christ and call them church, and we seek to bring about the kingdom of God. But we must never conflate the kingdom of church with the kingdom of God (as Leonardo Boff frequently reminds us). We must constantly strive to peel away the blinders and truly see *imago Dei* in each and every person we encounter, because our goal is full communion with each other around the table of Christ. The path to vision is an ongoing process:

1. Have difficult and vulnerable conversations
2. Listen to those around us
3. Recognize our blind spaces
4. Repent and seek healing and reconciliation
5. Pray a lot
6. Take the next faithful step
7. Rinse and repeat

As bishop, I serve my people and remind them of that to which we are all called. My episcopal task is not coming up with the next great scheme or figuring out how to "fix" my congregations or my diocese. I have no secret gnosis. The vision that God is revealing for The Episcopal Church in Colorado will come as we humble ourselves, as we seek God's face, as we follow our Lord and Savior. The vision, the real, divine vision, will come as we take the next faithful step as the body of Christ, acknowledging our blindness and shining the light of Christ into every dark corner of our world.

CHAPTER 12

Themes That Challenge Episcopal Leadership

Diana Akiyama

A day or so after my consecration I had this waking dream: I am kneeling as the consecrating bishops put their hands on my head and shoulders. After the consecrating prayer, they remove their hands. My phone buzzes; someone has texted me. I look at the screen and read, "Diana, Congratulations on your consecration. LMAO, Rusty."

Rusty Kimsey knew, as seasoned bishops have told me recently, you don't know what it is to be a bishop until you are a bishop. It's easy to be on the sidelines criticizing and offering gratuitous advice to the bishop; it's a whole other thing to be the bishop: on point, in the public eye, and vulnerable to the temptation to offer wisdom or a vision, only to be pushed back for having done so. In the early years of my priesthood I generously shared my unsolicited comments and advice with my bishop, and now I'm quite sure Bishop Kimsey is very amused.

I am in the early days of this work, which makes writing anything about the episcopacy a true work in progress. The frame that keeps coming back to me as I consider what it means to serve as a bishop in 2021 is one that is both abstract yet achingly relevant. The current reality of our world, our nation, our church, and our dioceses is one of grave urgency. Yet within this unrelenting sense of urgency are undeniable places and times of grace. Time. Place. Relationship. This is my frame and one I did not choose. It chose me.

Time

Why would anyone want to be a bishop now? The church is "dying," as some would say. Death and dying language is helpful to me only if we are talking about taking the time to grieve alongside the new kind of living we are being called into. I miss the days when the church nave was so full the ushers scrambled to set up folding chairs in the aisles—both sides and center. But honestly, I don't miss the days when girls couldn't serve as acolytes, women could not be ordained to the priesthood, and my family was one of two Asian American families in our church. It is true that membership in many of our congregations is getting smaller, not larger. But this has been a fact far longer than we are willing to admit. The difference now is that we have run out of distractions from the fact: the church is changing. For some that means it's dying.

From my perspective, this is a great time to serve as a bishop. I say this not because I have the answers but because I am energized by the questions and the talents that are emerging in response. In 1988, I wondered, after conversations with students, faculty, and staff, what it would take for us (The Episcopal Church) to imagine church differently? Several years later, I wondered when we would begin to talk about our faith in a way that served as vibrant and vital counternarrative to the biblical literalists. As I started creating programs to highlight religious diversity, I also wondered how we could tell our Christian story in a way that had integrity and was life-giving as society became more religiously diverse. We are now engaging many questions like these. It would be ill informed to say The Episcopal Church has finally "seen the light" as if we only now figured out that racism is evil, or that poverty has roots in corporate capitalism. Over the years, we've been pretty good at identifying the issues God has set before us and invites us to engage. We're just not so good at diving into the work and staying in the deep end. And even that observation is no news flash. Humans, in general, are loath to spend time developing the habits that will change us and therefore change the world. And so the question I have carried around with me for decades and the reason I obeyed the call, and now sit here typing out this piece as a newly consecrated bishop, is, Why does my faith as an Episcopalian matter, in light of the latest upheavals and downfalls in our church and the world?

My faith matters now more than ever as my particular denomination is undergoing dramatic change because I can see only one way through—one way forward—and that is in and with the risen Christ. There is no other way. It is remarkable, and I continue in these early days to reflect on this, to be elected bishop after a long priesthood serving in the mission field of the "unchurched."

Speaking objectively, this form of priestly ministry may not seem very unique. I would simply remind us of the preference our church has (and might wistfully want to continue) for full-time priests we can proudly call "rectors." One conversation with a clergy colleague, early in my ministry, said it all: "So Diana, when are you going to get a real job and join the church?" Odd. I thought I *was* in a real job serving the church.

After I recovered from that comment, I reflected on "why" I was happily moving about a college campus often never recognized as a priest. In short, the life in that environment was vibrant, intellectually stimulating, and full of great questions—*big* questions. I was partnering with all manner of teams comprised of staff, faculty, and students as we tackled diversity, women's equity, gay rights (the term back then), and religious diversity. I preached regularly at the university chapel, always seeking new and creative ways to help folk understand the intersection between intellect and soul—the ways that faith can move us to think expansively and question soulless applications of data. It was fun to swim in those waters. It was also challenging. My colleagues and I were often facing an upstream swim as the biblical literalists and self-righteous Christians swept through campus in swarms of self-satisfaction, leaving us the cleanup work as students eventually defected when the hate, judgmental attitude, and groupthink became too much. This led me to wonder why our campus ministries, including Canterbury, were so anemic. Our Episcopal theology, scripture study, and engagement of social justice are perfect for campus settings. Why so underfunded? Why so focused on our own? What other models are possible?

Thinking about the church from this new vantage point, I also wonder how we can reverse the on-again/off-again approach we've had toward our young adults. The funding, in the vast majority of cases, has been, at best, second tier. Yet, the ongoing and ageless concern continues: "How can we get young people to join us?" We do need to pay attention to fields we left fallow and that we dismissed as being "not really in the church." Young adults need the companionship of a clergy person and a faith community who will simply walk with them, help them stay with the hard questions, and remind them again and again they are loved. They need help learning and practicing the habits of our baptismal vows because this is how we remind ourselves that we have God-given agency, that we are woven into God's purpose, and our actions reflect the hope of transformation in and through Christ. Our campus programs cannot remain the privileged domain of Episcopalian students—if *we* thrive in these faith waters, surely there are others who would delight at being invited in. Now is not the time to pull back. Now is the time to really press on in new ways.

The questions I've been asking all these years have likely played a role in my sense of urgency today as I take the measure of the church. As the singer Tracy Chapman sings, "If not now, when?" Action seems to be the order of the day. We've been given the metrics and scenarios about the future church. It looks different, very different. I wonder about the way in which we deliver the news. Has inciting fear and grief in a people ever worked out well? Certainly, the prophets can be read as gloom- and doomsayers, but that's not what they were intending. Their purpose was to wake up the people from living in ways that were not life-giving, that were dehumanizing for others. Striking fear into their hearts was not the goal; striking focus and serious intentionality centered in faith most certainly was.

My sense of urgency has to do with the metrics, for sure. But even more, it has to do with an opening that has been created by this moment in history. Or perhaps more theological, it has to do with the resurrection that we know follows an anguished death. But, as I said previously, the language of death and dying is most helpful within a frame of living anew. I would add that the part of the church that is dying might very well be the part of the church that has distracted us from the gospel. Which is to say, the part of the church that has been seduced by security and the work involved in keeping it. The death of *that part* is creating the opening—the possibility of something new and alive with gospel urgency.

I wonder about our capacity to enter into the kind of dying we are being called into. Will these be "good" deaths? Will we do the work of our baptismal vows in order to resist blaming and shaming? Will we do the work to build our capacity to grieve in order to move forward?

Outside the empty tomb, Jesus said to Mary, "Don't cling to me." That passage has come to mind frequently since my consecration. We *are* clinging and it's hard not to do so. Those were happier days, we tell ourselves. I'm sure they were—for those who were secure in that world. Back then, the homeless weren't sleeping against our doors, the city wasn't trying to control our feeding ministries, the racial homogeneity of the church wasn't considered an obstacle to living the Good News.

"Don't cling to me." The church, the body of Christ, might be trying to say that to us now. There is more that needs to be given to God before we can see and fully understand. My sense of urgency is not centered on finding the next new way to build security if it is simply trying to do the same thing using different tools. The urgency is about the soul-work urgently needed to become the people God already sees but that we only glimpse. Such a faithful people do not live in fear; do not act out of fear. Such a faithful people do not point fingers at others; instead we reflect long and hard and then prepare to confess in order to be reconciled to one another.

Relationship

We are living in a time when relationships are being heavily curated and styled. Folks gravitate toward associations and loyalties based on sameness. Social media allows us to style ourselves—despite what is actually true—to represent an ideal of ourselves rather than the whole person, warts and all. This reality runs counter to what we teach about being members of Christ's body. The diversity of humanity is the glory of God and is the very thing we filter out with our curated circle of friends and our carefully styled posts on social media.

The irony here is that we are also more full-throated than ever about racial justice; we are urging each other to do business with how we "other" those who are not like us. We are going deep with this too, as we talk about our histories, our ancestors, our laws, and practices—all the ways we have made security a right of the privileged race. I worry, though. This is hard work for everyone and in different ways. In our humanness, the temptation will be to "other" the work of racial justice and reconciliation. This kind of "othering" might look like scholarly engagement to investigate the roots of the issue, easily objectified by the intellectual pursuit of evidence. It might look like blaming others while remaining blind to the work we each must do. It might look like just another power shift as the "mighty are thrown down." These are discouraging examples of racial justice work avoidance, but far more discouraging is the loss of perspective of the reason for this work. Why ought we to care about racial justice? We ought to care because we have been created for relationship with each other. This artful creative work of God's has placed us in each other's midst, and although we may attempt to curate who is in our circle, this would be a departure from God's dream. We are all members of Christ's body. It's an awfully uncomfortable truth, if we're honest. This is why reconciliation is central to this work.

We all know the work that is waiting for us when we promise to be reconciled to one another. There is no shortcut. Many of us bear the wounds of not having done the work, or of doing it poorly. A church of security will not engage the work of reconciliation willingly. It will need to be dragged there when all other options have closed.

Reconciliation requires love, which means we are vulnerable to the other. The kind of love that fuels reconciliation work is the heartbreaking love from a God who knows our "coming in and our going out" and still loves us. It is borne from knowing God loves us because of God's mercy. We know this. So why is reconciliation work so hard?

Barely a bishop for a year, I have run into the temptation to be all-knowing and all-advising. It's a trap for those who yearn for lives to be transformed through love and the requisite vulnerability. There is a kind of modeling that bishops do—I wonder how often it's conscious. Exercising leadership as a bishop from a place of "Father knows best" is a trick-bag not only for the obvious reasons of paternalism and power-over but also because we don't become models of transformation without being in authentic relationship. If we are not embodied models of reconciliation, we are not living into the story of how we live together as one body.

Reconciliation requires preparation and spiritual discipline. It's hard to confess without mutual trust and respect. It's hard to forgive without mutual respect and trust. We can't get very far with this commitment to racial reconciliation if we don't have the basic building blocks in place. I wonder how often the Confession has been central to us in this work. A careful and slow meditation on the theology of the Confession ought to bring us to our knees—without any kind of rubric telling us to. It's all there. "Almighty and merciful God, we confess we have sinned against you in thought, word, and deed. By what we have done and by what we have left undone." No one is exempt: thought, word, and deed. That's pretty much all of what it means to be human. I believe reconciliation work must be life-giving for everyone; otherwise, it's self-righteousness parading as a spiritual practice. Racial reconciliation needs to be engaged from a place of humility not labeling, assigning, or predetermining the outcomes. For some it's a short journey; for others it's a much longer journey. We ought to commit to walk in faith with each and every one in this work, no matter the twists and turns.

Place

There are a few of us new bishops who were leading congregations when the pandemic forced us into lockdown. This experience gives me a particular perspective of one who felt the numbness, disorientation, and hard pivot to keep the congregation together in worship. I managed the anger and frustration of parishioners at being disconnected from the Eucharist. I stood in the crosshairs as some accused me of being unreasonable: the protocols and restrictions became my fault—something I had somehow manufactured. At my most frustrated and discouraged, it was my bishop who brought clarity, calm, and cover. Now, as bishop myself, I have an even fuller understanding of the manner in which he pastored the diocese by being on point. In particular, the Eucharist became the lightning rod. In short order, it began to seem as though our entire sense of being "church" culminated in the Eucharist. If we couldn't celebrate and receive the Eucharist, we weren't having church . . . we weren't engaged in the heart of worship. Priests asked me to allow all sorts of adaptations to the Eucharist in order that their people could receive both bread and wine. It seemed to me as though our theology of the Eucharist was now being held captive by pastoral needs and concerns of unhappy parishioners. Fears that people would leave the church if they couldn't receive the Eucharist were real, and, in some cases, people left the congregation, saying, "I'll come back when you start celebrating the Eucharist again."

This moment in our faith life is excruciating because it makes me wonder how well we've trained our priests about the theology of the Eucharist, but even more it has me wondering about the *power* of the Eucharist in the life of the church. What is going on for us in the Eucharist? Why does this particular part of our liturgical life carry so much significance and weight? What are the stories people need to share about their life as eucharistic people?

We can't walk away from these difficult moments around the pandemic and the Eucharist, simply discounting them as misdirected anger or fear. In truth, there is something happening at our Eucharist, and it is thick with power and promise. The anger and frustration over ceasing the Eucharist during the pandemic are telling us something about who we are as Episcopalians—as liturgical Christians. I don't remember who said this, but it came to me as I reflected on this challenge and opportunity: we are *homo eucharisticus*. We are a eucharistic people—we are made to stand in the presence of this great mystery, to return again and again, seeking a deeper understanding of its power. One of the things I believe is true about liturgy and ritual is that it allows us to say things that cannot otherwise be said. What are people hearing and saying in the Eucharist? What is different because of it?

The pandemic protocols imposed on us a form of physical remoteness that will have lasting effects for many. The need to regard the bodies of others as potential sources of impurity and danger is primal and ancient. The need to protect ourselves and each other today requires us to absorb this as a necessary scientific fact in order to survive. How is this necessity shaping our conversation about the Eucharist? In what ways has the Eucharist undergirded our faith as embodied and mysterious? Although I have wondered about the thoroughness of teaching around our theology of the Eucharist, I have also observed people's anger and frustration as more than a form of "you aren't the boss of me." The emotional responses tell me that this liturgy is tapping into the spiritual depths of the faithful—there is an increasing spiritual hunger people are experiencing the longer we cannot share the Eucharist. Rather than stop here and agree that these are strange times calling for strange answers, so go ahead and put a cluster of grapes and a stalk of wheat on the altar, we seem to be called into a crystallizing moment in which we can, corporately, ask the question, Why is the Eucharist important for us as the body of Christ? How is God's mystery, experienced in the Eucharist, revealing to us a new creation—the next part of our faith journey as a people? My concern here is about the way in which we have missed the corporate part of the Eucharist. If folks are simply participating in it as an individual practice for individual purposes, we know the work ahead of us is to explore the ways in which the rite is working in us and upon us as a people, not simply as individuals with privileges and rights. We cannot ignore this moment because virtual realities are only becoming more a part of our lives. Is it possible to experience ourselves as one in the body of Christ while sitting in our separate spaces, seeing each other virtually and drinking from individual cups? What is the difference that drinking from the common cup makes?

From Where I'm Standing: Time | Relationship | Place

I'll be honest. The next nonpandemic bishop who says to me, "I'm so sorry you were consecrated in the pandemic. My consecration was so wonderful and I'm sorry you didn't get that," might get something for which I will need to ask forgiveness. Yes, of course we all wished it had been different. But it is not. What I find annoying is not only the obvious assumption but also the suggestion that a consecration is more akin to a coronation than a sacred moment in which the Holy Spirit is swirling and alighting. The pity bestowed upon me (and my peers) has nothing to do with affirming the truth: the Holy Spirit came among us and dwelt with us the same.

Timing is everything, goes the adage. God's time is like that; I have spent as little time as I can wondering, Why this time? I will admit that I don't have a great deal of time to actually entertain that question because serving as bishop in these times seems to differ dramatically in terms of time, relationship, and place from serving fifteen years ago. I have a sense of urgency that does not come from small worry-flurries but from a church that is facing decisions that cannot be delayed: budget constraints, congregations that ought to have been allowed to close years ago, transitions in congregations that are troubled by a shortage of interim priests, dramatic shifts in clergy formation and training, and so forth. Although these have been identified and discussed before, I find that the work waiting for me was for immediate and pastoral action. There has been little time to ponder the various facets of the pros and cons of closing a congregation. The building has been empty and neglected and is now a danger. Decision time.

Some of the best advice I've received in these early days has been in the form of text messages from bishops who've been eager to help me. One of my favorites was from Bishop Fitzpatrick the morning after my consecration. He was heading to the airport to return to Hawaii and I was getting ready for the seating liturgy at the cathedral. I realized the "in the moment on the ground" stuff of the miter and the crozier was not clear, so I texted him. His response was deeply pastoral—and by that I mean *fast and succinct*. After running through the basics and an easy way to remember them, he said, "And Diana, remember, no one will be concerned, and you are the bishop!"

My point is this: the things I need to know, the questions I have, are so often time sensitive. I would love to have the leisure to reflect and talk for even two hours about things. But I daresay, the magnitude of the work is different today. Although the detail of much of what crosses my stand-up desk is familiar to all bishops, the pace is relentless. For those of us who do not have budgets that allow us to have the diocesan staff of our dreams, we are doing far more than we'd imagined.

Earlier in this chapter I referenced the fact that I am among those few bishops who were priests leading congregations when the pandemic hit. Now as bishop, I can easily recognize the look of weariness, exhaustion, and overwhelm of our active clergy. The way the pandemic has stressed our clergy leadership remains largely unexamined. This worries me. To the extent that our clergy are running on empty, our congregations will experience the effects, and while I understand the ongoing conversation about Holy Eucharist in the pandemic, I have an even larger concern for the spiritual and physical well-being of our clergy. Do we really know how they are handling this? Do we know what they need? Do they?

The clergy are on the front lines, and those who are paying attention are acutely aware of the dramatic changes before them. The creative and innovative clergy are looking for colleagues with whom to share ideas. They know that the terrain up ahead will be mostly uncharted, risky, and fraught with setbacks. They were not trained for this in seminary, and they are adapting. I see that my responsibility is to help them prepare to adapt. And I am doing this at the same time that I am shaping a reality that requires change at a pace this diocese will need in order to adapt successfully.

My questions and the demands of this work do wake me up in the middle of the night. It's not worry as much as it is wondering, envisioning, and hoping. Some might think this is a crazy time to be called to this work. That might be true. But from where I'm sitting, it's a crazy awesome kind of opportunity to do work that will shape the church of the future. God had a plan all those years ago, it seems, placing me in a curacy that was not "a real job in the church." We would do well to trust God in all things, that we are being wonderfully made for this time, this place, and particularly to be reconciled one to another.

CHAPTER 13

The Authority of Episcopal Bishops and Resolution 2018-B012

Joan C. Geiszler-Ludlum

What Is Authority?

In common usage, authority, power, and control are terms often used interchangeably. Authority and control are better understood as different shades of the same thing: power. Power connotes control and coercion, the ability to force one's will on others. Sociologist Max Weber[1] has given us a different way of viewing power: the possibility of an individual or a number of individuals realizing their own will in a communal action, even against the resistance of those who are participating in the communal action.[2] Key to Weber's definition of authority is the operation of the individual in the community, built on relationships.

Weber identifies three sources of authority, which will likely have a familiar ring to Episcopalians: traditional, legal-rational, and charismatic. Weber favors legal-rational authority, idealized as the efficient and pure exercise of legal authority, permitting decision-making based on facts and rational thinking. He consequently favored bureaucracy as the best means to enact efficient systems for implementation of legal authority.

Traditional authority arises from social action founded on shared beliefs, customs, and values, and is held through hereditary mechanisms, such as monarchy. Weber viewed traditional authority as a barrier to the development of rational economic and political structures.

Charismatic authority arises from personal qualities of a leader, a form of authority that Weber viewed with discomfort as inherently fragile and revolutionary. The charismatic leader emerges in a time of crisis and turmoil when other leadership structures and institutions appear to be failing and advocates for dramatic systemic change. Weber finds charismatic authority unstable, lasting only so long as the charismatic leader can hold power, or the crisis continues. The charismatic organization lacks rational criteria and formal rules, disrupts and dismantles established administrative organs, and ignores precedents to guide new judgments. Charismatic authority, while a factor in all leadership, tends toward authoritarian rule.

Legal-rational authority is the legal order flowing from society's rules and laws, reflected in governmental structures and rules. Legal-rational authority gains its legitimacy from its relationship with accepted processes for enacting rules and laws. What Weber calls legal-rational authority underpins modern democracies.

As scholars have worked with Weber's concepts of authority over the century since his work first appeared, the common view is that authority typically requires all three elements. Nowhere is that perhaps clearer than in the role of bishop in The Episcopal Church today.

Bishops in Tradition

The traditional role of bishops comes down to us through the ages from the Roman Catholic Church through the Church of England, as interpreted in The Episcopal Church. The tradition evolved through the centuries, from the Roman Catholic view of the solo and absolute authority of bishops to the shared model of authority among bishops, clergy, and laity found today in The Episcopal Church.

From its founding in 1789, The Episcopal Church pursued a separate polity from the Church of England: The governing General Convention included clergy and laity; coequal houses consisting of bishops and deputies; and local selection of bishops.[3] At the same time, The Episcopal Church retains a tradition dating from the Council of Nicaea in 325 CE requiring the act of three bishops to ordain and consecrate a new bishop.[4] Traditional roles have been redefined throughout the history of The Episcopal Church by enacting, amending, and repealing portions of the Constitution and canons of the General Convention.

Nonetheless, traditional understandings may remain alive in custom and lore, the oral history of the church. These traditional and contemporary understandings of the authority of bishops have entered into the General Convention's action to implement access to marriage for same-sex couples, bringing to light important differences of opinion about the role and authority of bishops in liturgical matters that have hampered discussion, decision-making, and implementation of Resolution 2018-B012, Authorizing Trial Liturgies for Same-Sex Marriage.

This chapter reviews those different opinions, attempts to clarify the status of bishops' authority in current church law, and reviews the Hearing Panel's decision in the document "In the Title IV Disciplinary Matter Involving the Rt. Rev. William H. Love."[5]

Authority of Bishops in Authorizing Rites for Same-Sex Marriage

In the evolution of the General Convention's decision on same-sex marriage, the view of the role of bishop in authorizing liturgies for same-sex relationships—first the blessing liturgy authorized by the General Convention in 2012 followed by authorizations of liturgies for same-sex marriage in 2015 and 2018—also evolved. Civil law regarding same-sex marriage began to change rapidly in 2000 with the Vermont legislature's recognition of civil unions and a court decision in Massachusetts in 2003 recognizing same-sex marriage as a right under state law. By 2012, fifteen states had authorized either civil unions or marriage for same-sex couples.[6] In parallel, building on work begun by the General Convention in 1976 to recognize equal protections and access for LGBT people, appeals for the development of authorized rites of blessing and marriage for same-sex couples continued. Resolution 2009-C009 called for the Standing Commission on Liturgy and Music to "collect and develop theological and liturgical resources" for blessing same-sex relationships, undertaken by what became the Blessings Project. Review of the wide range of liturgies written by couples and, in some cases, clergy that were collected pushed forward the need for an authorized liturgy that reflected the theology of marriage as well as liturgical values. This work led to the question of how to implement the liturgies and who is authorized to do so. Resolution 2012-A049 proposed to authorize the liturgies "for use," following the legislative approach to authorizing other liturgies, such as Rites for Care of

Animals (Resolution 2012-A054) and Daily Prayer for All Seasons (Resolution 2012-A055), intending to permit parish clergy to make the decision as to their use without consultation with their lay leadership. As amended in the House of Bishops, the authorization was modified to "provisional use . . . under the direction and subject to the permission of the bishop exercising ecclesiastical authority," a phrase that has no constitutional or canonical foundation as to its meaning, but interpreted by some to mean something short of authorized use.[7] Based on statements made later, it appears the intention of this amendment was to ensure that the bishops exercising ecclesiastical authority would retain their traditional authority, as they understood it, to control use of liturgies outside the Book of Common Prayer, an authority derived from one of the promises made in the service for the ordination of a bishop: "to guard the faith, unity, and discipline of the Church,"[8] and the admonition in the same service to "solemnly engage to conform to the doctrine, discipline, and worship of The Episcopal Church."[9] Both were cited by bishops who declined to allow use of the blessings liturgy. Bishops were also encouraged to provide for use of the liturgy as a generous pastoral response in meeting the needs of members of the church. Resolution 2012-A049 passed the House of Bishops on a roll call vote of 111 ayes, 41 nays, and 3 abstentions; and the House of Deputies on a vote by orders, in the lay order, 86 yes, 19 no, and 5 divided, and in the clergy order, 85 yes, 22 no, and 4 divided, both margins of more than two to one.

Over the next triennium, the Task Force on the Study of Marriage worked to, among other things, find a way forward on authorizing rites for same-sex marriage. Twenty states recognized same-sex marriage by the end of the triennium. Federal courts were also finding a basis in the US Constitution for expanding marriage to same-sex couples, culminating with the US Supreme Court's decision in *Obergefell v. Hodges*,[10] ruling that same-sex couples have a fundamental right to marry under the Due Process and the Equal Protection clauses of the Fourteenth Amendment of the Constitution, and therefore, absent a compelling basis, no state could block same-sex couples from marrying. The Task Force monitored these secular legal trends while pursuing its mandate "to address the pastoral need for priests to officiate at a civil marriage of a same-sex couple in states that authorize such."[11] Because the goal became finding a path to incorporate one or more liturgies for marriage for use by any couple seeking to marry, attention turned to examination of the existing provisions in the Constitution and canons to amend the Book of Common Prayer (BCP) and authorize other liturgies for use. Article X of the Constitution, *Of the Book of Common Prayer*, requires use of the authorized book in all dioceses; sets out a procedure to alter or add to the book by adopting a resolve at one meeting of the General Convention, giving notice to all the diocesan conventions, and adopting the same wording at the following regular meeting by vote of a majority of all bishops entitled to vote in the House of Bishops, and a vote by orders in the House of Deputies, with an affirmative vote in each order by concurrence by the majority of dioceses entitled to vote. Article X also provides a separate procedure, requiring a vote of one General Convention, voting by orders:

> Authorize for trial use *throughout this Church*, as *an alternative* at any time or times to the established Book of Common Prayer or to any section or Office thereof, a proposed revision of the whole Book or of any portion thereof, duly undertaken by the General Convention.[12]

These provisions refuted several arguments against recognizing same-sex marriage. One argument pointed to the constitutional process for amending the BCP, the provisions for amending the BCP as set out in Article X, contending that the bishops controlled whether a liturgy may be used anywhere in their diocese if it was not a part of the BCP. A corollary of this argument seemed to say that by extension this means that a liturgy authorized for trial use is not, by definition, a part of the BCP and therefore the consent of the bishop was required. There was enough question about this position that Resolution 2015-A054, as submitted to the General Convention, retained the requirement that the bishop give permission to use the same-sex marriage liturgies, in modified form: "under the direction of the bishop exercising ecclesiastical authority." Through the legislative process this language reverted to its 2012 form, "Trial use is only to be available under the direction and with the permission of the Diocesan Bishop," as a compromise to ensure continued use of the same-sex marriage liturgies. But in 2015 the General Convention prefaced this condition with another: "Bishops exercising ecclesiastical authority or, where appropriate, ecclesiastical supervision will make provision for all couples asking to be married in this Church to have access to these liturgies."[13] In placing this language first, the intent was to convey the preference for access over restriction. This line of reasoning overlooks the separate provisions of Art. X (b) setting out a procedure for trial use. Reliance on this provision was muddled by authorizing "provisional" use in place of "trial" use in 2012 but was deliberately corrected in the language of 2015-A054.

Another argument put forth by those who objected at the time to the church authorizing same-sex marriage relied on the definition of marriage in Canon I.18, the rubrics, and the catechism, which contained the language that marriage is between a man and a woman or referenced husband and wife. Rubrics[14] are all directions and instructions contained in the BCP, and all tables, prefaces, rules, calendars, and other contents thereof. Violation of the rubrics subjects clergy to Title IV discipline. The catechism describes marriage as

> Holy Matrimony is Christian marriage, in which the woman and man enter into a life-long union, make their vows before God and the Church, and receive the grace and blessing of God to help them fulfill their vows.[15]

At the same time, the canons do not define marriage based on a description of the people to be married, instead giving deference to how the state regulates marriage, except in the Declaration of Intention to be signed by the couple:

> We, A.B. and C.D., desiring to receive the blessing of Holy Matrimony in the Church, do solemnly declare that we hold marriage to be a life-long union of husband and wife as it is set forth in the Book of Common Prayer.

> We believe that the union of husband and wife, in heart, body, and mind, is intended by God for their mutual joy; for the help and comfort given one another in prosperity and adversity; and, when it is God's will, for the procreation of children and their nurture in the knowledge and love of the Lord.

> And we do engage ourselves, so far as in us lies, to make our utmost effort to establish this relationship and to seek God's help thereto.[16]

Resolution 2015-A036 amended canon I.18 to, among other things, revise the Declaration of Intention to remove the focus on the gender-referential terms, husband and wife, and emphasize the purposes and promises of marriage in the vows taken:

We understand the teaching of the church that God's purpose for our marriage is for our mutual joy, for the help and comfort we will give to each other in prosperity and adversity, and, when it is God's will, for the gift and heritage of children and their nurture in the knowledge and love of God. We also understand that our marriage is to be unconditional, mutual, exclusive, faithful, and lifelong; and we engage to make the utmost effort to accept these gifts and fulfill these duties, with the help of God and the support of our community.[17]

One of the perceived and intended benefits of the amendments to canon I.18 was expanding potential use of the new marriage rites to dioceses in the twenty states where same-sex marriage was legal.

During the 2015–2018 triennium, the church saw a substantial expansion in the authorization of same-sex marriage rites within the domestic dioceses.[18] The reauthorized Task Force on the Study of Marriage, surveying the dioceses in 2017, reported to the 2018 General Convention that the same-sex marriage rites were authorized, with or without conditions,[19] in 93 of the 101 domestic dioceses. In the other eight domestic dioceses, bishops with jurisdiction prohibited use of the authorized rites for same-sex marriage, citing, among other reasons, that same-sex marriage violated their sincerely held personal beliefs that same-sex marriage violates the doctrine of the church, subjecting them to Title IV discipline. This position relied on the contentions discussed above but leaves open the question whether personal beliefs ought to control in making this determination. The tradition of this church is to discern in community, which includes the General Convention and diocesan councils.

Hoping to open access to the trial liturgies in all dioceses, the Task Force proposed this language in Resolution 2018-A086:

Resolved, That bishops exercising ecclesiastical authority or, where appropriate, ecclesiastical supervision, will make provision for all couples asking to be married in this Church to have reasonable and convenient access to these trial liturgies.[20]

The language intended to charge the bishops with finding a way to give same-sex couples access to their home churches to marry did not overcome the objections of individual rectors who cited canon III.9.6 (a), which gives the rector authority over and responsibility for worship in the parish and full control over the use of the church and parish buildings.

One week before the opening of the seventy-ninth General Convention, Bishops Provenzano of Long Island, McConnell of Pittsburgh, and Knisely of Rhode Island introduced Resolution 2018-B012, Authorizing Trial Liturgies for Same-Sex Marriage.

The key provision in the resolution proposed a new application of Delegated Episcopal Pastoral Oversight (DEPO), a novel procedure that the House of Bishops adopted in 2004 to address unrest between some bishops and congregations in their dioceses following the 2003 General Convention giving consent to the consecration of Gene Robinson, an openly partnered gay priest elected as bishop of New Hampshire. In its original iteration, DEPO allowed congregations who disagree with their bishop on issues of human sexuality to consult with the bishop to seek reconciliation. If reconciliation is unsuccessful, the rector and two-thirds of the vestry, or, in the absence of a rector, two-thirds of the canonically designated lay leadership, may request, or the bishop may suggest, alternative oversight through which the diocesan bishop invites another bishop to provide care while remaining otherwise in relationship with the congregation. Oversight is defined in the response as "the episcopal acts performed as part of a diocesan bishop's ministry either by the diocesan bishop or by another bishop to whom such responsibility has been delegated by the diocesan bishop."[21] In its application after adoption, congregations that disagreed with their bishop's vote, whether for or opposed to consent to the consecration of Bishop Robinson, requested oversight. Contrary to the hopes of the House of Bishops in adopting DEPO, it did not prevent members of congregations and dioceses, including some bishops and clergy, from leaving The Episcopal Church to join other Anglican provinces and, later, creating extraprovincial organizations of like-minded clergy and laity on matters of human sexuality.

The proposal to apply DEPO in the context of authorizing liturgies raised many concerns. Some felt it elevated the role of bishops in marriage decisions beyond their canonical role limited to matters of remarriage after divorce.[22] Some felt it undermined the canonical role of rectors in liturgical decisions, giving new authority to bishops, and setting a bad precedent. Some felt applying DEPO conveyed the impression that the church was teetering on the edge of schism, similar to the sense of the context into which it was first introduced.

The Legislative Committee to Receive the Report of Resolution A169[23] deleted the DEPO paragraph and added a paragraph that limited use of DEPO to cases under canon 19 addressing remarriage after divorce. The House of Deputies adopted a further amendment in an effort to make clear in the seventh Resolve that the decision to use the trial liturgies rests with the local congregations and worshipping communities "under the direction of the Rector or Member of the Clergy in charge," and reinstated DEPO in a new eighth Resolve to apply where bishops "hold a theological position that does not embrace marriage for same-sex couples," the stated goals being "allowing all couples to be married in their home church" and "to fulfill the intention of this resolution that all couples have convenient and reasonable local congregational access to these rites."[24] This version then went to the House of Bishops, where one additional amendment added this language to the seventh Resolve: "provided that nothing in this Resolve narrows the authority of the Rector or Priest-in-Charge given in Canon III.9.6 (a)."[25] After passing as amended in the House of Bishops by a voice vote, the amended Resolution 2018-B012 returned to the House of Deputies for concurrence, which occurred by wide margins on a vote by orders.

One important difference between Resolution 2015-A054 and 2018-B012 was the wording around honoring theological diversity and protecting clergy who supported or opposed the actions of the General Convention from Title IV consequences. Resolution 2015-A054 contained intentional language that proposed to shield clergy from Title IV disciplinary consequences:

> *Resolved*, That this convention honor the theological diversity of this Church in regard to matters of human sexuality; and that no bishop, priest, deacon or lay person should be coerced or penalized in any manner, nor suffer *any canonical disabilities*, as a result of his or her theological objection to or support for the 78th General Convention's action contained in this resolution.[26]

Resolution 2018-B012 contained very different and more limited language:

> *Resolved*, That this Church continue to honor theological diversity in regard to matters of human sexuality.[27]

Following the seventy-ninth General Convention, the trial liturgies for use by any couple seeking marriage as authorized by Resolution 2018-B012 went into effect on the first Sunday of Advent, December 2, 2018, as prescribed. As anticipated, the majority of domestic dioceses proceeded with use as determined by the rectors or priest-in-charge of congregations and worshipping communities. As anticipated, Province IX dioceses did not implement the liturgies for use, due to same-sex marriage being civilly barred in their jurisdiction. It was for this reason that the blessing rites, "The Witnessing and Blessing of a Marriage" and "The Celebration and Blessing of a Marriage 2," were authorized for continued trial use as a means of blessing same-sex relationships where marriage is not civilly allowed. As anticipated, seven of the eight dioceses that had not implemented 2015-A054 did allow the trial liturgies of 2018-B012 to become available, utilizing DEPO in five dioceses. The bishop of Albany, William Love, refused to implement 2018-B012 and refused to utilize DEPO, resulting in Title IV charges, discussed further below. Three dioceses implemented 2018-B012 in parishes only, and restricted use by missions, asserting that missions are under the pastoral leadership of the bishop who holds theological objections to same-sex marriage. This position is explored further below.

Diocese of Albany

Bishop Love issued a pastoral direction on November 10, 2018, anticipating the effective date of the requirements of Resolution 2018-B012, to all canonically resident and licensed clergy in the diocese, prohibiting them from presiding over marriage rites for same-sex couples and requiring compliance with Albany Canon XVI, which provides:

CANON XVI—MARRIAGE
16.1—Celebration or Blessing of Marriages by Clergy

Members of the Clergy Resident in or Licensed to Serve in this Diocese shall neither officiate at, nor facilitate, nor participate in, any service, whether public or private, for the Celebration or Blessing of a Marriage or any other union except between one man and one woman. Unions other than those of one man and one woman in Holy Matrimony, even if they be recognized in other jurisdictions, shall be neither recognized nor blessed in this Diocese.

16.2—Marriages on Church Property
Properties owned, controlled, managed, or operated by this Diocese, or
any Parish of the Diocese, or any legal entity established by the Diocese
or a parish of the Diocese, shall not be the site for any service, public or
private, for the Celebration or Blessing of a Marriage or any other union
except those between one man and one woman.[28]

Bishop Love based his pastoral directive on his belief that same-sex marriage
violates scripture and the official teaching of the church. In response, Presiding
Bishop Michael B. Curry issued a partial restriction on ministry to Bishop Love,
prohibiting him from engaging in the church's disciplinary process in the Diocese of Albany against any member of the clergy involving issues of same-sex
marriage and from penalizing in any way any member of the clergy, any laity,
and any worshipping community arranging for or participating in any same-sex
marriage in the Diocese of Albany. After investigation, The Episcopal Church
found that Bishop Love's pastoral direction violated the Title IV Disciplinary
Canons by failing to abide by his ordination promises and vows, citing canon
IV.4.1 (c). Specifically, the pastoral direction violated the discipline and worship
of the church as mandated in Resolution 2018-B012, and as mandated by canon
I.18. The matter then went to the Hearing Panel for a coronavirus-delayed hearing on June 21, 2020. The Hearing Panel issued its findings on October 2, 2020,
concluding that Bishop Love violated his ordination promises and violated the
discipline and worship of the church.

The Hearing Panel's decision carefully analyzed these questions in its report and offered answers to a number of important and recurring questions about
the authority of bishops and the General Convention in liturgical authorization
and use.

A. Is Resolution 2018-B012 Permissive or Mandatory?

There is an ongoing debate about the effect of a resolution adopted by the General Convention. It is fair to say that it depends on what the resolution says. Some
resolutions serve as memorials, a petition to the General Convention asking for
action or for use by the General Convention in guiding its deliberations on a
matter of great importance. Some resolutions convey the mind of the General

Convention on a current issue and may advise or direct further action. And some resolutions give direction to the church or require specific action by a named person, group, or agency of the church. Resolution 2018-B012 is a resolution of direction, giving rise to a perennial question: Is its direction permissive or mandatory? The Hearing Panel considered the contentions of The Episcopal Church that it is mandatory, requiring dioceses and clergy to offer same-sex marriages, a mandate that Bishop Love violated. Bishop Love contended that B012 lacked sufficient elements that required considering it a mandate because the liturgies were not explicitly offered as proposed revisions to the BCP; it lacked specification of duration of trial use and direction as to publication of the authorized rites; and its drafters and other commentators stated, prior to final passage, that it intended to offer additional rites, not revisions to the BCP.

Article X does several things:

- It sets the Book of Common Prayer, as established or amended, as the exclusive source of liturgy to be used in this church.
- It sets out the two–General Convention process for adopting alterations or additions to the BCP.
- It sets out an additional one–General Convention process for (a) amending the Table of Lessons, all Tables and Rubrics related to the Psalms, and (b) for authorizing trial use throughout this church, as an alternative to the BCP or any section or Office, a proposed revision of the whole Book or any portion of it.

Canon II.3.6 adds specific additional requirements for BCP amendments. The enabling resolution must specify the period of trial use, the precise text, and any special terms or conditions applying to trial use. The Hearing Panel found that B012 met all the criteria expressed in the plain language of the Resolution:

Resolved [1], the House of Deputies concurring, *That the 79th General Convention authorize for continued trial use, in accordance with Article X of the Constitution and Canon II.3.6,* "The Witnessing and Blessing of a Marriage" and "The Celebration and Blessing of a Marriage 2" (as appended to the report of the Task Force for the Study of Marriage to the 79th General Convention); and be it further

Resolved [2], *That the 79th General Convention authorize for trial use, in accordance with Article X of the Constitution and Canon II.3.6,* "The

Blessing of a Civil Marriage 2" and "An Order for Marriage 2" (as appended to the report of the Task Force for the Study of Marriage to the 79th General Convention), beginning the first Sunday of Advent, 2018.[29]

Bishop Love contended that B012 must contain the magic formulation, "proposed revision to the Book of Common Prayer." The Hearing Panel disagreed, finding that referencing Article X and Canon II.3.6 is sufficient to make it plain and clear that B012 is addressing a proposed revision to the BCP. Citing the history of liturgical revision over the past more than fifty years, the Hearing Panel makes note that the trial liturgy provision was added to Article X in 1964, at the outset of the work leading to the adoption of the 1979 BCP. Trial use recognizes the value of testing the performative aspects of liturgy. The General Convention has shown appreciation for the distinctions between authorizing trial liturgies and authorizing optional observances, such as *Lesser Feasts and Fasts*, and supplemental liturgical options, such as *Enriching Our Worship*. The Hearing Panel took note of the General Convention's "careful adherence" to the requirements of canon II.3.6: setting the period of use "to continue until the completion of the next comprehensive revision"[30] to the BCP; setting a specific starting date on the first Sunday of Advent 2018; appending the liturgical texts to the report of the Task Force on the Study of Marriage; including special conditions requiring the availability of translations in the four primary languages of this church; including directions on electronic publication and availability at no cost; directing a process (DEPO) to allow dissenting bishops to step aside and invite other bishops to support local access to the liturgies and counsel for remarriage; and finally, directing rectors or members of the clergy in charge to provide access to the marriage liturgies in their local congregations or worshipping communities without narrowing the authority of the rector or priest-in-charge under canon III.9.6 (a). The Hearing Panel concluded,

> In its final form, Resolution B012, on its face, contained all the necessary elements to ensure its canonical validity, thus mandating it "shall be in use in every Diocese in the Church." Art. X. Thus, Bishop Love's metaphor that Resolution B012 was like a truck painted on the outside advertising that it was carrying oranges, when its cargo was something entirely different, is misplaced. The B012 truck was carrying all the oranges that it was required to carry to be canonically enforceable.[31]

B. Did Bishop Love's Refusal to Abide by B012, a Resolution, Violate the Discipline of the Church?

While acknowledging his noncompliance with B012, Bishop Love neverthe-less contends that noncompliance cannot be a Title IV disciplinary violation because B012 was not an amendment to the Constitution, the canons, the rubrics of the BCP, or the ordinal. This line of argument has its origins in Res-olution 1994-B005, which proposed to avoid the perceived danger of subjecting clergy to disciplinary action by running afoul of vaguely written resolutions by requiring the inclusion of an explicit "intent to interpret and/or apply any pro-vision of the Constitution or Canons of the Church." The proposal was not adopted and instead was referred to the Standing Commission on Constitution and Canons (SCCC) for report back to the seventy-second General Conven-tion in 1997.[32]

The SCCC declined to put forward the contents of B005, anticipating un-foreseen and unfortunate consequences of equating the direction of a resolution to canon without thorough seriousness and scrutiny, and instead added defini-tions of doctrine and discipline to Title IV, which were carried forward in the subsequent Title IV revision. The SCCC further declined to hinge clergy dis-cipline on the inclusion of "magic words" in a resolution. Bishop Love contends this handling of B005 is proof that discipline applies only in instances of viola-tion of the canons or Constitution. The Hearing Panel rejects this argument by pointing to the express language of Article X and Canon II.3.6, which, when properly followed and invoked as it was in B012, gives the resolution canonical effect. Bishop Love is thus subject to discipline for his admitted failure to com-ply with B012.

C. Did Bishop Love's Pastoral Direction Violate the Discipline and Doctrine of the Church?

Discipline and doctrine are defined terms found in canon IV.2:

> *Discipline* of the Church shall be found in the Constitution, the Canons and the Rubrics and the Ordinal of the Book of Common Prayer.

Doctrine shall mean the basic and essential teachings of the Church and is to be found in the Canon of Holy Scripture as understood in the Apostles and Nicene Creeds and in the sacramental rites, the Ordinal and Catechism of the Book of Common Prayer.[33]

The catechism in the Book of Common Prayer contains this exchange:

Q: What is Holy Matrimony?

A. Holy Matrimony is Christian marriage, *in which the woman and man enter into a life-long union*, make their vows before God and the Church, and receive the grace and blessing of God to help them fulfill their vows.[34]

The Hearing Panel addressed each cited provision separately.

1. Is the Language in the Commentary "Concerning the Service" in the BCP and the Catechism in the BCP an Impediment to B012 Being Afforded Canonical Authority?

Bishop Love relies on what he sees as conflict between the rubrics of the BCP rite "The Celebration and the Blessing of a Marriage" and the catechism, where marriage is set in the cisgender context of one man and one woman. The Hearing Panel found that there is no conflict by recognizing that the rubric in "Concerning the Service" attaches only to the service that follows it. The rites authorized in B012 each contain their own rubrics, which do not restrict the use of the service by defining who the couple may be. In addition, Liturgical Resources 2 proposes an amendment for the BCP marriage rite that opens with "Christian marriage is a solemn and public covenant between two people in the presence of God."[35]

B012 referred the proposed change to the Standing Commission on Liturgy and Music (SCLM) "for serious consideration as they engage in the process of revision of the Book of Common Prayer."[36]

The Hearing Panel drew a similar conclusion regarding the catechism, which is prefaced by its own rubric, describing the catechism as "intended for use by parish priests, deacons, and lay catechists, to give an outline for instruction. It is a commentary on the creeds, but is not meant to be a complete statement of belief and practice."[37]

The Hearing Panel also considered the application of canon I.18.1 as amended in 2015, and canon I.17.5. Canon I.18.1 requires "every member of the clergy" to follow the laws of the state and the canons in solemnizing a marriage using any liturgical forms authorized by the church. Nowhere in Canon I.18 is a description of the couple.[38] Canon I.17.5 states,

> No one shall be denied rights, status or access to an equal place in the life, *worship*, and governance of this Church because of race, color, ethnic origin, national origin, marital status, sex, sexual orientation, *gender identity and expression*, disabilities or age, except as otherwise specified by Canons.[39]

Acknowledging the canons as the higher authority, the Hearing Panel concludes that the rubrics and the catechism must be read in harmony with the canons, not the reverse; that prohibiting access to the marriage rites authorized by canon I.18 and B012 violates the intent of canon I.17; and that B012 must be interpreted as consistent with the two canons.

2. Does Compliance with Resolution B012 Violate the Rubrics of the Church?

Bishop Love next contends that compliance with Resolution B012 forces him to violate other canons, specifically canon IV.4.1 (b), requiring clergy to conform to the rubrics of the BCP, and canon III.9.6 (a), subjecting a rector's authority over worship to the Constitution, canons, the rubrics, and the ordinal, and the pastoral direction of the bishop. The Hearing Panel refers back to their reasoning in section 6.A. of their decision, discussed in section A above, to conclude that B012 does not conflict with the BCP rubrics.

3. Does Compliance with B012 Violate the Doctrine of the Church?

Bishop Love next contends that Resolution B012 lacks canonical backing because the General Convention failed to change the current doctrine of this church when it did not address the definition of who may marry in "Concerning the Service" and the catechism. The Episcopal Church responds with two contentions. First, the *Righter*[40] decision effectively eliminated the rite of marriage from the doctrine of the church. Second, the 2015 revision of canon I.18 to allow for same-sex marriage effectively changed the doctrine of the church.

The Hearing Panel summarily rejected the first line of argument. While the *Righter* decision may provide guidance and reference, it is not a binding precedent in future cases. That is not the polity of this church. In this church, canon law and resolutions enacted through the legislative process of the General Convention are the primary sources of law. In response to *Righter*, the next General Convention enacted a precise definition of the doctrine of the church in Resolution 1997-A014 (see canon IV.2 [2018]). This definition determines the outcome. B012 enacts multiple separate marriage rites with separate rubrics that are not governed by the commentary "Concerning the Service." Likewise they are not "constrained by a Catechism that expressly states it is meant to be an 'outline' of instruction and not a 'complete statement of belief and practice.'"[41] Citing the fifth resolve of B012, the Hearing Panel correctly assesses the directive to the SCLM to attend to revision of "Concerning the Service" for the BCP rite for marriage, the proper prefaces, and the catechism as part of a comprehensive revision of the BCP, at which time the trial rites are anticipated to be incorporated into the BCP, as addressed in the third resolve as the period for trial use.

4. Did Bishop Love Violate Canon I.18, and If So, Did The Episcopal Church Prove That His Pastoral Direction Enforcing the Albany Canons Was Prohibited by Title IV?

Bishop Love's pastoral direction of November 10, 2018, to the clergy of the Diocese of Albany prohibited all clergy in the diocese—canonically resident, resident, and licensed—from using any of the trial liturgies authorized by Resolution B012; and required all clergy to comply with Diocese of Albany canon XVI, which restricts marriage to heterosexual couples ("one man and one woman"), prohibits all clergy from officiating or blessing same-sex unions, and prohibits the use of diocesan, parish, and institutional property for the conduct of any marriage other than one between a man and a woman. Bishop Love contends that he cannot be found to have violated canon I.18.1 because it makes the trial liturgies optional and not mandatory.

Bishop Love's reasoning is mistaken. Canon I.18.1 recognizes and reinforces B012 in that it recognizes that the church may authorize other liturgical forms for the solemnization of marriage beyond what is contained in the BCP. The Hearing Panel has already held that B012 has canonical effect in its authorization of the trial liturgies, having followed the provisions of Article IX (b) to the letter. B012 mandates that bishops provide access for same-sex couples to the marriage rites within their congregation or worshipping community by stating explicitly that a bishop who holds a theological position opposed to same-sex marriage must stand aside and invoke DEPO by inviting another bishop to minister to the couple, the member of the clergy, and the congregation or worshipping community "in order to fulfill the intention of this resolution that all couples have convenient and reasonable local congregational access to these rites."[42] This provision overrules the provision Bishop Love cites from Resolution 2015-A054, which made use of the previous form of the trial rites for same-sex marriage subject to authorization by the bishop. Resolution 2018-B012 intended to overrule Resolution 2015-A054 and did so explicitly.

Bishop Love asserts that diocesan canon XIV takes precedence over Resolution 2018-B012, citing canon IV.3.1 (a), which subjects a member of the clergy to discipline for "knowingly violating or attempting to violate, directly or through the acts of another person, the Constitution or Canons of the Church or of any Diocese."[43] His contention is based on his mistaken reading of canon I.18.1 as permissive, thereby failing to see that there is any conflict between The Episcopal Church canon and the diocesan canon. This view runs afoul of the clear requirement of Article V.1 of the Constitution, which requires that the diocesan constitution contain "an unqualified accession clause to the Constitution and Canons of this Church."[44] Article IX of the Constitution of the Diocese of Albany seems to conform to this accession requirement but is hardly an unqualified accession, stating, "The Convention may adopt Canons and Rules of Order consistent with this Constitution or the Constitution and Canons of the General Convention."[45]

5. Is B012 Unenforceable in That It Seeks to Impermissibly Restrict the Jurisdiction of an Episcopal Bishop?

Bishop Love asserts that Resolution B012 improperly restricts the jurisdiction and authority of a duly elected diocesan bishop, in violation of Article II.3 and Canon III.12.3 (e).[46] Article II.3 states,

A Bishop shall confine the exercise of such office to the Diocese in which elected, unless requested to perform episcopal acts in another Diocese by the Ecclesiastical Authority thereof, or unless authorized by the House of Bishops, or by the Presiding Bishop by its direction, to act temporarily in case of need within any territory not yet organized into Dioceses of this Church.[47]

Canon III.12.3 (e) states,

No Bishop shall perform episcopal acts or officiate by preaching, ministering the Sacraments, or holding any public service in a Diocese other than that in which the Bishop is canonically resident, without permission or a license to perform occasional public services from the Ecclesiastical Authority of the Diocese in which the Bishop desires to officiate or perform episcopal acts.[48]

Bishop Love asserts that B012 requires the diocesan bishop to relinquish episcopal authority, cloaked as a permissive act. He contends that a bishop's diocesan jurisdiction is a "fundamental tenet of episcopal governance [that] dates from the ancient ecumenical councils of the Christian church."[49] The Episcopal Church's response is that B012 neither nullifies nor requires a diocesan bishop to relinquish his or her authority.

B012 places the decision to offer the trial liturgies for same-sex marriage with rectors or priests-in-charge who are designated by canon to make decisions regarding the conduct of worship[50] and secures their access to church and parish buildings in order to carry out their functions and duties. While bishops point to their ordination vows charging them with responsibility for the doctrine and discipline of the church, the canons restrict this authority when it comes to worship in parishes and missions. B012 offers the bishop with theological reservations in conflict with their rectors and priests-in-charge on same-sex marriage an alternative in the form of DEPO, to separate themselves and their consciences from the local decision. Note that B012 also requires a rector or priest-in-charge with similar theological reservations to allow access to parish or mission buildings to make provisions "for all couples desiring to use these marriage liturgies in their local congregation or worshipping community."[51] What was envisioned here is that the rector or priest-in-charge would allow another member of the clergy to preside and provide pastoral care for the couple, a common practice where any couple may choose someone other than their rector or priest-in-charge to preside at their marriage.

The Hearing Panel supports this option by noting the delegation to another bishop is narrow in scope, limited to providing pastoral support and in appropriate cases, performing the bishop's duties under Canon I.19 when remarriage is involved. DEPO does not authorize the invited bishop to perform any episcopal acts. And finally, the diocesan invites another bishop of the bishop's choosing to take on these duties by her or his own choice. While not a factor to the Hearing Panel, it is important to recall that B012 in its final form was initiated by bishops themselves who saw DEPO as a solution and it passed both Houses of the General Convention by a wide margin.[52]

D. Does Respondent's Pastoral Direction Violate the Worship of the Church?

Bishop Love contends that his pastoral direction to the clergy of the Diocese of Albany conforms with the worship of the church, defined narrowly as the Book of Common Prayer, proposed revisions of the Book of Common Prayer, and "special forms of worship," which has a specific meaning in Article X. He builds this contention on his previous failed assertion that Resolution B012 is extracanonical.[53] The Episcopal Church contends that B012's authorized marriage rites for same-sex couples are included within Bishop Love's definition of worship because the rites are proposed revisions to the Book of Common Prayer. The Episcopal Church further states,

> The Authorized Marriage Rites rest upon a foundation of prayerful corporate discernment in The Episcopal Church that extended over a period of decades and are validated by actual use by the People of God in all domestic dioceses of The Episcopal Church other than the Diocese of Albany.[54]

The Hearing Panel correctly understands that both parties agree that if Resolution B012 was properly constituted as a canonical proposed revision to the BCP in accordance with Article X (b), then it properly forms the worship of the church. The Hearing Panel properly concludes that Bishop Love's pastoral directive prohibiting use of the B012 authorized marriage rites violates the worship of this church.

The Hearing Panel reached the conclusions that Bishop Love's pastoral directions to diocesan clergy to refrain from performing same-sex marriage and to enforce diocesan canon 16 violate Title IV as violations of his ordination vows; that Resolution 2018-B012 has the same enforceability as a canon adopted by the General Convention because of its language and its adherence to the requirements of Article X (b) and Canon II.3.6; and Resolution 2018-B012 preempts diocesan canons, which are in conflict with it pursuant to the accession clause requirement of Article V.

What's Next?

Two questions remain for the marriage rites for same-sex couples in The Episcopal Church. First, do the rites continue in limited use in several dioceses where the bishop has prohibited their use in mission congregations under the bishop's asserted control? Second, what is the future state of incorporation of these rites into a revised Book of Common Prayer?

The traditional role of bishops in a mission is one of tighter control than in parishes. However, the relationship between a bishop and a mission, in particular between a bishop and a priest-in-charge, has undergone changes through the canons. Can the bishop who has appointed a priest-in-charge according to canon III.9.3(b) preempt the priest-in-charge's right to "exercise all the powers of a rector outlined in Canon III.9.6 subject to the authority of the bishop"?[55] What does "subject to the authority of the bishop" mean in this context? Are bishops subject to the meaning of "member of the clergy" where Resolution B012 in resolve 7 requires "provision will be made for all couples desiring to use these marriage liturgies in their local congregation or worshipping community"?[56] In the mission congregation context, is "the bishop exercising ecclesiastical authority who holds a theological position that does not embrace marriage for same-sex couples, and there is a desire to use such rites by same-sex couples in a congregation or worshipping community," also required to "invite, as necessary, another bishop of this Church to provide pastoral support to the couple, the Member of the Clergy involved and the congregation or worshipping community in order to fulfill the intention of this resolution that all couples have convenient and reasonable local congregational access to these rites"?[57] What is the status of canons in other dioceses that define marriage as applying to only relationships between one man and one woman, and prohibiting use of church buildings and property for use of the B012-authorized rites? These are some of the questions that the Hearing Panel was not asked to address in the Bishop Love Title IV action.

And finally, what is the future of the rites authorized in B012? Resolution B012, resolve 3, sets the period of trial use to continue "until the completion of the next comprehensive revision of the Book of Common Prayer."[58] Article X (b) envisions trial use as an alternative for use as "a proposed revision of the whole book or any part thereof."[59] Some resistance remains in the church to any incorporation of the B012 marriage rites into the Book of Common Prayer. For some, any such official recognition of marriage rites for same-sex couples remains anathema to their reading of scripture. There is also considerable resistance to undertaking revision of the Book of Common Prayer. Some do not wish to revisit the rancor that surrounded the 1979 book's adoption. Some like the theology of the 1979 book and do not want to risk its loss in a revision. Some do not want to undertake the work or dislike the process or misunderstand the process. And some do not want to incorporate the B012 marriage rites by stand-alone legislation so that a new printing of the BCP is required when the form of the BCP moves to digital publication. Failure to add these marriage rites, in their current form or with refinements evolving from use, to the BCP gives same-sex marriage second-class status, something that the Task Force on the Study of Marriage, alongside many LGBTQ+ Episcopalians and their allies, has fought hard to change. The title given to the authorized trial liturgies, *Liturgical Resources 2: Marriage for the Whole Church*, says it all.

CHAPTER 14

The Future of the Episcopacy and Relational Leadership

Jennifer Baskerville-Burrows

I n 2018, the General Convention of The Episcopal Church received thirty-four resolutions from the Task Force for the Episcopacy, a group of bishops, clergy, and laypeople created in 2015 to "study the election, appointment, roles, and responsibilities of the episcopate" and propose a new process for forming and electing bishops.

Nearly all the task force's proposals failed. This was not the church's first attempt to reconsider the formation and ministry of bishops, but it was a moment of reckoning that confirmed what many on the task force and beyond suspected: the challenges inherent in the future of the episcopacy have become, in many quarters, what leadership consultants call "undiscussable issues." In some parts of the church, the willingness to address the challenges presented by an old model of the episcopacy is commonplace. In others, it's barely possible to have a conversation about them.

Although the Task Force on the Episcopacy proposals failed—many of them in the House of Bishops—some of the issues it sought to address, like the need for more diversity in the House of Bishops, have been taken up at the grassroots of the church to good effect. Since 2016, seven dioceses—all overwhelmingly white—have elected Black women as diocesan bishops, while another diocese has elected the church's first openly gay Black bishop, who is also an immigrant. These eight historic elections represent about 20 percent of the domestic diocesan bishop elections held in the last five years. The concern about unsustainable dioceses electing bishops is being addressed, at least in some places, with diocesan partnerships, reunifications, and other forms of collaboration. But other issues raised by the task force, including a churchwide discernment process and more support for dioceses in transition, remain unaddressed. Regardless of the increasingly apparent needs, the initiative to create bishops for the future of the church has not come from the General Convention.

But even though the General Convention has so far been unable to create the change we need, this recent wave of more diverse elections tells us about both where in the church initiative can be found and how this new generation of bishops has found its way. To understand what is happening today, we need to understand what happened a generation ago, when I and many of today's new bishops were first learning to be leaders in the church.

Beginning in 1998, a series of conferences and retreats called Gathering the NeXt Generation brought together Episcopal clergy (and later lay leaders) under age thirty-five to explore how to be church in the postmodern era. At that time, fewer than three hundred of The Episcopal Church's priests and deacons—a fraction of its more than eight thousand active clergy—were part of the Gen X generation. We understood then that The Episcopal Church was shrinking, and though we were small in number, we saw our role as being a bridge from the boomers to the generation coming after us. We created preaching conferences and think tanks on adaptive change and postmodernism, wrote books, and self-published journals. We sought to change the church from within, using existing church structures, and from without, by creating new networks and relationships with the emergent church movement beyond The Episcopal Church.

As we came together to explore new models of ministry and leadership, we learned to value our relationships with one another and to understand their power to help us transform the institutional church. The 1998 Lambeth Conference heightened and created conflict and anxiety in The Episcopal Church, and we sought to lead, transform, and hold the church together as it began to fracture over human sexuality and definitions of orthodoxy. Bishops and heads of major Episcopal institutions were concerned about the future leadership of the church and were supportive of our efforts to gather for fellowship and to strategize to transform it. But often, on the ground, the local church seemed uninterested in our voices, perspectives, and desire for change.

As Gen X leaders, we spoke often of the need for parallel development. We sought to create the church we hoped and longed for while working within the institutional structures to provoke change. The large increase in younger people with vocations to ordained ministry that began in the early aughts can be traced to our efforts to get elected to commissions on ministry, standing committees, and General Convention deputations. At the same time, it is perhaps no accident that movements such as the Chicago Consultation, Episcopalians for Global Reconciliation, Ashes to Go, and church plants, such as Church of the Apostles in Seattle and The Crossing in Boston, were either created or fronted by GenXers. We experimented with liturgical forms, spirituality conferences, and expanded intentional living communities that were the precursor of Episcopal Service Corps, and we supported the generation coming up behind us by serving as campus chaplains. And because we were young and hopeful about what the church could be, we spoke often of how it would be if we were in charge.

Fast-forward two decades, and many of us who were part of Gathering the NeXt Generation—the X a play on Generation X, the demographic cohort that was then young—are now bishops, rectors, and leaders of Episcopal organizations and institutions. Those of us in the original cohort are still connected and continue to gather from time to time. But we have also stepped aside and provided support and encouragement to the millennial generation of clergy as they engage the ministry challenges of today as a generational cohort.

Those of us who have been called as bishops know that we have taken up this vocation at a time when we must realize our youthful dreams of changing the institutional church. We are being called to hold the institutional church together just long enough to change it radically, and for us, the future of the episcopacy is rooted in the quality of the relationships we form and sustain both with one another and with the people we serve and the structures—the containers—we can create to hold and nurture them. My decades of involvement in Gathering the NeXt Generation has been pivotal to my understanding of leadership as a function of relationship.[1]

New Structures, New Neighborhoods

When I became bishop of Indianapolis in 2017, I quickly realized that my call was not just to be a pastor or a chief operating officer, although those are important aspects of my role. My first job was to develop structures, systems, and networks—or to find the people who could—that can hold the church as we now understand it together while we discern God's dream for us. Within those structures, we are finding new ways of relating to one another and making new room for the Spirit to move among us.

In the Diocese of Indianapolis, we began by considering how we could restructure and reimagine our life together in ways that would address both a long-standing divide between congregations in metropolitan Indianapolis and in the small towns and rural areas of central and southern Indiana and also the isolation that many congregations in those rural places experienced. I heard repeatedly in listening sessions I conducted shortly after becoming bishop that we had a desire for closer connection with one another, and an understanding that our current structures weren't serving us very well in that regard. We also realized that we needed time to experiment with new ways of organizing ourselves before we committed to a permanent structure.

In 2018, the diocese's Executive Council submitted to the convention a resolution that gave it temporary power to change the composition of the diocese's long-standing geographic divisions, the deaneries, "in order to allow experimentation with developing regional structures to advance God's call for this diocese." At the time, I said, "This is a public declaration that we intend to experiment [with]."[2]

That resolution resulted in new regional groups in our diocese, which we call neighborhoods. We use the term purposefully, because it helps us refocus on our neighbors both in the church and in the communities our congregations serve. "What might your life in Christ look like if you understood your call to be about letting those in your neighborhood know that they are loved and are capable of loving?"[3] I asked the convention in 2019, after neighborhoods had begun their pattern of meeting twice each year, focusing on helping delegates and clergy know each other better, developing the leadership of convention delegates, and broadening participation in diocesan decision-making and initiative-taking.

Our neighborhood experiment, codified in our diocesan canons by convention in 2020, has inspired other forms of structural innovation that help us tend our relationships more actively. In particular, restructuring the diocesan budget and organizing ourselves for racial justice and education work have freed us up to face openly the ways that disparities of both resources and privilege have shaped our past and how our future might be different. These two initiatives are part of what I think of as a dance that has been happening since the day I arrived in Indianapolis—listening, and then trying to keep a conversation going to move us along on a particular initiative. When I arrived, I remember thinking that the work before me was about money and about race, and now, five years in, we are organized and energized to address that work.

We Could Have Money but No Church

The conversation about money—or rather, at times, the lack of conversation about money—is in many ways borne out of the privilege conferred on the Diocese of Indianapolis and several of its parishes by endowments created in the mid-twentieth century by Eli Lilly, a pharmaceutical titan and faithful Episcopalian. For decades, that money has insulated the diocese from the worst repercussions of global recessions, depopulation, economic transitions, and the decline of mainline Protestantism. But by resting in that safety, we have also at times been reluctant to innovate, to risk, and to face the holy endings that we must grieve well before we can find the courage to make holy beginnings.

In 2019, as our new neighborhood structures were making deeper conversation about our common life possible, the Executive Council, led by a budget formation committee of talented lay and clergy leaders, took the first step in a multiyear process of aligning the diocesan budget with our new mission strategy. The new budget concentrated resources on programs and initiatives to promote congregational vitality and community engagement and categorized programmatic expenses according to the area of mission strategy they support. We call those categories Serve as Beacons of Jesus Christ, Offer a Generous Invitation and Welcome, Stand with the Vulnerable and Marginalized, Connect Within and Outside the Church, and Develop Clergy and Lay People to Lead.

The 2020 budget continued the realignment of resources and began to tackle what had, for some time, been an undiscussable issue in the diocese: the cash aid provided to congregations that were no longer sustainable. With the leadership of the Executive Council, we began the shift to a new system by which all congregations in the diocese were provided with the opportunity to develop new mission initiatives and apply for grant funding to support them. Parishes currently receiving direct aid have the opportunity to seek particular support, including participating in congregational vitality programs that provide intensive resources for ministry. In short, we moved from simply aiding parishes with the implicit assumption that they would continue doing what they were doing until the people were gone to working together with their clergy and lay leaders to provide both financial and practical resources. At the same time, self-sustaining congregations are also able to imagine new initiatives and ask for support from the diocesan budget to try them out.

"You have heard me speak with some urgency about our need to do and be church differently," I said when introducing this change to the people of the diocese. "I truly believe that all of our congregations have the possibility to become healthy and thriving communities of faith. I trust that this new budget structure developed by Executive Council will reshape our ability to use our resources to bring about the flourishing that God desires for our common life."[4]

I won't pretend that changing the way we think about, use, and talk about the diocese's considerable resources is always easy. Particularly in congregations where a few faithful people are struggling to maintain the congregation where they grew up, raised their children, and where they hope to go to God, the reduction of cash aid can seem like a blow they have no strength left to withstand. But because our diocese is blessed with money we can invest in ministry, we are also faced with the specter of having money but no church. By tending our relationships and trusting one another enough to have hard conversations we are moving toward more authentic, more radical investment in God's mission and a vision of the church's future that is life-giving and energized.

"We Wonder Why . . . We Are So White"

As if hard conversations about money weren't enough, we have also been working on racial reconciliation, part of one of our mission pillars that commits us to standing with the vulnerable and marginalized to transform systems of injustice. Some might suspect that emphasis was imported to the heartland of Indiana by this Black, New York–born and –raised bishop, but the truth is that the determination of Episcopalians in Indiana to wrestle with racial reconciliation is what drew me to the diocese in the first place.

Back in 2016, when I was asked to consider entering the discernment and election process for bishop of Indianapolis, I had more than my fair share of presumptions of what Indiana was like. Stories about the Ku Klux Klan loomed large in my initial understanding of Indiana history, and those stories weren't exaggerated. As the ABC affiliate in Indianapolis, WRTV, reported a few years ago, "There was a time in the 1920s when being seen as a good, upstanding Hoosier meant joining the Ku Klux Klan. At its peak, the Klan counted among its members the governor of Indiana, more than half of the state legislature and an estimated 30 percent of all native-born white men in the state."[5]

But when I finally read the profile for what the diocese was searching for in its next bishop, I discovered that things, at least in The Episcopal Church, had changed. One sentence in large black type caught my eye: "We wonder why when we gather at diocesan convention we are so white." I thought, any diocese that is willing and able to wonder about that out loud is a diocese I want to know more about.

Fast-forward five years, and we are talking about race everywhere. That isn't to say that it's easy, and that isn't to say that everyone is willing. Like all conversations about race and white supremacy, what we are doing in the Diocese of Indianapolis is profound and challenging work. As a Black woman in authority helping to provide, nurture, and sustain the relationships and spaces where a majority white community can have these conversations, I find the work liberating, exhausting, and transformative.

The changes in the political and social climate since 2017 have not made this work easier, and trust can be harder to come by when having conversations about race and diversity. But those challenges are why I think our diocese is required to be about the work of having these conversations, both inside our congregations and outside our doors in our communities. And when we do, we do so in a way that centers the relationships we have grown in the crucibles of our new structures, speaking about race and racial injustice with a vocabulary that binds us together as Christians, that keeps us focused on seeking reconciliation and deepening relationship across racial differences.

Our work on building new structures for mission has helped us get clear that the work of dismantling racism and white supremacy is not a program or initiative. Rather, it is central to our faithful discipleship. As we build new systems and structures, including our new racial justice and education team, we must be intentional and relentless in recognizing the ways that racism shows up in the structures and systems that sustain it.

These are hard conversations, and they can strain our hard-won relationships sometimes to the breaking point. But as my friend and fellow bishop Bonnie Perry of Michigan says, the church is not audacious enough in its hope. We need to stop being afraid of committing to the work of dismantling systemic racism and white supremacy and talking about it out loud with each other. We need to learn and understand how it operates inside The Episcopal Church and in the world, and we must be clear about our intent to do so. When I go to the webpage of Ben & Jerry's Ice Cream, it is clear that they are about selling ice cream and dismantling white supremacy. I want our church to be that clear, and to do so, we need to keep having conversations with one another even—especially—when it gets hard.

Stay Focused, Stay Clear, Stay in Relationship

As we have faced the increasingly urgent need to imagine and bring about a new dream for our church, I have come to understand that my ministry as bishop of Indianapolis must be rooted not in old institutional structures that are passing away, but in the relationships that I can build and the practices that sustain them. As we begin to emerge from the COVID-19 pandemic, the essential nature of these relationships, strained by many months of isolation, has never been clearer to me.

The church, as we all know, can call all kinds of people, and nothing else we hope or imagine for The Episcopal Church in our context will be possible unless my highest priority is to build relationships and stay in them even—especially—when it is hard. I have to make this work the center of my ministry, and the canons with whom I serve must do the same. As we have sought to put relationship-building and tending at the center of our work, we have learned that staying clear about our priorities and focused on our mission helps build the trust without which nothing else can happen.

We got to practice this kind of clarity early in my episcopacy when we constructed our diocesan mission statement, mining from the diocesan profile and other search materials words, phrases, and ideas that could help people get clear about what they loved, what they longed for, and what they feared. We wrestled with those words, asking one another, "Is that what you are really saying? Do you mean it? What are you afraid of?"

The mission statement that emerged from those conversations is expressed in relational terms: Grounded in God's love in Christ, the Episcopal Diocese of Indianapolis and its people:

- Serve as beacons of Christ in central and southern Indiana and beyond
- Offer a generous invitation and welcome
- Stand with the vulnerable and marginalized to transform systems of injustice
- Connect with other Episcopalians, ecumenical and interfaith partners, and advocacy groups
- Develop clergy and laity to lead the church of today and tomorrow

As we seek to embody the mission statement, we often speak of offering radical welcome and making bold witness to God's love. Inspired by Dr. Catherine Meeks of the Absalom Jones Center for Racial Healing, who borrowed poet David Whyte's language for the church, we seek to be "half a shade braver" as we reach across divides and difference to know our neighbors more fully.[6] In conversations with lay leaders, I hear both the deep desire to be able to show up in real and authentic ways at church and the fear of meeting new people or experiencing new circumstances. In these conversations, I encourage congregations to name the desire for change while also expressing our reticence about both change and the costs of staying the same. It is a privilege to have the kind of relationship between bishop and people that makes these kinds of conversations possible.

In those kinds of hard, heartfelt conversations, my outsider status can sometimes jump-start the work. I remind vestry members at visitations to introduce themselves to me, and I introduce myself to them by saying "I'm from New York. I don't do Indiana nice. I rely on you to tell me the truth, and I will tell you the truth, including if I can't tell you something for pastoral or confidential reasons." I tell them that if we can't be truthful with each other, then we can't be in authentic ministry together. And sometimes I even tell them, "If you're not truthful with me now, then I'm just going to have to come back until we do have enough trust and enough relationship for you to tell me the truth. But we are about God's mission, and we really don't have time to mess around." And perhaps most importantly, I try to say those things just as often at parishes with multimillion-dollar endowments as at congregations that are struggling to pay their priest.

My sense of urgency about change is strong, but I have learned that it takes time to loop people into the big conversations, and that we can either invest that time at the beginning or waste it cleaning up the mistrust that is created when people feel disconnected. We spend a lot of time figuring out ways to flatten the distinctions between metropolitan Indianapolis and the more rural parts of the diocese, continuing to invite people into leadership and going to them, over and over again. We try to create islands of trust in places where trust had been broken, and then use them like lily pads to make leaps to people and congregations where we need to rebuild relationships.

In leading this work, I also try to stay clear that I must continually use the emotional capital we are building to move our diocese toward the future God has in store for it. As much as I value relationships, I know that I cannot be invested in being liked all of the time and that I will make mistakes. I remind myself and the people with whom I serve that fear of failing cannot stop us from trying new things or taking risks. I prioritize the physical and spiritual practices that help me stay centered and available for this work and keep me clear that it is not, in the end, about me.

And finally, none of this would be possible without focused discipline, which can be the hardest practice of all in these overwhelming times. Supported by the canons with whom I serve, I work hard to stay focused on our mission and on the relationships that make it possible. We try to make sure that the things to which we say yes are aligned with our mission and have the potential to keep these new structures we are building engaged and connected. We are blessed with more opportunities for collaboration and connection than we can hold, and we try to choose wisely to be sure we can sustain our work and ourselves over the long haul. These relationships with my team are the most important ones I have, and they help make it possible to set the tone for the entire diocese, ensuring that people are building trust not just with me personally but also with the office of the bishop and all the people who support it.

As we emerge from the pandemic, I marvel at everything we have accomplished in the first five years of my episcopacy under such challenging circumstances. Spending 2020 largely distanced from one another, we are clear that we must double down on creating new relationships and deepening the ones of long standing. But as devastating as the pandemic has been, I long for more of the transformation it has prompted for the church. As I said, via Zoom, to our diocesan convention in 2020, "We have seen the difference it makes when we are forced to let go of the vestments, and the buildings, and the trappings of imperial church as we cultivate a deeper faith lived on the margins of power and privilege. In the devastations of this pandemic, we are centering our lives around what matters most. Like you, I look forward to postpandemic times when it will be safe to gather again and see one another face to face. But until then, I pray that we would continue to be present to the people, the challenges, and the opportunities that are in front of us right now, because the church that is rising up in the Diocese of Indianapolis during 2020 is actually the church I want to be in. Right now. Let us not fear the future, and may nothing get in the way of us becoming the church God needs us to be."

Conclusion

When I think about Episcopal leadership, it is helpful for me to remember that bishops are ordained not just to an order but also for a place. The model of leadership that I exercise in the Diocese of Indianapolis is attuned to my personal leadership style, the practices I learned as a young Gen X clergy leader, and the personality and culture of this diocese. But I am convinced that some elements of this way of leading a diocese transcend both numerical size and structural complexity:

- Deep investment in building and maintaining emotional capital through trust and appropriate vulnerability
- Commitment to centering voices and perspectives on the margins
- Curiosity about and willingness to learn from those on the outside of the institutional church
- Willingness to discover and discuss the "undiscussables"

- Enough love for the instructional church to be willing to critique it and experiment boldly to change it.

If we can invest in helping bishops, both new and experienced, adopt these practices and stick with them over time, I believe that we can help the wider church face this age of institutional church decline, social change, and spiritual longing with care and hope for the future God has in store for us.

CHAPTER 15

Learning to Think Institutionally and Lead Adaptively

Sean Rowe

I n 1951, Easter came early, and the next day, March 26, the Rt. Rev. Henry Knox Sherrill, presiding bishop of The Episcopal Church, appeared on the cover of *Time* magazine. In the illustration, he rises up over a towering cross and throngs of people meant to represent every Christian in the United States who was not a Roman Catholic. The accompanying article hailed Sherrill as the man who could unite all Protestants and as "a kind of personification of what every boy's mother wants him to be when he grows up: fair-minded, respected, a good mixer, and an unswerving steerer down the middle of the road."[1] The occasion for the publicity was his election as the founding president of the National Council of Churches.

As the admiring article recounts, Sherrill had prepared for the episcopacy in the right way. He had attended Hotchkiss, Yale, and Episcopal Divinity School, and then served in World War I, after which he became rector of a succession of prestigious parishes and married "pretty Barbara Harris, daughter of a prosperous Brookline businessman."[2] When he was elected the ninth bishop of Massachusetts on the first ballot in 1930, at age thirty-nine, his mentor, Bishop William Lawrence, the seventh bishop of the diocese, received news of his election "at a meeting of the Harvard Corporation. Leaving the meeting at once, he accompanied Sherrill to the convention meeting at St. Paul's."[3] Sherrill served in Massachusetts for seventeen years before being elected presiding bishop unanimously in 1947.

Sherrill was the first presiding bishop elected after the 1943 canon change that required presiding bishops to resign their previous jurisdictions, and although he bore the burdens of institutional leadership well, they weighed on him nonetheless. "The real job is to be a pastor to people," he said. "No one ought to look forward to an administrative position. It is a trial to be out of touch as far as I am."[4]

"The most immediate danger," he went on to say of the new National Council of Churches, "is that [the organization] may be so complex and diffuse that it may turn into a machine operating without the life of the spirit. The real task is to make the spirit live in this complicated machinery."[5]

This new kind of corporate Christianity had its challenges, to be sure, but at least in the pages of *Time* magazine, it was regarded as the only possible way to respond to the gathering storm of "a new, anti-Christian faith that is moving against the very basis of Christianity."

"How will Christianity—how will the Christian churches—meet the crisis?" the article asks in its concluding paragraph. "The answer, in large part, will depend on Bishop Sherrill and his Christian cohorts. If their united Christian effort can meet and master the challenge, Christendom may experience a rebirth of life and light that will mark an age in history."

Twenty-first-century bishops reading this article may well feel as if they have entered a time machine. Many of the terms and titles are the same as we have today, but for those of us increasingly accustomed to the institutional church's cultural marginalization in the last seventy years, such minute attention to Episcopal Church and mainline Protestant politics is almost jarring—as is its optimism about a golden age of Christianity on the horizon.

And yet, the legacy of the institutional church over which Bishop Sherrill presided is ours today. It has provided the staging ground for the ordination of women, the full inclusion of persons who identify as LGBTQ, and our strides toward becoming the Beloved Community. At times, our institutional steps toward justice have been brought about by pressure from grassroots leaders who were able to call the institution to account and force a change in policy. When the Philadelphia Eleven were ordained after two failed attempts to change the ordination canon at the General Convention, the resulting furor forced the following convention to take action. At other times, leaders who see a particular need before it becomes an institutional priority simply act, expecting the grassroots of the church to catch up. This was the case with the General Convention Special Program approved in 1967, which directly confronted the issue of race and the urban underclass and represented "an enormous break with the status quo and past leaders—black and white."[6]

Whether change originates at the grassroots or grasstops, it is the institution that makes the incarnation of these changes and achievements more visible and more relevant to the world in a way that 1.2 million individuals—about the number of people who claim to be Episcopalians—never could on their own. A basic understanding of modern communication indicates that, without institutional legacy, no one would have any reason to listen to or to care what The Episcopal Church is doing at any given moment. In fact, it is precisely the legacy of the institution of our sister Church of England that gave our presiding bishop, one of the finest evangelists of our day, the platform on which to electrify the world with his royal wedding sermon.

But in moments like that one, when we glimpse the extraordinary possibilities that our Christian message has for the world around us, we also see the limitations and constraints that result from the decline of our institutional structures brought about by our refusal to think institutionally in the last half century. Even as we recognize the power of the presiding bishop's message to spread the gospel and transform the world, we are forced to acknowledge that if he preached to the average Sunday attendance of our three largest dioceses combined, he would still not reach the number of people that Joel Osteen reaches on a Sunday morning.

Institution vs. Mission: A False Choice

The fact is that we now face a significant lack of capacity at nearly every level of the church. That lack of capacity is not the inevitable result of the cultural decline of mainline Protestantism. Instead, it is directly related to institutional atrophy that is continually reinforced by rhetoric that points the finger at this separate thing we call the "institutional church." This rhetoric, it should be noted, is used most often by those of us who receive paychecks from this institution and who will be willing beneficiaries of that part of the institution we call the Church Pension Fund.

Today, predictions about the institutional church's horizon mostly involve speculation about the year in which it will finally disappear. In the face of the numerical decline we now face, it is tempting for church leaders to advocate jettisoning the church's institution in favor of its mission. In this way of thinking, the church's mission is a more pure, less political alternative to the institution that Sherrill and generations of bishops after him have loved to hate. And for bishops, one attractive aspect of this idea is that it serves to devalue many of the administrative and institutional aspects of our role for which we often find ourselves unsuited and ill prepared.

But we ignore the institution at our peril, and not just because its atrophy leads to disciplinary, human resources, and financial disasters. The idea that the church's institution and God's mission can be bifurcated ignores the fact that without a structure, we cannot develop, pursue, and scale mission in the ways that God calls us to do. When we construct a false choice between institution and mission, we end up with a weakened institution that loses the capacity to practice the values it is meant to embrace.

Those of us who serve as bishops in the twenty-first century have the opportunity to chart a different course. Together, we can create a strong, adaptive institution with deep capacity to participate in God's mission in the world. Doing so will require us to learn strategic organizational skills, to be fluent enough to navigate the complexity of our current environment, and perhaps most of all, to make a steadfast commitment to freeing the institutional church from the systemic racism that has shaped every era of its history and every aspect of its development. Embracing this model of the episcopacy requires us to understand ourselves as leaders whom God has called into uncharted territory—leaders who must resist the idea that just because the church we serve still bears some outward resemblance to the church Sherrill served, we can double down on the models and methods of his era of leadership to return the church to some kind of imagined golden age.

Learning to Be Adaptive

In the face of the daunting challenges inherent in the twenty-first-century episcopacy, it can be a relief to understand that the five key behaviors required for bishops to be adaptive leaders can be learned. No matter their age, the number of years since their ordination as priest or bishop, the number of ministry calls or size (average Sunday attendance, or ASA) of parishes served, bishops can learn to be successful adaptive leaders who exhibit these five key behaviors:

- Creative problem solving
- Ability to handle unexpected emergencies or crises
- Interpersonal adaptability
- Effort in training and learning
- Ability to manage work stress

What is more, research tells us that these five adaptive behaviors correlate with bishops' psychological well-being. In other words, the more adaptively a bishop performs, the lower her level of emotional exhaustion in ministry and the higher her level of satisfaction in ministry. In particular, a bishop's ability to manage stress determines whether she can maintain interpersonal adaptability, which is characterized by working on teams, collaborating with others, and adjusting to the needs and demands of the laypeople and clergy with whom she serves. Interpersonal adaptability, in turn, results in a higher level of satisfaction in ministry. Likewise, a bishop's ability to solve problems also contributes to her satisfaction in ministry.

But research also provides bishops—particularly those of us who have served for many years—one significant caution. The longer bishops serve in office, the less interpersonally adaptive they become. This is true no matter how old the bishop is or how long he has been ordained. The more years we bishops serve in office, the less we exhibit the kind of interpersonal adaptability required to lead effectively and achieve satisfaction in our ministry. This ongoing loss of interpersonal adaptability is problematic at best, and too often, it has catastrophic consequences for the dioceses of the church.

Currently, there are few organizational resources available for bishops who need to learn the key adaptive behaviors that help us face the complex work required of us. Worse still, the pressure from the systems in which we operate is often to narrow our focus, double down on current strategies—regardless of whether they are working—and escape any institutional disequilibrium that would make people anxious, unhappy, or resistant.

But to reshape the office of bishop in ways that will allow us to be effective, we need to learn to foster these key behaviors that equip us to work in deeply collaborative ways. We must move beyond the collegiality that is so central to our identity as bishops and become truly interdependent with one another and the people we serve. Otherwise, we will be undermined by an all-too-tempting sense of learned helplessness and the perception that the external cultural forces we face are insurmountable, these all too often lead our diocesan systems to practice work avoidance disguised in theological terms. Instead, we should be willing to create what organizational development scholars call "learning organizations"—ones that value experimentation, innovation, and a clearer focus on impact—for the sake of the gospel.

Thinking Institutionally and Leading Adaptively

As bishops embrace the new skills and behaviors that adaptive leadership requires, we become better able to shepherd both our dioceses and the church-wide structure through what organizational development scholars call "midlife issues." These issues, commonly faced by institutions that have atrophied or are in decline, include the need to shed obsolete or dysfunctional aspects of their cultures and to integrate and align institutional subcultures with one another. Making these changes requires the stakeholders of an organization to take ownership of the issues and the solutions. And today in the church, this means doing so with a healthy respect for the institution as a necessary part of God's mission.

The challenge of taking on these issues at this point in The Episcopal Church's history is significant. As bishops, it means that we must exercise more of our leadership in what Ron Heifetz, the Harvard scholar who pioneered the concept of adaptive leadership, calls "the productive zone of disequilibrium."[7]

In short, the productive zone of disequilibrium is a range in which systems—in our case, dioceses and other institutional church structures—are unsettled enough that people are motivated to be creative and take on adaptive work. If the level of disequilibrium is too low, people stay complacent, but if the level is too high or the anxiety too much to bear, people can easily become overwhelmed, panic, and engage in work avoidance. This diagram illustrates the term:

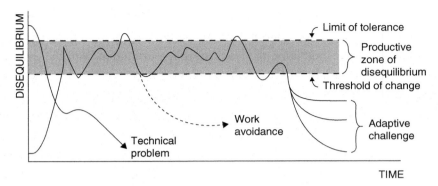

SOURCE Adapted from Ronald A. Heifetz and Donald L. Laurie, "Mobilizing Adaptive Work: Beyond Visionary Leadership," in *The Leader's Change Handbook*, eds. Jay A. Conger, Gretchen M. Spreitzer, and Edward E. Lawler III (San Francisco: Jossey-Bass, 1998).

Work avoidance behavior is especially evident in the church when diocesan governance bodies like councils and conventions delegate work to committees or task forces that have no real ability to enact the change. This is not always intentional or conscious. Take, for example, the Task Force to Reimagine The Episcopal Church (TREC), authorized in a nearly unanimous voice vote by the General Convention in 2012. At that time, the first decade of the new century had proven challenging in ways we had neither anticipated nor were prepared to face. The idea of a task force to explore new ways of being and governing made sense and could have worked well. In retrospect, though, the church simply relegated the problem to a group that lacked the authority to enact the change or inspire the commitment to change in those who did hold the authority. Once TREC was convened, the stakeholders no longer owned the problem—a key of adaptive change—and the project was doomed. In 2015, the General Convention largely rejected the larger, more fundamental changes recommended by TREC. Work avoidance is an old story for us in the church, and we see it repeated each convention in which we fight hard about liturgical texts or an obscure canon while the real adaptive work languishes or, worse, is not even acknowledged.

Learning to lead adaptively will not return us to the days of institutional reverence or cause us to embrace a nostalgic twentieth-century institutionalism. Instead, when we are thinking institutionally and behaving adaptively, we reclaim the notion of the institution as an agent of mission. When we dismantle the false choice between mission and institution, we are freed up to identify opportunities for experimentation using the resources of the institution, with the goal of participating more fully in God's mission. We are freed up to create space for adaptive conversations and discernment about where God might be leading us in our dioceses and communities. And we are liberated from old institutional norms and expectations that keep us from discussing the undiscussable issues, especially those that keep us mired in a fundamentally white vision of the institutional church with meager carve-outs for people of color, for dioceses outside the United States, and for women and LGBTQ+ people.

Toward a Sustainable Institution

So if, as bishops, we learn the adaptive behaviors we need to lead in this time, and we accept that a strong institution is essential for our participation in God's mission, then how should we proceed in changing the church's values about the institution?

One of the early and most influential organizational behavior scholars, Edgar Schein, posits that when decline is underway, there are only two basic mechanisms for culture change. The first is bankruptcy/turnaround, which consists of eliminating parts of the culture and building new patterns that are more adaptive and might start a new culture creation process. The second is merger/acquisition, which consists of "destroying the organization and its culture through a process of total reorganization."[8]

While neither term is entirely comforting, there are elements of both in what both research and experience suggest we need to do.

First, as Christian leaders, we need to agree on what we are trying to do. The urgent need—the essentially Christian nature of this work of thinking institutionally—is to define the outcomes we are seeking as a vision of the kingdom of God and build and adjust the institution to achieve those outcomes.

Second, we need to decide how we will measure the impact of what we are doing so we know if the elements of the institution we are retaining or building are contributing to our ability to reach the vision we have set forth. This is not a simple cause-and-effect analysis. Solving adaptive problems requires creating the space for innovative people and production-oriented people to collaborate, to leverage resources, to experiment with interventions and measure their impact, and then to try again. And again. Along the way, we will inevitably change and update our vision of what success looks like, but we need to start with a common goal.

Third, we need to organize our institutional structures to achieve the impact we want. This will involve focusing the institution on creating and fostering grassroots churchwide networks to help dioceses to do what they cannot do on their own and serving as a catalyst for initiatives throughout the church. Institutional staff structures and budgets would all need to be aligned to these ways of working and the results they could achieve.

This sounds much, much more benign than it is. The legacy of systemic racism, colonialism, and discrimination in our church has resulted in a structure created in part by hard-won and righteous battles by people of color, women, and LGBTQ people to have an institutional voice of any kind. Essential to the work Schein and others recommend related to integrating and aligning various subcultures would be deep and painful anti-racism work that would require a complete restructuring with diversity, equity, and inclusion at its core. This would be essential for us to become a church with people of color, LGBTQ people, and women invested at all levels rather than pursuing a primarily white vision of the institution with minor accomodations for people the church has historically disenfranchised.

To transform the institution in this way would require us to have what entrepreneur Susan Scott calls fierce conversations, and to ensure the psychological safety to do what is called "discussing the undiscussable." Only through these kinds of difficult conversations can organizations adapt and transform themselves. In fact, one of the early and primary theorists of the learning organization, Peter Senge, argues that "nothing is more limiting to a group than the inability to talk about the truth."[9]

Today in The Episcopal Church, we have a host of issues that are preventing us from transforming the institution. Some of them, like systemic racism at the churchwide level that keeps us locked in a structure where the ministry of people of color is restricted to a particular desk or office, we have begun to address. Others are still undiscussable. A partial list of those third-rail issues might include the fate of unsustainable dioceses; the size of our churchwide governance structures; our aversion to setting goals and defining metrics for success; the ways in which our guilt about the past keeps us from defining mission strategy for the future; and the vast inequity of salaries and benefits between lay and clergy employees and among clergy and bishops based on geography, gender, and other demographic factors.

Both organizational theory and lived experience tell us that The Episcopal Church has not yet reached the level of psychological safety necessary to have all these conversations—to discuss the undiscussable. Psychological safety is essentially the freedom to speak without fear of retribution, make a mistake in public and not be "cancelled," and share honestly within the organization what does and does not work. Research indicates that a sense of psychological safety is not a personality difference but a feature of the workplace that leaders can and must help create.

As bishops, we can create and sustain the psychological safety we need to have these hard conversations only when we commit to tending the organizational and institutional mechanisms that make them possible. It is not enough to love one another, nor to form deep relationships, although those things are essential. And we cannot avoid tackling these issues by claiming exceptionality, by insisting that because we are the risen body of Christ in the world, we are exempt from wrestling with the hardest institutional issues that confront us.

We will never return The Episcopal Church to the days of Henry Knox Sherrill. But as we seek to tackle adaptive problems with creativity and a sense of psychological safety, we must think and act institutionally—but not out of nostalgia or magical thinking, or as a way of avoiding the ministry to which we have been called. To survive in the twenty-first century as anything more than a relic, The Episcopal Church must reclaim and reinvent our institution precisely because it is the only way that we can participate faithfully in God's mission and be the body of Christ in a world that badly needs our witness.

CHAPTER 16

The Beauty Way

Cornelia Eaton

What in our sacred stories draws you to think of the episcopate in a new and different way, not as one with hierarchy over the people but one to be invited to see a bishop and people together as a community of the baptized? How might one be invited to create a holy space of hope and healing in the faith of Jesus's very Word for all of God's people through the work of the hospitality of the Holy Spirit? How might I invite the episcopacy to a ceremony of the Diné Hózhójíí, the Beauty Way?

1. SET CONFLICT RESOLUTION GROUND RULES:

Recognize whose lands these are on which we stand.

Ask the deer, turtle, and the crane.

Make sure the spirits of these lands are respected and treated with goodwill.

The land is a being who remembers everything.

You will have to answer to your children, and their children, and theirs—

The red shimmer of remembering will compel you up in the night to walk
   the perimeter of truth for understanding.

As I brushed my hair over the hotel sink to get ready I heard:

By listening we will understand who we are in this holy realm of words.

Do not parade, pleased with yourself.

You must speak in the language of justice.[1]

US poet laureate Joy Harjo, of the Muscogee (Creek) Nation, inspired me with her holy realm of words, "Conflict Resolution for Holy Beings." Her words invited me to write an essay that would be like weaving a Diné (Navajo) traditional rug. My collection of words is offered in rhythms of stories and poetry,

207

hopes and dreams, in concert with the voices of my ancestors and elements of the universe—wind, fire, water, and earth. Just as you would find with one of our rugs, in this chapter you will find an effort to pay attention to our surroundings, to every good God has created, by way of reflection, awareness, insight, and reverence. Just as a traditional weaver uses the gifts of the sacredness of holy creation when she creates her story woven together in a traditional rug with design, color, and positivity, I want to share these gifts in weaving new ways, healing ways, of thinking about the episcopate.

In Diné spirituality, sheep wool is holy and using it properly is a sacred act. Before sheep wool is spun into fine yarn, first there is preparation. We invite First Thought to enter heart and mind, asking God for guidance and direction. God shows us where to find and choose sacred plants to create such a rug. First cedarwood is gathered for the fire to boil water in a large metal bucket. Then herbal medicine plants are picked from a sacred site and placed in the boiling water to dye the wool. The result is a beautiful creation.

The Beauty Way of thinking, which is the heart of Diné culture, can produce more than beautiful objects. It can produce beautiful, healed people. A community of relatives is gathered, like the sacred plants and herbs, to make this Harmony Way spirituality happen. In this way, I imagine my words are woven together with the voices in memory of my ancestors. They, too, help guide our thinking for the immediate needs of healing for God's creation and people. Healing, like weaving, happens through ritual and ceremony all done in prayerful listening and prayerful doing.

In *God's Church for God's World: A Practical Approach to Partnership in Mission*, a colleague and friend, Rev. James Stambaugh, and I co-authored a chapter titled, "Communion as a Discipleship of Mutuality." Philippians 2:1–11 was our guide. In the chapter, we write, "Stories and songs weave us together and help us to see our common humanity. Part of discipleship is learning how we are invited to be in relationship with God in our story so that we can also discern our common dependence on God and God's grace."[2] For us, Philippians is about emptying self in the act of humility to help a disconnected world to return in relationship with Jesus in faith in the Beauty Way.

Our stories are rooted in the spirals of spirituality of the Beauty Way, also known as the Blessing Way. It is a prominent ceremony of the Diné in which a patient in need of healing is restored in relationship with God and sacred creation. We believe that telling and listening to each other's stories is a way to strengthen us in partnership to participate in preparing for the coming of God's kingdom with a new and creative lens. In Philippians, Saint Paul encourages the church to be partners in ministry in humility and unity. As we learn about and from each other, we learn humility, inviting us to consider how we might be in relationship with each other and with creation. Humility is a primary virtue. Humility has the power to redeem and heal. Humility is sacred. As we learn each other's stories we may find we have much in common.

There are two prominent ceremonies that the Diné are encouraged to have every four years. These ceremonies are the Ash Blackening Way and the Beauty Way. The Ash Blackening Way is a ceremony offered by medicine chanters, who are gifted with particular sacred songs and prayers, for a person in disharmony with the physical and natural world. The ash that covers all of the person's body is a sign of protection for four days. During those four days, the patient is reflective and prayerful, being aware of and paying attention to the inner self where there is need of restoration. This discipline involves truth to bring brokenness to the surface. What follows after four weeks is the Beauty Way ceremony. The Beauty Way is also offered by medicine chanters who with the community gather to pray for harmony. The community sing creation songs with the universe in order to restore her. Those gathered learn how to live in relationship with creation again. At the closing blessing of a Beauty Way, the restored person stands in harmonious relation with creation and, facing the rising dawn, prays for the healing of the world, that all learn to walk in harmony, in Hózhó, in Shalom, in the Beauty Way. Diné spirituality is about healing and wholeness. Healing and wholeness are part of what God hopes for us and for the world. Thus, Diné spirituality connects with Christian spirituality.

Ceremonies of Hózhójíí (doing the Beauty Way) have been practiced over centuries through sacred songs and prayers and continue in the present time. For Diné Christians, Jesus is the center of the Beauty Way. Jesus, the Cosmic Christ, through God, incarnates and dwells among all of creation and all people. Jesus connects us to God's unity as a Beloved Community of faith. Hózhó—peace and harmony—connects us through stories of hope and relationship where the holy Incarnate One dwells within us and all around us.

Because Diné ceremonies have parallels to the Book of Common Prayer rituals, it is not difficult to integrate Diné spirituality with the Episcopal liturgy. For example, the Diné, like most Native people, identify closely with the four directions prayer. Our ancestors offered prayers to the east, south, west, and the north, giving an order to the day similar to the services in the Book of Common Prayer. Seeing and connecting with similarities like this, having the gift of open-mindedness, offers many possibilities and opportunities for connection and communication, especially for those who are different from us. Meeting people of many cultures in their context is one part of doing justice. Jesus of Nazareth shows how he did this very well in his time, and I believe he is trying to show us how to do this in our time.

Reflection: *How might God be inviting the episcopacy to bring together God's people to do justice as we look toward being a new church for the future mission and healing ministry of a changing world through the lens of Native people's spirituality?*

I was born where an ancient and magnificent rock formation stands strong and firm to this day. Rock with Wings, in our ancestral language is pronounced as Tsé Bit' A'i, and was known to early English settlers as Ship Rock because it appeared to them like a sailing ship. Shiprock, New Mexico, the town named after the rock formation, is located in the four corners region of New Mexico, Arizona, Utah, and Colorado.

There are a variety of stories about Rock with Wings, depending on the geographic location where one is raised. Even though "our time immemorial" ancestral stories differ, all the stories point to hope, healing, and resilience and to prospering after hardships. This story is the one I learned as a child in our ceremonial home, repeatedly told by my elders.

Tsé Bit A'i is a reminder to Diné about the ancient Navajo twin warriors. These brave brothers, known as children of the Sun, battled an enormous bird that was devouring the People. The power of the Sun's bright beams was their spiritual guidance as they fought to save the People from perishing. They were also supported by ancient sacred songs and prayers that tirelessly echoed in the voices of the strong wind carriers. In the end, the bird was defeated. Today, the ancient, petrified rock, the figure of a bird with wings, standing as tall as a Manhattan skyscraper building, is a symbol of hope.

All around Tsé Bit A'i are blackish lava rocks. Geologists confirm Rock with Wings is an extinct volcano. According to the New Mexico Bureau of Geology and Mineral Resources, "an explosive eruption occurred 30 million years ago" and produced the rocks.[3] Ancestors of the Diné believed they were the dried blood of the bird and the Diné today hold fast to the story of this gigantic pinnacle as a monument to one of their ancient stories, reminding us of the spiritual journey that is a part of life. At the tip of Rock with Wings appears an image carved by the winds of an eagle, reminding us of her humility, strength, and harmony.

Not all of our stories are stories of hope and healing, however. Native people have a painful history from decades of the harmful impacts of colonialism created from nationalist creeds such as the "doctrine of discovery" and "manifest destiny." Too often, these creeds gave support to campaigns of expansion that resulted in not only the grabbing of Native American lands but also attempts to erase Indigenous people's language, culture, tradition, and spirituality. The author of *Post- Colonial Theology*, Robert S. Heaney, associate professor of Christian mission and director of Anglican Communion Studies at Virginia Theological Seminary, describes the way the dominant society tells its side of the story of colonization as a "romance" in which pioneers created a "better" land. In America, this has led them to claim the stolen land as part of a "sweet land of liberty"—a place of opportunity and equality for all. But while this is "the story told by a dominant culture around thanksgiving tables, under fireworked skies, and beneath white flag poles, for many people, such tables, such skies, and such flag poles stand not for remembering, but for *dis*membering. They signify limbs cut off; voices silenced. Some cannot breathe. For Native Americans dismembering meant dispossession, schemes for assimilation and genocide."[4] This story must be acknowledged, and was also part of the story of the church.

The impacts of how this nation settled remain real today in the twenty-first century. If we hope to build a new community, then we must take on the revealing truths that will take us on a journey through history, seeing the past with courage. This journey will not be easy.

The ministry of reconciliation that I envision involves not only human relations but also our relationship with the total body of creation. I feel the spirit of Jesus inviting us toward greater connection with creation and with each other regardless of title, class, race, and _____. Humanity has forgotten how and why we are to care for and love Mother Earth and all the relatives who live upon her. In *Returning to Mother Earth*, Wati Longchar says, "A theology that addresses humanity alone and leaves the rest of the cosmos unaddressed is an incomplete theology."[5] My native elders shared how necessary it is to acknowledge creation because they help us stay spiritually balanced. When we listen to the elements of creation we can hear the sacred soil, the movement of the winds and waters, and the rays from the sun being formed by the body of the Incarnate One. We may feel this in our own bodies as well. The cosmos is trying to tell us that by way of returning to the earth we also learn reconciliation and to be part of the redemptive work of God.

Reflection: How might God be inviting the episcopacy to perceive organic interrelation as a way of balance and healing the earth and peoples as one body of creation in Hózhó, the Beauty Way?

I was raised in two faith communities. My parents and elders of the church are people of ritual—the Episcopal ritual and the Diné ritual. It is customary for an infant's dried umbilical button to be placed, by elders of the community, where the baby will be raised within the Four Sacred Mountains in Navajoland. When my infant umbilical button dried, my parents and the elders placed this sacred part of my being in the earth, in front of the eastern doorway of St. Michael's Episcopal Church. This giving back is one of the spiritual practices of Hózhójíí. When I tell this story it helps me to remember the soil of which I come and this sacred soil will call me home in the faith practice of the Beauty Way.

I was also raised at a sheep camp in a ceremonial octagonal hogan made of cedar logs plastered with mud. For the Diné, this location of my family camp is known as Bikooh Hó Tsaa, translated as At the Edge of Big Sandstone Canyon Wash. It is where my paternal grandmother and grandaunt lived. They were Episcopalians and renowned ceremonial elders in the community. I recognized them as reflective, humble, and slow to speak, but when they did speak wisdom flowed like water in their voices. Their voices carried strength. Now that I remember, it was very beautiful to see.

I went to and from these two places and learned to embody the manner of life in the Beauty Way.

Randy S. Woodley in *Shalom and the Community of Creation: An Indigenous Vision*, states, "The Harmony Way consists of a sense of unity and diversity that recognizes an individual, not just for how they continue the family's survival, but for their uniqueness and giftedness as an individual person."[6] Woodley invites us to prepare the way for community from every tribe, welcoming diversity through their gifts and values. Harmony, like the Beauty Way, is the very essence of our commonality as Native people. We hope for this for all divine creation. We must keep finding a way to welcome the beauty of diversity in liturgy, in unity, and in harmony, which is essential for us to move toward healing together. We are called to look toward the horizon of hope with the active continuation of doing justice. Justice is healing work that moves us toward the ministry of reconciliation.

Reflection: How might we build and strengthen our partnership as we are called to practice Hózhójí—doing Jesus's shalom?

Connectedness brings us home to the sacred heart of God. There God shows us what we must do together to build the kingdom of God. As a community of faith, a people of God, we should be about seeking to invite all people of faith to the table and listen. My father and mother used to tell me how my paternal grandparents joined The Episcopal Church because the church in Navajoland invited them in such a way that they didn't have to abandon their traditional ceremonies and their stories were valued. Connecting our faith traditions is a blessing way. In our worship, we use cedar juniper as our incense to purify sacred elements at the altar, Baptism, and special ceremonies. We bring water from sacred lakes and rivers for Baptism, and we remember Ash Wednesday as the Ash Blackening ceremony to keep us prayerful during the Lenten season.

At my ordination to the diaconate, a Beauty Way medicine man offered the blessing of the corn pollen ceremony to my ordination. Corn pollen is gathered in the early morning before sunrise during harvesting time. It is very sacred. In the Beauty Way, the corn pollen is placed on the tongue and the top of the head, and then sprinkled gently toward the firmament, acknowledging its holiness in our midst.

Our Episcopal and different community of faith visitors in the pews were amazed by how the order of service began not with the words and direction of a bishop, but with the chanting voice of the medicine man. The medicine man was also amazed with the use of cedar as our incense in the ceremony. His exact words, as we nodded in agreement, were, "This is nizhoní, very beautiful. I had not known this is the practice of your church." I often wonder how a part of himself must have healed in seeing both traditions honored in one ritual.

In the community of the Diné, reverence for the sacred corn pollen ceremony takes precedence over church liturgy. In this recognition of an ancient ceremony within another ancient ceremony, humility was present and it was very beautiful and holy for all people present, both the Diné and non-Native peoples.

My elders model connectedness well. Most are not financially wealthy, but are rich in experience through our practice of spirituality, faith, culture, traditions, and ritual. I remember my grandmother having stew simmering on the stove regularly. One day I asked Grandmother, "Why is there a whole pot of stew while we are so far away from relatives?" She replied with a smile, "Because we do not know when one of them might arrive and we must be ready to feed our relatives." Her intuition of hospitality was always right on. We would receive visitors occasionally, and after their visit with Grandmother over a dish of stew and coffee. After the meal, they showed their gratitude with these words: "Now my being is whole and well again. It is good." It is a beautiful example of discipleship. Jesus, too, fed the body as well as the soul.

Another principal part of Diné spiritual life is raising sheep. We believe sheep are healers. In tending them, they teach us how to love, care, feel, and pray, and we offer these aspects of self to God with gratitude. Sheep are our spiritual sustenance and they sustain our mind, physical being, and soul. Sheep keep the Diné connected to the Creator, land, medicine plants, sage and juniper brushes, rocks and trees, and all living creatures on the earth. Learning from both four-legged creatures and organic creation invites us to rethink our relationship with the earth and with God and how we might reconnect to our earth mother. As God's people, in the twenty-first century, we have forgotten how to practice organic relationship in the face of the greatness of creation where we encounter God's organic grace and love.

I am not surprised to learn sheep fat was my first taste when my infant belly was ready for something new. To this day when I am without the sacred meal of lamb for a time, I long for the sacred meal as a way to bring blessing and restore joy. My mother said sheep fat would bring healing and that this healing was to be craved. This is part of the faith of my ancestors my parents shared with me. Lamb is, to this day, offered at family gatherings, ceremonies, weddings, and funerals, so that all are fed. Lamb is a delicacy created for the Diné to carry forth with resilience, to keep us balanced in the healing nutrients of fragments of divine gift.

Sheep offer many ways of healing. When I used to have time to herd sheep, I would pay attention to them closely. I would recognize how some wandered far off from the others and I'd go after them and herd them back into the fold. When the sheep were all back together, this felt holy and loving—a blessing and restored joy.

Sheep are always hungry, and it is amazing to watch them find nutrients to satisfy their hunger. Sometimes I got weary walking all around the open land to find them, but interestingly the crows were a good help. They led me to where the sheep had wandered. Sometimes I wondered if I was the lost one. Lost because of my lack of attention to the sheep I was tending. But the birds helped with finding my way back to them. I didn't realize the birds were offering hospitality. My ancestors saw this kind of connection. It has taken time to come to this awareness and realize my ancestors' wisdom, listening even now to what they have to say. Wisdom comes to us through deep listening and attention.

Sheep wool was also handled with tenderness and care and used for many purposes. Weavers would prepare and spin wool into fine yarn and a sheep creation song accompanied the ritual. The weavers sang because their own stories intertwined with the fabrics and tapestries of the woven rug. There are countless Navajo rugs and blankets with songs and prayers of beauty interwoven in them for the purpose of healing.

Native people love to share moving stories of hope and resilience. We are spiritual people grounded to the elements of holy creation. We are relatives to water, wind, fire, and earth. We are earth people rooted in our sacred land where the umbilical cord of our ancestors is grounded. In this groundedness, we are all related and it is how we experience healing and reconciliation.

Reflection: *How might God be inviting the episcopacy to practice and acknowledge interrelatedness by paying attention to the stories in your surroundings?*

God is certainly at work in these current times through the Holy Spirit. God is shifting us toward a different way of embodying God's vision, of preparing for the coming of the kingdom. God is showing us how to learn from the historical experiences of how Native peoples embodied the earth as ways of healing among creation relatives. Native peoples are rooted in the land where we can name every living organism as our relatives. On our sacred lands, which we share together with those living organisms and each other, we are in relationship with the gifts the holy Creator is providing to sustain us. We do not separate self from the elements of the universe—earth, sky, fire, water, air. We are part of the elements because they dwell within us. This kind of connectedness is necessary to share for the future of the church. Jesus of Nazareth was very attuned to the elements. In scripture we hear how he went to the mountain to pray and stayed near the waters. He looked to the heavens and offered himself in obedience to God, always giving thanks and praise. I imagine the elements as Jesus's clans. I imagine Jesus saying to us daily, "Ya'ah'tééh (Greetings from Sky, and from within Me, to You, all is beautiful). I am Jesus, I am water clan, born for my father, the fire clan, my paternal grandfathers are the wind clan and my maternal grandfathers are the earth clan; this is how I am me." Jesus is our relative and holy brother. Here I imagine how Jesus embodies the Beauty Way and teaches us how to be a people intertwined in our sacred stories.

In Navajoland Area Mission along with the Episcopal Diocese of Northern Michigan, we are hoping to weave a dream together by revisiting *The Dream: A Church Renewed*,[7] by the Rt. Rev. Wesley Frensdorff, former interim bishop of Navajoland (1983–1985). Bishop Frensdorff was one of many bishops to share God's dream with the Diné. I knew Bishop Frensdorff for a very short time in my teenage years. I have experienced his concern, love, and care for the Diné and his desire to help us flourish in our uniqueness of spirituality and how we envision becoming a Diné church in the Beauty Way.

To this day, I am still very moved by the vision of *The Dream*. We all have dreams. These visions of the future are born out of pains and sufferings in the past and the present, our awakenings before dying, our joys and praises, our disappointments and inspirations in living, and in the tension of balancing our reality with our hopes for new life to emerge.

The mission and ministry of Navajoland Area Mission is emerging in a new way of becoming church, spiraling outward beyond the Four Sacred Mountains. This awareness of mission and ministry is being born out of the pains of the pandemic. The people of Navajoland are making their way into the field beyond ourselves to make Christ's love known, even in the midst of vulnerability. During the pandemic we stayed as closely connected as best we could to the values of sacred stories both in Christianity and Diné. We shared our losses and uncertainties, but we learned in our vulnerable grief, where hope remains. Coming to this awareness and understanding of the people has taken time. However, the result is born from the elements of Jesus. Jesus is the emergence who invites and enables us to dream God's dream and hope for God's hope.

Over centuries the prayers, ceremonies, rituals, and stories of the Diné never ceased to be repeated. The Old Testament and New Testament stories, psalms, parables, and prophecies also continue to be remembered and repeated. It is absolutely important to hear and listen to the voices and stories of Native peoples and include their sacred words with ours. They have much to tell us about resilience, survival, and hope. Bishop Steven Charleston, of the Choctaw Nation, in his essay "The Old Testament of Native America," shares his vision of how in the next century, the Christian church is going to need to be open to becoming a new way of being a church. Charleston states, "The Church will experience a second major reformation. In this becoming there is a need of balance. The leaders of the coming reformation will be women. They will be from Africa, Asia, Latin America, and Native America. They are being born right now and that one of the major shifts in theology of the second reformation will be attuned with the stories of the Old Testament of Native America."[8]

Prophetic voices have been a gift of Native elders for centuries. Our ancestors looked to the sky, waters, trees, and animals of divine creation and by paying close attention to them were able to see how the future is shifting. A traditional herbalist elder and mentor, who lived the Beauty Way throughout her life identifying medicine plants, was aware of change happening around her. She ceremonially picked medicine plants most of her life and grew to know these plants intimately expressed through prayers and gratitude. She picked these sacred plants for healing for the people. I recall recently she acknowledged certain plants didn't bloom where they used to and how they were hard to find. She called this change relocation. The seeds of the plants moved to a community where another clan kinship is valuing their presence with prayers and gratitude. The last holy realm of words my elder left with us, before COVID-19 took her life in early March 2020, was a reminder about how "we must remember we are earth and the earth is us. Our earth mother shares the same spirit and breath we breathe." This one spirit weaves us together through the four sacred elements. She continued, "We need to talk to the earth, to the sky, to the stars, and to acknowledge their presence because they acknowledge and pray for us daily. These holy things provide us with healing medicines. But now we have forgotten these sacred living things and how to give thanks for their presence. These holy creations teach us how to pray and depend on Diyín, the Holy, and will help us to pay attention to our surroundings." We are all part of sacred creation. Her final teaching is a gift and I believe we are given a responsibility to take care of this gift and share it as hope and healing.

I invite the episcopacy to prayerfully seek new ways of being Christian in the Beauty Way. Connecting our two traditions offers us a new path. The Beauty Way is a beautiful and sacred ceremony. In the process is life, ritual, and emergence toward healing and wholeness. The journey is difficult and challenging; however, we will come to a new horizon, an Easter if you will, a new birth from the womb of our Earth Mother. This journey has much in common with the Christian journey.

The world we share is in need of healing and reconciling and recovery from historical trauma. I am finding the Beauty Way offers a way to achieve this. Reconciliation requires truth and trust. The difficulties and challenges of trust after the repeated and present experiences of colonialism are understandable, but we cannot allow ourselves to be hopeless. Indigenous communities are undergoing traumas from seven generations of colonialism, structural and systemic racism resulting in genocide, ethnic cleansing, dislocation, and the effects of globalization, that afflict us all. We have to find a way to help the wounded heal, both people and our earth mother. As my elders said, "We need a cleansing and healing ceremony." In *Post-Colonial Theology*, Heaney writes, "Given the trauma associated with colonialism and coloniality, on the land and in the people of the land, the idea of 'redemption in Christ' is associated with a renewal of interconnectedness to creation and decolonization."[9] Heaney goes on to convey how shalom is the bringer of the kingdom through redemptive atonement—being one with God, all part of God's family.

The world has wandered from being relatives with one another. I feel that, as The Episcopal Church, the Holy Spirit is leading us to pray about how we might improve relationships. But we have much work ahead of us. The history of harm done to Native people cannot be undone, but we can begin by raising up healers and leaders for the generations before us. We are in a very holy liminal time, being invited by the Holy Spirit to raise up Native voices and invite them to the table, to listen to them and find solutions to do justice and heal Earth Mother and all peoples who live with her.

Reflection: How might God be inviting the episcopate to reach out to Native voices to partner and assist the church toward a ministry of decolonization, recovery, and healing for wounded people in our communities?

In 2015, I left my homeland to attend seminary in Virginia for three years. Even for that short course of time, I felt my being was too far away from the four sacred mountains. However, through the sacred prayers I was taught in my mother tongue, the company of solitude got me through difficult days. In my second year at seminary, on a fall weekend, my relative and colleague Rev. Leon Sampson and I went to a festival in the outskirts of Alexandria, where we met Virginia Natives. We ate their frybread. We dipped frybread in sweet berry syrup, which was new for us as Diné, and God led us there to remind us we are not alone. When God invites us into a new culture of people, where we get to know God's life in theirs, God shows us, as followers of Christ, that after all we do have something in common. We are all beings created from the one sacred soil of God's creation.

We can learn much from Native people. Our relatives, in their vulnerability, teach us through their songs and prayers how to be with divine creation.

They can teach us what it means to be connected with each other and creation with compassion and humility. I am one of many to share my culture and stories of my elders and ancestors for my community, and future generations. Our children and youth need to hear our stories so they learn the truth, and do justice. God is placing in our hands the responsibility to become our ancestors' voice, voices as healers and harmony. We use our blessings, and we are told to take care of them, so that we can share our blessings. This is how Native people heal.

Divine love brings people closer in relationship of togetherness to lead the baptized toward healing and wholeness. Listening, trust building, and acknowledging the historical past are some of the highest points of moving toward restoring relationships and healing. Listening and paying attention deeply to every voice are important; even the trees, plants, waters, insects, and four-legged creatures are trying to tell us how to heal, and when we sit quietly and truly listen, the answers will come. God will show us where God is leading. The answers are in such liminal times.

I pray and hope for The Episcopal Church to continue strongly in advocacy for justice for healing of all God's creation. I am honored to serve on the Presiding Officers Racial Justice committee, of "Truth, Reckoning, and Healing." This sacred journey will be a process paved with how we the church are called to reckon the harm of colonialism and its history. I feel the Holy Spirit continues to move us ultimately toward God's reconciliation and redemption. As God's beloved people, we have touched the surface of racial justice and we have a long way to move toward deep reconciliation. Over centuries, Native people and many people of color have been silenced, and we must actively work to invite all voices to speak around God's table.

Let us continue to celebrate the languages, dances, food, and history of various cultures through listening to one another's stories, which bring us all into the fold so that we all heal together. I realize and understand reconciliation might not be complete right away for many, but we must keep on trying and moving forward, and simple gestures, such as showing hospitality, do make a difference.

God is inviting us all to God's table as one people united in the heart of Christ, the sacred heart of love, in the new breath of creation to be the words that should guide us in our paving the way for the Lord. Each day at dawn is a new birth and opportunity in Diyín—the Holy—to do the Beauty Way and it is good, it is very good.

Reflection: How might God be inviting us to offer hospitality in hopes to move us toward God's dream in the ministry of reconciliation?

Notes

Introduction

1. This is drawn from a brilliant quote by Hilton Als, who is reflecting on the intercultural bias of communities in an interview with musician PJ Harvey. He writes, "Racism seduces us with its desire to categorize, shutting out the living and breathing and 'different' world all around us." See Hilton Als, "New Again: PJ Harvey," *Interview*, January 7, 2015, retrieved August 7, 2020, https://www.interviewmagazine.com/music/new-again-pj-harvey.

Chapter 1

1. *The Book of Common Prayer: And Administration of the Sacraments and Other Rites and Ceremonies of the Church: Together with the Psalter or Psalms of David* (New York: Church, 2007), 517. Hereinafter *Book of Common Prayer* (1979).

2. See, e.g., Wolfhart Pannenberg, *The Church* (Louisville, KY: Westminster: John Knox, 1983).

3. The image was a favorite of Karl Barth's.

4. This was a point made by Professor Sonderegger of Virginia Seminary at the conference on disagreement in the church in January 2020.

5. This is the title of the statement of the Toronto Anglican Congress of 1963.

6. See Kathryn Tanner's *God and Creation in Christian Theology* (New York: Fortress Press, 1988).

7. See, e.g., Anglo-Catholics and Christian socialism, or Evangelicals and the anti-slavery movement in England.

8. I offer a similar argument for the particular identity of the ordained, as they display what is distinctive of the church in general, in respect to the office of the presbyter, in my book *Being Salt* (Eugene, OR: Wipf and Stock, 2007).

9. On this, I have profited from reading the essays by Bishops Griswold and Borsch in the edition of the *Anglican Theological Review* devoted to the episcopate. *Anglican Theological Review* 71, no. 1 (January 1989).

10. Erik H. Erikson, *Young Man Luther* (Gloucester, MA: Peter Smith, 1994).

11. *Book of Common Prayer* (1979), 517.

12. Ibid., 518.

Chapter 2

1. Anglicans already showed their recognition of the importance of college work in America in the late seventeenth and early eighteenth centuries, when Anglican commissary James Blair founded the second American college (the College of William and Mary, 1693) and Society for the Propagation of the Gospel missionaries succeeded in convincing most of the faculty of Yale College to leave the Congregational Church and join the Church of England (1722).

2. See *Journal of the General Convention of the Protestant Episcopal Church in the United States of America Held in Honolulu, from September Fifth to Fifteenth, Inclusive, in the Year of Our Lord, 1955* (n.p.: W.B. Conkey, 1955), 249–50, 252. In the 1890s Bishop Charles Henry Brent argued that overseas mission was vital to the success of the local parish: "The Church is strong when she is daring, and only then; her strength rises and falls with her courage—victory is faith. What an inspiration to every parish, the lowest and poorest as well as the numerically strong and financially rich!—the uttermost part of the earth is within the reach of its influence: ay, more than that, is in need of its prayers and its labours. Work for foreign mission is the climax and crown of Christian life, not a sluggish tributary to it. And a parish will be in the vanguard of God's forces or far in the rear, according as it rises to its responsibility in this direction or not" (Charles H. Brent, *With God in the World* [New York: Longmans, Green, 1902], 119). The General Conventions of 1955 took this idea seriously, and its 1956 budget devoted 39 percent to overseas mission. Individual dioceses and such groups as the Episcopal Churchwomen also devoted significant funds to foreign mission.

3. The General Convention's efforts to dismantle segregation began as a response to an Episcopal election in Arkansas in 1932. The House of Bishops declined to endorse the election, because racist campaigning had played a role. In the 1940s all dioceses except South Carolina dissolved their separate Black convocations. During the 1950s segregated Episcopal colleges integrated. It would not be until the 1960s that Episcopal secondary schools in the South were integrated.

4. *The Book of Common Prayer: And Administration of the Sacraments and Other Rites and Ceremonies of the Church: Together with the Psalter or Psalms of David* (New York: Church, 1979, 2007), 517. Hereafter *Book of Common Prayer* (1979).

5. *Book of Common Prayer* (1979), 298.

6. *Book of Common Prayer* (1979), 322, 354.

7. The Standing Commission for Liturgy and Music created traditional language Rite I services for Morning and Evening Prayer, the Eucharist, and burial. The

decision not to offer a Rite I form for the services of Baptism, confirmation, and ordination meant that when bishops presided in local parishes they always had to use services that were entirely or in part in Rite II contemporary language.

8. Title III, canon 20 of the 1976 Constitution and canons explained that "the control of the worship, and the spiritual jurisdiction of the Parish, are vested in the Rector, subject to the Rubrics of the Book of Common Prayer, the Canons of the Church, and the godly counsel of the Bishop." The language had been in the canons since 1904, and is now found (with slight emendations) in Title III, canon 9.6 (a).

9. The bishop was Bishop Suffragan John A. Baden.

10. This was a problem for both "high-church" and "evangelical" bishops. Interestingly, both parties had the greatest trouble controlling those with whom they were in the closest agreement. High-church bishops were able to stop changes by evangelical clergy but could not stop Anglo-Catholic clergy from introducing the unauthorized Benediction of the Blessed Sacrament or using the Anglican Missal (an edited form of the prayer book to which elements of the Roman Catholic liturgy were added). Evangelical bishops were able to curb the behavior of some high-church clergy but not to stop the more gradual adoption of Catholic liturgical elements by evangelical and broad-church rectors.

11. The General Convention authorized the use of the first of the trial liturgies, *The Liturgy of the Lord's Supper*, in 1967. Unlike the later *Services for Trial Use* and *Authorized Services*, this first liturgy contained only a revision of the Eucharist.

12. Richard Fabian, "Plan for the Mission of St. Gregory of Nyssa," St. Gregory of Nyssa Episcopal Church, December 1977, 3–4, accessed September 14, 2021, https://www.saintgregorys.org/articles.html.

13. The practice of inviting the unbaptized to receive the Eucharist contradicts title 1, canon XVII.7: "No unbaptized person shall be eligible to receive Holy Communion in this Church." This canon, adopted as title I, canon XVI.7 in 1982, clarified the understanding of Baptism shared by the members of the Standing Liturgical Commission, who had drafted the 1979 edition. It was only after the adoption of the 1979 edition that it became clear to them that their proposal to remove an earlier rubric limiting communion to the confirmed or those "ready and desirous to be confirmed" (*Book of Common Prayer* [1928], 299) was being interpreted by some to mean that Baptism was unnecessary for reception. The text of the prayer book they prepared had not stated explicitly that Baptism was necessary, but it did imply it strongly. For example, new rubrics in the baptismal service called Baptism "full initiation . . . into Christ's body the Church," and directed that the prayers of the people and the

Eucharist follow Baptism (298, 310). It also explained in the catechism that the Eucharist strengthened "union with Christ" that had been given at Baptism (858, 860), an explanation that assumed that Baptism preceded reception.

14. *Journal of the General Convention of . . . The Episcopal Church, Indianapolis, 2012* (New York: General Convention, 2012), 728–29.

15. *The 1892 Book of Common Prayer* (Lewiston, NY: E. Mellen Press, 1993), vi.

16. The 1928 edition of the Book of Common Prayer expanded this provision in three ways. Devotions could be taken not only from the prayer book but also from the Bible or from forms "set forth by lawful authority within this Church." The latter source was a reference to the *Book of Offices: Services for Certain Occasions Not Provided for in the Book of Common Prayer*, which had been issued in 1917 by the authority of the House of Bishops. The requirement that Morning and Evening Prayers be said was amended to say that such devotions could be used "in place of the Order for Morning Prayer, or the Order for Evening Prayer." Finally, the 1928 text made a new distinction between missions and parishes. The clergy of missions needed only to be "subject to the direction of the Ordinary" to use such devotions, while those in parishes and cathedrals needed to be "expressly authorized by the Ordinary." This difference may have reflected the recognition that mission clergy—and especially those in non–English language settings—needed more flexibility. The 1979 prayer book reworked the note slightly and dropped the distinction between missions and parishes. See *The 1928 Book of Common Prayer* (Oxford: Oxford University Press, 1993), vii, and *Book of Common Prayer* (1979), 13.

17. Edwin Augustine White and Jackson A. Dykman, *Annotated Constitution and Canons for the Government of the Protestant Episcopal Church in the United States of America Otherwise Known as the Episcopal Church*, 1981 edition (New York: Seabury Press, 1982), I:131, 135 (emphasis added).

18. White and Dykman, *Annotated Constitution*, I:464.

19. *Constitution & Canons*, General Convention Office, 2018, https://extranet.generalconvention.org/staff/files/download/23914. See *Constitution*, Preamble.

20. The specific term used in the diocese was "Lichty's boys." Bishop Lichtenberger went on to become presiding bishop (1958–1964). See Robert Benjamin Tobin, *Privilege and Prophecy: Social Activism in the Post-War Episcopal Church* (Oxford: Oxford University Press, forthcoming), 75.

21. George Henry Jack Woodward, conversation with the author, 1994.

22. A personal example of how the system was intended to work is my clergy profile from the 1970s that included the following details: I had established and served a Spanish-speaking congregation, I had served on a diocesan and a local ecumenical

committee, and I was pursuing a PhD in church history. Every time a certain Episcopal congregation in Latin America that hosted an ecumenical service and was linked to a school of theology sought a clergy person, the deployment office suggested my name. Though the openings never coincided with my own availability, I visited, preached, and lectured at the parish and the linked school of theology multiple times.

23. *Constitution & Canons 1982*, Episcopal Church Archives, 1983, https://www.episcopalarchives.org/sites/default/files/publications/1982_CandC.pdf. See canons IV.3.14, IV.4.2, and IV.4.3. For the different procedure to be followed in matters of doctrine, see canon IV.4.2.

24. *Constitution & Canons 1982*, canons IV.3.1, IV.3.2–13, and IV.4.1.

25. The 1994 revisions limited the possibility of a complaint by a single person to cases of sexual misconduct. The 2009 revisions expanded this possibility to cover all types of complaints.

26. See the definitions for "sexual behavior" and "sexual misconduct" in *Constitution & Canons 2009*, canon IV.3. Curiously, the canon makes no exception for the spouse of a clergy person, who could conceivably be a volunteer or employee in the congregation in which that person's spouse served. See *Constitution & Canons 2009*, Episcopal Church Archives, 2010, https://www.episcopalarchives.org/sites/default/files/publications/2009_CandC.pdf.

27. The address of the page is https://www.titleiv.org/title-iv-structure-and-proce dures (accessed September 17, 2021). To reach it, navigate from episcopalchurch.org in the following manner: The Episcopal Church > About Us > Church Governance > General Convention > Title IV Website (one of the choices from a list in small print at the bottom of the page) > Structures and Procedures. A site search for "title IV structure" on the initial page does not bring up the "Title IV Structure and Procedures" page.

28. Canon IV.17.2 explains that "in all matters in which the Member of the Clergy who is subject to proceedings is a Bishop . . . Intake Officer shall mean a person appointed by the Presiding Bishop," and the "Bishop Diocesan shall mean the Presiding Bishop." See *Journal of the General Convention of . . . The Episcopal Church, Anaheim, 2009* (New York: General Convention, 2009), 227–66.

29. *Constitutions & Canons . . . 2006*, 154, and Edwin Augustine White and Jackson A. Dykman, *Annotated Constitution and Canons for the Government of the Protestant Episcopal Church in the United States of America Otherwise Known as the Episcopal Church, 1789–1979* (New York: Church Publishers, 1997), I1:1082.

30. See, e.g., the 2015 address of Bishop Bob Duncan to the Annual Convention of the Anglican Diocese of Pittsburgh, in which he cited the Jeremiah 29:11 passage about God's plans "to give . . . a future and a hope." The passage served as the theme for a 2005 gathering critical in the decisions of the diocese to leave The Episcopal Church. Duncan called the passage a "prophetic promise" that had "more than been fulfilled." See David W. Virtue, "Pittsburgh: Anglican Bishop Robert Duncan to Retire in 2016," November 8, 2015, accessed September 20, 2021, https://virtueon line.org/pittsburgh-anglican-bishop-robert-duncan-retire-2016-many-parishes-still -legal-limbo.

A long period of litigation followed, with both the departing dioceses and the loyalists who remained in The Episcopal Church in reconstituted dioceses resorting to the courts to claim property and assets. Courts reached different decisions in different states. As of September 2021, The Episcopal Church retained assets of the Dioceses of Pittsburgh and San Joaquin, those leaving The Episcopal Church retained property in the Dioceses of Quincy and Fort Worth, and the matter continued in litigation in South Carolina.

31. *Book of Common Prayer* (1979), 517–18.

32. See chapter 13 of this volume for Joan C. Geiszler-Ludlum's in-depth discussion of the trial of Bishop William H. Love of Albany for his refusal to follow General Convention Resolution 2018-B012, which would have made same-sex marriage available in his diocese. Earlier General Conventions allowed for greater diversity in diocesan policies. Resolutions such as 1991-A104 ("General Convention . . . affirms that the teaching of The Episcopal Church is that physical sexual expression is appropriate only within the lifelong monogamous 'union of husband and wife in heart, body, and mind' intended by God for their mutual joy; for the help and comfort given one another in prosperity and adversity and, when it is God's will, for the procreation of children and their nurture in the knowledge and love of the Lord' as set forth in the Book of Common Prayer," but "continues to work to reconcile the discontinuity between this teaching and the experience of many members of this body") and 2000-C008 ("We . . . commit ourselves to continue the process of mutual sharing, study, and discernment concerning human sexuality, so that we remain open and connected to one another despite our differences, and so we can permit the Holy Spirit to act in our midst") attempted to keep members of the church of differing opinion in discussion with one another. In contrast, 2018-B012 required bishops who did not "embrace marriage for same sex couples" to "invite another bishop of this Church to oversee the consent process." Bishop Love of Albany was tried and convicted in a church court

for failure to follow this provision. See *Journal of the General Convention of . . . The Episcopal Church, Phoenix, 1991* (New York: General Convention, 1992), 746; *Journal of the General Convention of . . . The Episcopal Church, Denver, 2000* (New York: General Convention, 2001), 244; and *Journal of the General Convention of . . . The Episcopal Church, Austin, 2018* (New York: General Convention, 2018), 659–60.

33. I heard this quip by Bishop Lawrence from Charles P. Price (1920–1999).

Chapter 3

1. Personal in this context means that these relationships are constituted and sustained by the gift of self, of one's person. This dynamic personal relationship is grounded in the ecstatic dimension of the *imago Dei* at the core of our essence as human beings. Personal *ecstasis* reflects the nature of God as ecstatic, as demonstrated in God's self-revelation culminating in Jesus. God's *ecstasis* continues as self-gift in love, which we call grace. It is how we know in living our Baptismal Covenant that we do so, "with God's help." *Ecstasis* is therefore the personal nature of the core of our being manifested in living the *mandatum* of Jesus in John 17:12.

2. Genesis 1:1–2:25.

3. The concept, theologically, is also reflected in the doctrine of Trinity, Christology, soteriology, theological anthropology, and the theology of participation.

4. For our purposes here, it is not necessary to get into the weeds of the various, and somewhat inconsistent, uses of terms for the various designated ministries we see in the New Testament. In the end, the ministry of "oversight" became the ministry of the bishop.

5. The life and work of a bishop have also, at times, become more controversial in The Episcopal Church, with a move toward social, cultural, and ecclesiastical egalitarianism from the late 1970s forward, especially as seen in the debates and struggles around the ordination of women as priests and bishops, the politicization of the diaconate as a full and "equal" order, the efforts to democratize holy orders and lay ministry as especially manifested in the variously named "mutual ministry movement," racism, and the rights and ordination of LGBTQ persons.

6. *Baptism, Eucharist and Ministry* (The Lima Document) (Lima: World Council of Churches, Faith and Order Paper No. 111, 1982).

7. *The Book of Common Prayer* (1979) (New York: The Church Hymnal Corporation and The Seabury Press, 1977), 511–524. The Constitution and canons of The Episcopal Church provide further explication and application of the order. In the

Anglican tradition, the primary meaning is to be found in the texts of the prayers by which the church invokes the Holy Spirit to make a deacon, priest, or bishop.

8. Ibid., 308.

9. Ibid., 513.

10. Ibid., 514.

11. Ibid.

12. Ibid., 517. See also "The Examination," 518. The ministries of the bishop identified in the exhortation at the beginning of "The Examination" also form the substance of the questions that follow, to which the bishop-elect responds (518).

13. Ibid., 513. See also "The Consecration of the Bishop": "Therefore, Father, make *N.* a bishop in your Church. Pour out upon *him* the power of your princely Spirit . . ." (521). In the prayer of the church, the office and ministries of the bishop, by the grace of God in the Holy Spirit, become inherent in the man or woman who is made a bishop. The prayer here does not reflect a kind of docetic view of ordination, nor does it in the ordination of a priest (533) or a deacon (545).

14. Ibid., 517.

15. This brief sketch could apply to the theology of the polity of the Orthodox, Roman, and Anglican traditions. However, in the Anglican tradition, such a reading of order would be controversial, depending on where on the Anglo-Catholic–Protestant spectrum one begins.

16. Richard Hooker, *Of the Laws of Ecclesiastical Polity*, Book 1 (Cambridge, MA: The Belknap Press of Harvard University Press, 1977). This theological understanding of order decently lived is grounded, as noted earlier, in the biblical concept of righteousness as a rightly ordered relationship.

17. It is essential to remember that our ecclesiology and polity speak structurally and institutionally in symbolic language and acts. Therefore, to speak of the bishop as the center around whom the diocese gathers is to speak symbolically. The bishop, in one sense, may be understood to stand in the community both *in persona Christe* and before God *in persona communitatis*. This understanding of the role and function of the bishop neither intends nor means, in any sense, a displacement of Christ as the head of the body.

18. The ecclesiological assumption I am making throughout this chapter is based on Paul's image of the body of Christ in 1 Corinthians 12:12–31 and Romans 12:4–8. The image supports both the catholic polity of The Episcopal Church and a theology that embraces the great breadth and depth of diversity created by God for our participation in the *missio Dei* in this life. The ecclesiological perspective of doing all things

decently and in order is the dynamic underpinning of a participatory, collaborative network of righteousness for the good of God's beloved and the greater glory of God. This model weaves together inextricably functional, concrete action in service in this world with the vision of our final eternal life in God in the kingdom.

19. St. Benedict's *Regula* is both an ideal and a practical model for the life and work of a community at the individual and corporate levels. Its continued influence in monastic life across the range of religious orders as well as in organizational and congregational theory and practice bears witness to its strength and effectiveness. It is not perfect. Nonetheless, it is a good model and lens for understanding and implementing a life committed in faith to doing all things "decently and in order."

20. The life of the *Regula* was not only applied to life within the monastery. The *Regula* was, and is, the way a Benedictine lives wherever she or he is. The day is ordered around the *ora et labora* where one is, with whom one is, in the circumstances and conditions of this people and place.

21. This balance is explicit in the Benedictine motto "*ora et labora*." The *coordinating* conjunction, "*et*," is intentional.

22. It of course must be said that this process of development took time, indeed centuries. By the seventh century, St. Benedict had a much easier time forming an ordered and decently operative community than did the church. The point here is what did emerge both ideally and functionally. It was not perfect in the first or the seventh century, nor is the model or implementation of episcopacy perfect in the present. The work of the Spirit in the church and in/through the episcopate is always in a dynamic process of discernment and development. Hence, there is a sense in which the episcopate, as the church, is always adapting to the people, times, places, conditions, and circumstances in which we find ourselves.

23. It is beyond the scope of the present essay to explore in detail the pneumatological dimensions and implications of doing all things decently and in order. I note it here as a point for further study and examination. This dimension of the episcopate, as well as the life of all God's beloved, is, at the least, something of the consequences of being "sealed by the Holy Spirit" when we are anointed with chrism at Baptism.

24. *Book of Common Prayer* (1979), 517.

Chapter 4

1. I have previously discussed William White in these additional articles: "William White's Example," *The Living Church* 214, no. 5 (February 2, 1997): 14–15;

"Conciliarism and Convention's Authority," *The Living Church* 243, no. 7 (September 25, 2011): 18–25; "Conciliarism and the Ecclesiology of The Episcopal Church: A Review of Resources on the Authority of the General Convention," *Sewanee Theological Review* 61, no. 2 (Easter 2018): 447–494. For this current chapter I am deeply indebted to Judy Stark for her advice and improvements.

2. On Absalom Jones and White, see George Freeman Bragg, *History of the Afro-American Group in the Episcopal Church* (Baltimore: Church Advocate Press, 1922), 42–60; and Harold Lewis, *Yet with a Steady Beat: The African American Struggle for Recognition in the Episcopal Church* (Valley Forge, PA: Trinity Press International, 1996), 27–29.

3. On Leavington and St. James', Baltimore, see Lewis, *Yet with a Steady Beat*, 32–33, and Bragg, *History*, 91–94.

4. On White and the Methodists, see Robert Bruce Mullin, "Methodists and Episcopalians in American History," 1–18; and Thomas Ferguson, "Caught in the Parent Trap: Anglicans and Methodists in the USA," 19–30; both in *That They May Be One? The Episcopal-United Methodist Dialogue*, ed. C. Franklin Brookhart and Gregory V. Palmer (New York: Church, 2014). The correspondence of White and Coke can be found in William White, *Memoirs of the Protestant Episcopal Church in the United States of America* (New York: 1836), 343–348.

5. On White and Bible societies, see Arthur Lowndes, *A Century of Achievement: The History of the New-York Bible and Common Prayer Book Society for One Hundred Years*, 2 vols. (New York: 1909).

6. For my interpretation of White's *Case* here I am indebted to an unpublished paper prepared for the dialogue toward full communion between The Episcopal Church and the Evangelical Lutheran Church of Bavaria by the suffragan bishop of the Convocation of Episcopal Churches in Europe: Mark D. W. Edington, "Episcopal Views of Episkope: Sources, Significance, and Expression," Paris, France, January 2021.

7. William White, *The Case*, quoted in Edington, "Episcopal Views," 13.

8. On conciliarism in the ecclesiology of The Episcopal Church, see Raymond W. Albright, "Conciliarism in Anglicanism," *Church History* 33, no. 1 (March 1964): 3–22; and Franklin, "Conciliarism and the Ecclesiology," 470–471.

9. White, *The Case*, quoted in Edington, "Episcopal Views," 18.

10. Ibid.

11. Ibid., 11.

12. William White, *Memoirs*, quoted in Edington, "Episcopal Views," 17.

13. "Collect for the Commemoration of William White," in *Holy Women, Holy Men: Celebrating the Saints* (New York: Church, 2010), 467.

14. The most thorough discussion of this theological evolution of The Episcopal Church is Robert Bruce Mullin, *Episcopal Vision/American Reality* (New Haven & London: Yale University Press, 1986). See also Robert Prichard, "Rational Orthodoxy (1800–1840)," in *A History of the Episcopal Church* (Harrisburg: Morehouse, 1999), 105–135; and David Hein and Gardiner Shattuck, "Unity, Diversity, and Conflict in Antebellum America," in *The Episcopalians* (New York: Church, 2004), 62–83.

15. The classic overview of the rise of the "popular denominations" can be found in Sydney E. Ahlstrom, "The Golden Day of Democratic Evangelism," in *A Religious History of the American People* (New Haven & London: Yale University Press, 1972), 388–510.

16. The American Colonization Society as an instrument of white supremacy is discussed in David W. Blight, *Frederick Douglass: Prophet of Freedom* (New York: Simon and Schuster, 2018), 238–240.

17. The evolving understanding of the authority of bishops within the three orders of ordained ministry in the nineteenth century, and before and after, within Anglicanism and in contrast to other denominations is discussed in R. William Franklin, *Anglican Orders: Essays on the Centenary of Apostolicae Curae 1896–1996* (London: Mowbray, 1996).

18. The American version of the "Articles of Religion," established by the General Convention, can be found in the 1979 edition of *The Book of Common Prayer*, 867–876.

19. A thorough discussion of the theology of White's "Course of Ecclesiastical Studies" is found in Mullin, *Episcopal Vision*, 13–22.

20. By a Protestant Episcopalian, *Bishop White's Opinions on Certain Theological and Ecclesiastical Points Being a Compilation from the Writings and in the Words of The Rt. Rev. Wm. White, D.D.* (New York: Henry M. Onderdonk, Church, 1846).

21. Protestant Episcopalian, *Bishop White's Opinions*, 152.

22. Ibid., 83.

23. Ibid., 153.

24. Ibid., 73–74.

25. Ibid., 54.

26. Ibid., 61.

27. Ibid., 62.

28. Ibid., 59.

29. Ibid., 58.

30. Ibid., 65.

Chapter 5

1. Gardiner Shattuck, *Episcopalians & Race: Civil War to Civil Rights* (Louisville: University Press of Kentucky, 2000), 29.

2. Raymond Albright, *A History of the Protestant Episcopal Church* (New York: Macmillan, 1964), 494.

3. Robert L. Crewdson, "Bishop Polk and the Crisis in the Church: Separation or Unity?" *Historical Magazine of the Protestant Church* 52, no. 1, 1983, www.jstor.org/stable/42973930.

4. Ibid., 43.

5. Ibid., 51.

6. James M. Donald, "Bishop Hopkins and the Reunification of the Church," *Historical Magazine of the Protestant Episcopal Church* 47, no. 1 (1978): 73–91, www.jstor.org.stable/42973598.

7. John Henry Hopkins, *Bible View of Slavery* (Burlington, VT: Papers from the Society for the Diffusion of Political Knowledge, January 30, 1861), 43.

8. T. Felder Dorn, *Challenges on the Emmaus Road: Episcopal Bishops Confront Slavery, Civil War and Emancipation* (Columbia: University of South Carolina Press, 2013), 295.

9. Henry Shanks details Hopkins's maneuver just prior to the 1865 Convention in his essay, "The Reunion of the Episcopal Church, 1865," *Church History* 9, no. 2 (1940): 120–140, www.jstor.org/stable/3160350.

10. Ibid., 122.

11. Ibid.

12. Ibid.

13. Ibid.

14. Dorn, *Challenges*, 346–355.

15. *Journal of the Proceedings of the Bishops, Clergy, and Laity of the Protestant Episcopal Church in the United States of America Assembled in a General Convention 1865*, Episcopal Church Archives, 1865, 195, https://www.episcopalarchives.org/sites/default/files/publications/1865_GC_Journal.pdf.

16. Ibid., 157.

17. Dorn, *Challenges*, 351.

18. Ibid., 351.

19. Ibid., 353.

20. Ibid.

21. Ibid., 354.

22. Locket Mason, "Lower Cape Fear Historical Society: The Latimer House: Wilmington NC." Lower Cape Fear Historical Society, October 1992, uploads/1/1/9/8/119823026/bulletin_oct_1992.pdf.

23. *Episcopal Recorder* 43, no. 31 (October 28, 1865): 245. Quoted in Dorn, *Challenges*, 357.

24. Shattuck, *Gardiner*, 8.

25. Herbert Thompson, "A Black Bishop's Journey to Reconcile, to Heal, to Liberate, to Serve," *Anglican and Episcopal History* 74, no. 4 (2005): 355–481, www.jstor.org/stable/42612920.

26. Michael J. Beary, *Black Bishop: Edward T. Demby and the Struggle for Racial Equality in the Episcopal Church* (Urbana: University of Illinois Press, 2001), especially 16–47.

27. Robert A. Bennett, "Black Episcopalians: A History from the Colonial Period to the Present," *Historical Magazine of the Protestant Episcopal Church* 43, no. 3 (1974): 231–245, esp. 233, www/jstor.org/stable/42973424.

28. Harold T. Lewis, *Yet with a Steady Beat: The African American Struggle for Recognition in the Episcopal Church* (Valley Forge, PA: Trinity Press, 1996), 86.

29. Ibid., 86–108. The West Indian influence in The Episcopal Church and on African American Episcopalians deserves even deeper research and study of its own.

30. Beary, *Black Bishop*, 83.

31. Ibid., 22–23.

32. Ibid., 25.

33. Ibid., 37.

34. Ibid., 39.

35. Harold Lewis, "Unapologetic Apologetics: The Essence of Black Anglican Preaching," *Anglican Theological Review* 101, no. 1 (2019): 55.

36. *Journal of the Proceedings of the Bishops, Clergy, and Laity of the Protestant Episcopal Church in the United States of America Assembled in a General Convention 1877*, Episcopal Church Archives, 1877, 529, https://www.episcopalarchives.org/sites/default/files/publications/1877_GC_Journal.pdf.

37. William Brown is better known as the first bishop to be tried and deposed for heresy since the Reformation.

38. "Diocese of Arkansas Journal 1902." Hathi Trust. Episcopal Diocese of Arkansas, May 14, 1902, 75–78, https://babel.hathitrust.org/cgi/pt?id=nyp.33433070785187&view=1up&seq=9.

39. *The Church Advocate*, May 1907, 2.

40. E. C. Gailad, "A Negro Suffragan—A Puppet Bishop," *The Church Advocate*, 1916, 3.

41. George Bragg, *Arkansas Churchman*, December 15, 1925, 3.

42. Lewis, *Yet with a Steady Beat*, 79.

43. Ibid., 78.

44. "Diocese of Arkansas Journal 1902," 48–51.

45. Beary, *Black Bishop*, 149.

46. In Exodus 5, when Moses confronts the pharaoh for the first time to let his people go, the pharaoh responds by saying, "You shall no longer give the people straw to make bricks, as before; let them go and gather straw for themselves" (Exod. 5:7).

47. Beary, *Black Bishop*, 199.

48. Ibid., 243. For a more detailed study of the missionary district plan, see David M. Reimers, "Negro Bishops and Diocesan Segregation in the Protestant Episcopal Church: 1870–1954," *Historical Magazine of the Protestant Episcopal Church* 31, no. 3 (1962): 231–42, http://www.jstor.org/stable/43748127.

49. *Journal of the Proceedings of the Bishops, Clergy, and Laity of the Protestant Episcopal Church in the United States of America in a General Convention 1835*, Episcopal Church Archives, 1835, 475–78, https://www.episcopalarchives.org/sites/default/files/publications/1835_GC_Journal.pdf.

50. Ibid., 143–252.

51. Ibid., 181.

52. This letter is quoted in full in Beary, *Black Bishop*, 201.

53. *New York Churchmen*, August 17, 1932, quoted in Beary, *Black Bishop*, 206.

54. *Arkansas Democrat* (Little Rock), August 15, 1932.

55. E. J. Lunon's letter to William T. Holt, August 16, 1932, quoted in Beary, *Black Bishop*, 213.

56. W. T. Capers to W. T. Holt, August 23, 1932, quoted in Beary, *Black Bishop*, 215.

57. Ibid.

58. Demby, *Off the Record*.

59. Ibid., 255–258.

60. Ibid., 258, 161–62.

61. Ibid., 255.

62. *Holy Women, Holy Men* (New York: Church, 2010), 326.

Chapter 6

1. 1 Tim. 2:12 and 1 Cor. 14:34–35.
2. See "Feminae: Medieval Women and Gender Index," Inpress Library University of Iowa, The University of Iowa Libraries, 2014, https://inpress.lib.uiowa.edu/feminae/DetailsPage.aspx?Feminae_ID=37095, and Paul Collins, "'Theodora the Bishop': Pope Francis and Women Deacons," June 1, 2016, http://www.paulcollinscatholicwriter.com.au/blog/blog_2016.06.01.html.
3. Ally Kateusz, "Feminine Euphrasiana Basilica," Divine Balance, https://www.slideshare.net/DivineBalance1/art-as-text-11-feminine-euphrasiana-basilica. Today the pallium is reserved for papal usage and the occasional gift.
4. Sara MacDonald, "Researcher: Artifacts Show That Early Church Women Served as Clergy," *National Catholic Reporter*, July 13, 2019, https://www.ncronline.org/news/theology/researcher-artifacts-show-early-church-women-served-clergy. Pallia (plural) are visible in several slides.
5. Gary Macy, "The Ordination of Women in the Early Middle Ages," *Theological Studies* 61, no. 3 (2000): 481.
6. "Italy Ecclesiastical," Worldwide Guide to Women in Leadership, January 31, 2009, accessed January 5, 2022, https://guide2womenleaders.com/italy_ecclesiastical.htm. See also Rogelio Zelada, "Almost a Bishop: The Abbess of Las Huelgas," Archdiocese of Miami, March 27, 2017, https://www.miamiarch.org/CatholicDiocese.php?op=Blog_148882306520331.
7. For a Roman Catholic perspective on the role of mitered abbesses, see "Of Mitres, Mitred Abbesses and Clerical Kings," Shrine of the Holy Whapping, February 14, 2006, http://holywhapping.blogspot.com/2006/02/of-mitres-mitred-abbesses-and-clerical.html.
8. Maeve Callan, "Ireland's Own 5th-Century Female Bishop: Brigid of Kildare," *Irish Times*, May 25, 2018, https://www.irishtimes.com/culture/books/ireland-s-own-5th-century-female-bishop-brigid-of-kildare-1.3504216.
9. John Paul, "Dame Elizabeth Shelley, Last Abbess of St. Mary's Abbey, Winchester," *Proceedings of the Hampshire Field Club & Archaeological Society* 23, no. 2 (1965), https://www.hantsfieldclub.org.uk/publications/hampshirestudies/digital/1960s/vol23/Paul.pdf.
10. Gary Macy, *The Hidden History of Women's Ordination: Female Clergy in the Medieval West* (New York: Oxford University Press, 2008).
11. Local taxation supported religious activity in most parts of the former colonies until the 1780s.

12. The history of diaconal orders is complicated by the church's refusal to recognize women as deacons. Beginning in 1885, they were "set aside," rather than ordained, and women were not recognized or ordained as deacons, rather than deaconesses, until 1970. Nevertheless, they were recognized as significant leaders in the church's ministry—e.g., "Deaconess Margaret S. Bechtol, Superintendent of the Episcopal Eye, Ear and Throat Hospital, Washington, D.C.," is noted as one of the "Deaconesses [Who] Effectually Head Church Institutions Caring For Those In Need" in: "The Deaconess and Her Ministry in the Episcopal Church," published by the Executive Committee of the National Conference of Deaconesses, 1949, http://anglicanhistory.org/women/deaconess1949.pdf.

13. She took up her priestly orders again in 1971, when two women were ordained as priests in Hong Kong.

14. Matt. 5:11–12.

15. Central Africa, Melanesia, Papua New Guinea, and Southeast Asia.

16. Aotearoa, New Zealand, and Polynesia; Australia; Brazil; Canada; England; Ireland; Scotland; Southern Africa; South India; South Sudan; The Episcopal Church, including Cuba; and Wales.

17. Bangladesh, Iglesia Anglicana de la Región Central de América, Japan, Mexico, North India, Philippines, Tanzania, and Uganda.

18. This chart is updated fairly frequently: "Ordination of Women in the Anglican Communion," Wikipedia, Wikimedia Foundation, December 26, 2021, https://en.wikipedia.org/wiki/Ordination_of_women_in_the_Anglican_Communion.

19. Nerva Cot Aguilera, Suffragan.

20. Griselda Delgado del Carpio, Diocesan.

21. An overview of the first few years of women bishops in the CofE: "Factsheet: Women Bishops in the Anglican Communion," Religion Media Centre, October 26, 2021, https://religionmediacentre.org.uk/factsheets/women-bishops-in-the-anglican-communion.

22. The Lords Spiritual are the twenty-six Church of England bishops who serve in Parliament's House of Lords.

23. "South Sudan Has a Female Bishop," Thinking Anglicans, February 14, 2018, https://www.thinkinganglicans.org.uk/7803-2.

24. "Province of the Episcopal Church of South Sudan & Sudan," International Anglican Women's Network, Anglican Communion Office, accessed January 6, 2022, https://iawn.anglicancommunion.org/around-the-world/south-sudan-and-sudan.aspx.

25. Litoral and Central, Colombia, Venezuela (and Curaçao), Virgin Islands (British and US), Cuba, Haiti, Dominican Republic, Honduras, Puerto Rico, and the Convocation of Episcopal Churches in Europe (Austria, Belgium, France, Georgia, Germany, Italy, Switzerland).

26. Women, BIPOC, LGBTQI+, children, immigrants, disabled people.

27. Told me by a friend in Oregon over twenty years ago.

28. "The Lausanne Covenant," Lausanne Movement, October 25, 2021, https://lausanne.org/content/covenant/lausanne-covenant.

29. Egan Millard, "Episcopal Clergy Entertain and Evangelize in the Virtual 'Town Square' of Tiktok," Episcopal News Service, August 20, 2021, https://www.episcopal newsservice.org/2021/08/20/episcopal-clergy-entertain-and-evangelize-in-the-vir tual-town-square-of-tiktok.

30. Egan Millard, "'Wild Church' in Northern Michigan Invites Spiritual Seekers into the Woods," Episcopal News Service, September 1, 2021, https://www.episco palnewsservice.org/2021/08/30/wild-church-in-northern-michigan-invites-spiritual -seekers-into-the-woods.

31. "Refugee Net Grew out of the Diocese of San Diego, Its Congregations, and Partners," RefugeeNet, Episcopal Refugee Network of San Diego, https://www.ref ugee-net.org.

32. David Paulsen, "Church Pantries Help Diocese of Indianapolis Step Up Food Ministries during Pandemic," Episcopal News Service, April 17, 2020, https://www .episcopalnewsservice.org/2020/04/16/church-pantries-help-diocese-of-indian apolis-step-up-food-ministries-during-pandemic.

33. See First Nations Kitchen, https://firstnationskitchen.org.

34. "Santa Fe Church Forgives Medical Debt in New Mexico and Arizona," Episcopal News Service, July 15, 2021, https://www.episcopalnewsservice.org/pressreleases/ santa-fe-church-forgives-entire-state-of-new-mexico-medical-debt.

35. Faith Rowold and Ximena Diego, "Caring and Compassion for People Living with HIV/AIDS," Episcopal Relief & Development, May 28, 2019, https://www.epis copalrelief.org/stories/caring-and-compassion-for-people-living-with-hiv-aids.

36. "Migrant Outreach," Hispanic Affairs Project, accessed January 6, 2022, https:// hapgj.org/migrant-outreach.

37. Some bishops identify with more than one ethnicity; these identities are not mutually exclusive.

38. At least in corporate boards, to which the House of Bishops has abundant similarities. Cf. Carolyn Wiley and, Mireia Monllor-Tormos, "Board Gender Diversity

in the STEM&F Sectors: The Critical Mass Required to Drive Firm Performance," *Journal of Leadership and Organizational Studies* 25, no. 3 (2018): 290–308, https://doi .org/10.1177/1548051817750535.

39. I haven't figured out how to estimate the racial diversity over the whole of The Episcopal Church, but I would begin by noting that Haiti is our largest diocese, with more than 5 percent of The Episcopal Church's members.

40. Tiffany Burns, Jess Huang, Alexis Krivkovich, Ishanaa Rambachan, Tijana Trkulja, and Lareina Yee, "Women in the Workplace 2021," McKinsey & Company, November 2, 2021, https://www.mckinsey.com/featured-insights/diversity-and-inclusion/ women-in-the-workplace.

41. Sarah Kliff, "The Research Is Clear: Electing More Women Changes How Government Works," Vox, July 27, 2016, https://www.vox.com/2016/7/27/12266378/ electing-women-congress-hillary-clinton.

42. This story is told by Walter Wink, *Jesus and Nonviolence: A Third Way* (Minneapolis: Fortress, 2003), 31.

43. "All God's Creatures," Celtic Thunder, 2011; "Lift Every Voice and Sing," James Weldon Johnson, 1900; "We're Marching to Zion," Isaac Watts, 1707.

Chapter 7

1. Mary Frances Schjonberg, "Women Are Joining the House of Bishops at Unprecedented Rate," *Episcopal News Service*, July 1, 2019, accessed March 1, 2021, https://www.episcopalnewsservice.org/2019/07/01/women-are-joining-the-house-of -bishops-at-unprecedented-rate.

2. Pamela W. Darling, *New Wine: The Story of Women Transforming Leadership and Power in the Episcopal Church* (Cambridge: Cowley Publications, 1994), 176.

3. Joy McDougall, "Weaving Garments of Grace: En-gendering a Theology of Call to Ordained Ministry for Women Today," *Theological Education* 39, no. 2 (2003): 150.

4. "Ordination of Women," Connections, August 29, 2017, https://www.dso connections.org/2017/08/29/ordination-of-women.

5. Pamela P. Chinnis, *Decently and in Order: On Being the Church as the Century Turns: Selected Reflections of Pamela P. Chinnis* (Cincinnati: Forward Movement, 2000), 137–138.

6. Valerie Bailey Fischer (scholar), in discussion with the author, August 13, 2021. Fischer's revisionist work on the history of women and ordination is in production for publication and is related to her dissertation: "From Deacon to Priest: An

Alternative Narrative of Women's Ordination in the Episcopal Church," ThD, the General Theological Seminary, 2019. Fischer argues the importance of the historically neglected 1970 Deacon's Canon in the history of women's ordination in The Episcopal Church.

7. Paula Nesbitt, "Why Gender Still Matters: Continuing the Toolkit into the Future," Executive Council Committee on the Status of Women, 2012–2015, accessed February 24, 2021, https://www.episcopalchurch.org/cast-wide-the-net/why-gender-still-matters.

8. Paula D. Nesbitt, "Why Gender Still Matters," Church Divinity School of the Pacific (CDSP), accessed April 17, 2021, http://cdsp.edu/St-Margaret's-visiting-professorship.

9. Ibid.

10. For a summary of these views, see Mark Chaves, "Multidenominational Movements—the Ordination Movement," in *Encyclopedia of Women and Religion in North America*, ed. Rosemary Skinner Keller and Rosemary Ruether (Bloomington: Indiana University Press, 2006), 947–950. Fiorenza quoted in Natalie K. Watson, *Introducing Feminist Ecclesiology* (Eugene, OR: Wipf & Stock, 1996), 1; Natalie Carnes, "Gender and Ecclesiology," in *T & T Clark Handbook of Ecclesiology*, ed. Kim J. Bender and D. Stephen Long (London: T & T Clark, 2020), 386.

11. Fischer, discussion.

12. Schjonberg, "Women," 1–3.

13. Alistair S-Schoos, email messages to author, February 9–10 and August 3, 2021. Comparative data from the Evangelical Lutheran Church in America, last reported in 2019, confirms that twenty-four individuals or 36 percent of the bishops in the ELCA are women. Email, Linda Post Bushkofsky to SKH, February 22, 2021.

14. Todd Ousley, email message to author, August 9, 2021.

15. Schjonberg, "Women," 7.

16. Todd Ousley, email message to author, August 19, 2021.

17. Chilton Knudsen, email message to author, August 2, 2021.

18. Church Pension Group, *The 2019 Episcopal Clergy Compensation Report*, 2020, https://www.cpg.org/globalassets/documents/publications/report-2019-church-compensation-report.pdf.

19. World Economic Forum, *Global Gender Gap Report 2021*, March 30, 2021, accessed January 6, 2022, https://www.weforum.org/reports/ab6795a1-960c-42b2-b3d5-587eccda6023/in-full/gggr2-benchmarking-gender-gaps-findings-from-the-global-gender-gap-index-2021.

20. "Sustainable Development Goals: Goal 5: Achieve Gender Equality and Empower All Women and Girls," United Nations, accessed August 13, 2021, https://www.un.org/sustainabledevelopment/gender-equality.

21. Schjonberg, "Women," 4–5.

22. Ibid., 4–5, 7. In the Anglican Church of Canada, fourteen of the church's forty-two dioceses are led by women bishops. Linda Nicholls, email message to author, March 24, 2021. Nicholls notes that the experience of women bishops in Canada is different than in The Episcopal Church. As the first woman primate, she felt more marginalization as a priest. When she entered the House of Bishops as one of the first three women bishops, the women did not feel the need to caucus because of gender issues.

23. Paula D. Nesbitt, *Feminization of the Clergy in America: Occupational and Organizational Perspectives* (New York: Oxford University Press, 1997), 133.

24. Paula D. Nesbitt, "Feminization of the Clergy and the Future: Sociological Reflections," in *Looking Forward, Looking Backward: Forty Years of Women's Ordination*, ed. Fredrica Harris Thompsett (New York: Morehouse, 2014), 9.

25. Ibid., 9, 19.

26. Ibid.

27. Nesbitt, *Feminization*, 133.

28. Catherine Wessinger, *Charisma and Credentials: Women's Religious Leadership in America*, Yamauchi Lectures in Religion (New Orleans: Loyola University, 2007), 18.

29. Paula Nesbitt, letter to the author, "Women's Ordination Research," August 13, 2021.

30. See Janet Shibley Hyde, Rebecca S. Bigler, Daphna Joel, Charlotte Chucky Tate, and Sari M. van Anders, "The Future of Sex and Gender in Psychology: Five Challenges to the Gender Binary," *American Psychologist* 74, no. 2 (February 2019): 171–93. It should be noted that many of the sources related to women and the episcopacy are examining gender from a binary (female/male) perspective. Scholars and researchers of gender from an intersectional feminist and critical race theory perspective would refute this position, arguing that binary gender definitions are oppressive and serve to reinforce both colonization and patriarchy. Research points to a diversity of gender expressions and applications. Western notions of what constitutes female or male are considered inadequate to address the gender expressions found in different cultures and across humanity. While members of the current House of Bishops may now reflect binary categories, there are

gender-nonconforming clergy and church members; thus the election of a nonbinary bishop is just a matter of time.

31. Quoted in Fredrica Harris Thompsett, "Women in the American Episcopal Church," in Keller and Ruether, *Encyclopedia*, 278.

32. Kimberlé Crenshaw, "Demarginalizing the Intersection of Race and Sex: A Black Feminist Critique of Antidiscrimination Doctrine, Feminist Theory and Antiracist Politics," *University of Chicago Legal Forum* 1 (1989): 139–67; "Why Intersectionality Can't Wait," *Washington Post*, September 24, 2015, accessed May 23, 2020, https://www.washingtonpost.com/news/in-theory/wp/2015/09/24/why-intersectionality-cant-wait; Grace Ji-Sun Kim and Susan Shaw, *Intersectional Theology: An Introductory Guide* (Minneapolis: Fortress Press, 2018), 1–17.

33. Gay Clark Jennings, "The Annual Melissa L. Kean Women's Lecture," Li Tim Oi Committee (Sewanee, August 13, 2021).

34. Ibid.

35. Ibid.

36. Westina Matthews, *This Band of Sisterhood: Black Women Bishops on Race, Faith and the Church* (New York: Morehouse, 2021), xiii.

37. Ibid., 37.

38. Ibid., 34.

39. Ibid., 36.

40. Ibid., 35.

41. Ibid., 37.

42. Cornel West, *Race Matters* (Boston: Beacon Press, 2017), xxiv–xxv.

43. Robin J. Ely and Deborah L. Rhode, "Women and Leadership: Defining the Challenges," *Handbook of Leadership: A Harvard Business School Centennial Colloquium*, ed. Nitin Nohria and Rakesh Khurana (Boston: Harvard Business Press, 2010), 1–3, 24.

44. Respondent 1, questionnaire.

45. See Matthew Price, "Conclusion," in *Called to Serve: A Study of Clergy Careers, Clergy Wellness, and Clergy Women*, Church Pension Group, 2011, https://www.cpg.org/globalassets/documents/publications/called-to-serve-a-study-of-clergy-careers-clergy-wellness-and-clergy-women.pdf.

46. Respondent 13, questionnaire.

47. Respondent 6, questionnaire. See Darling, *New Wine*.

48. Respondent 11, questionnaire.

49. Respondent 8, questionnaire.

50. Catherine S. Roskam, "Women and the Episcopate: Looking Backward and Looking Forward," in Thompsett, *Looking Forward*, 89.

51. Respondent 8, questionnaire.

52. Respondent 18, interview.

53. *Called to Serve: A Study of Clergy Careers, Clergy Wellness, and Clergy Women*, Church Pension Group, 2011, https://www.cpg.org/globalassets/documents/publications/called-to-serve-a-study-of-clergy-careers-clergy-wellness-and-clergy-women.pdf.

54. *The Book of Common Prayer: And Administration of the Sacraments and Other Rites and Ceremonies of the Church: Together with the Psalter or Psalms of David* (New York: Church, 2007), 518. Hereafter *Book of Common Prayer* (1979).

55. Respondent 21, questionnaire.

56. Respondent 8, questionnaire.

57. Respondent 9, interview.

58. Respondent 11, questionnaire.

59. Respondent 12, questionnaire.

60. Rebecca Lyman, "Women Bishops in Antiquity: Apostolicity and Ministry," in *The Call for Women Bishops*, ed. Harriet Harris and Jane Shaw (London: SPCK, 2004), 46.

61. Margit Eckholt, Dorothea Satteur, Ulrike Link Wirczorek, and Andrea Strübind, *Women in Church Ministries: Reform Movements in Ecumenism* (Collegeville, MN: Liturgical Press, 2018), 21, 183.

62. Respondent 13, questionnaire.

63. Respondent 18, interview.

64. Respondent 11, questionnaire.

65. Respondent 10, interview.

66. Respondent 4, questionnaire.

67. Respondent 9, interview.

68. Carnes, "Gender and Ecclesiology," 375.

69. Ibid., 384–386.

70. Respondent 17, questionnaire.

71. Respondent 15, interview.

72. Respondent 20, interview.

73. Respondent 16, interview.

74. Respondent 3, interview.

75. Respondent 13, questionnaire.

76. Respondent 7, questionnaire.

77. Shannon Hopkins, "How to Lead When Things Are Falling Apart," Faith & Leadership, Duke University, July 21, 2020, https://faithandleadership.com/shannon-hopkins-how-lead-when-things-are-falling-apart, quoted in Lawrence Peers, "Resilience and the Practice of Pivoting," Congregational Consulting Group, March 15, 2021, https://www.congregationalconsulting.org/resilience-and-the-practice-of-pivoting.

78. Respondent 10, interview.

79. Respondent 13, questionnaire.

80. Respondent 18, interview.

81. Ellen K. Wondra, "Problems with Authority in the Anglican Communion," in *Anglican Women on Church and Mission*, ed. Kwok Pui-Lan, Judith A. Berling, and Jenny Plane te Paa (New York: Morehouse, 2021), 24–25. Also see Ellen K. Wondra, *Questioning Authority: The Theology and Practice of Authority in the Episcopal Church and Anglican Communion* (New York: Peter Lang, 2018).

82. Respondent 1, questionnaire.

83. Respondent 12, questionnaire.

Chapter 8

1. This is a quote that Hélder Câmara was fond of using. Its provenance may be traced to a popular song by Brazilian singer Raul Seixas called "Prelude," on his album *Guita*, released in 1974. While not certain, this in all probability links to an interview with John Lennon, who credits Yoko Ono for the phrase. See John Lennon and Yoko Ono, "John Lennon's Last Interview (December 8th, 1980)," YouTube, June 13, 2021, https://www.youtube.com/watch?v=xsu-GihhQIY.

2. Rick Warren, *The Purpose Driven Church* (Grand Rapids, MI: Zondervan, 1995), 15.

3. Quoted in Jean D. Clift and Wallace B. Clift, *The Archetype of Pilgrimage: Outer Action with Inner Meaning* (Eugene, OR: Wipf & Stock, 2004), 169.

Chapter 9

1. *The Book of Common Prayer: And Administration of the Sacraments and Other Rites and Ceremonies of the Church: Together with the Psalter or Psalms of David* (New York: Church, 2007), 518. Hereafter *Book of Common Prayer* (1979).

2. See "Most Diverse States 2021," World Population Review, https://worldpopula tionreview.com/state-rankings/most-diverse-states.

3. Eric H. F. Law, *The Wolf Shall Dwell with the Lamb: A Spirituality for Leadership in a Multicultural Community* (St. Louis, MO: Chalice Press, 1993), and *The Bush Was Blazing but Not Consumed: Developing Multicultural Community through Dialogue and Liturgy* (St. Louis, MO: Chalice Press, 1996).

4. Rosa Say, *Managing with Aloha: Bringing Hawai'i's Universal Values to the Art of Business*, Second Edition (Waikōloa, HI: Ho'ohana, 2016).

5. *Book of Common Prayer* (1979), page 513.

6. James 1:19 CEB.

7. *Book of Common Prayer* (1979), 521.

8. Ibid., 305.

9. Canon Chun also recounts the story in his book *No Nā Mamo: Traditional and Contemporary Hawaiian Beliefs and Practices* (Honolulu: University of Hawai'i Press, 2011), 7–8.

10. "Haole" is the Hawaiian term originally used for any "foreigner," but has come to be applied throughout Hawai'i by all groups for "white" persons of European descent.

11. *Book of Common Prayer* (1979), 518.

12. Ibid., 521.

13. See ibid., "The Examination," 518.

14. Ibid.

Chapter 10

1. *The Book of Common Prayer: And Administration of the Sacraments and Other Rites and Ceremonies of the Church: Together with the Psalter or Psalms of David* (New York: Church, 2007), 532.

2. Ronald A. Heifetz, *Leadership without Easy Answers* (Cambridge, MA: Belknap Press, 1994), 15.

3. 1966 Gallup poll; 1968 Harris poll.

4. Walter Brueggemann, *Reality, Grief and Hope: Three Urgent Prophetic Tasks* (Grand Rapids, MI: Eerdmans, 2014), 1, 2, 77.

5. *Book of Common Prayer* (1979), 382.

Chapter 11

1. Edward Mote, "The Immutable Basis for a Sinner's Hope," 1834, https://www .riteseries.org/song/levs/1011.

Chapter 13

1. Max Weber, the late-nineteenth-/early-twentieth-century sociologist, historian, jurist, and political economist, is much maligned for his work describing his favored, ideal type for rational decision making, bureaucracy. Nonetheless, his ideas remain a key influence in the structure and organization of modern western society and institutions.

2. See "Max Weber on Authority," Sociology Guide, accessed January 6, 2022, https://www.sociologyguide.com/socio-short-notes/view-short-notes.php?id=44.

3. Edwin Augustine White and Jackson A. Dykman, *Annotated Constitution and Canons for the Government of the Protestant Episcopal Church in the United States of America Otherwise Known as the Episcopal Church: Adopted in General Conventions, 1789–1979* (New York: Church, 1981), 11, 51–52.

4. Ibid., 55.

5. The Hearing Panel's decision was entered on October 2, 2020, following a recorded Zoom hearing on June 12, 2020. The recording of the hearing is available here: Egan Millard, "In Disciplinary Hearing, Albany Bishop William Love Defends Prohibition of Same-Sex Marriage in His Diocese," Episcopal News Service, June 12, 2020, accessed August 30, 2021, https://www.episcopalnewsservice.org/2020/06/12/in-disciplinary-hearing-albany-bishop-william-love-defends-prohibition-of-same-sex-marriage-in-his-diocese. The decision is available here: https://www.episcopalchurch.org/wpcontent/uploads/sites/2/2020/11/bplove_Summary_Judgement.pdf.

As the Hearing Panel's decision notes, "hearing panels are not bound by any prior decision of a former Title IV panel or Ecclesiastical Court."

6. "The Church's Canon Law and the Laws of the States," Report of the Standing Commission on Liturgy and Music, in *Reports to the 77th General Convention Otherwise Known as the Blue Book* (New York: Church, 2017), 217, 218.

7. "The Acts of Convention," Archives of the Episcopal Church, https://www.episcopalarchives.org/cgi-bin/acts/acts_search.pl.

8. *The Book of Common Prayer: And Administration of the Sacraments and Other Rites and Ceremonies of the Church: Together with the Psalter or Psalms of David* (New York: Church, 2007), 518.

9. Ibid., 513.

10. Obergefell v. Hodges, 576 U.S. 644 (2015). The decision was released on June 26, 2015. The General Convention adopted Resolution 2015-A054 on July 1, 2015, authorizing trial use of marriage and blessing liturgies for same-sex couples.

11. *The Blue Book – 2012*, Archives of the Episcopal Church (New York: Church Publishing, 2012), https://www.episcopalarchives.org/e-archives/gc_reports/reports/2012/bb_2012-R014.pdf. See also "Task Force on the Study of Marriage—the Archives of the Episcopal Church," 2015, https://www.episcopalarchives.org/e-archives/gc_reports/reports/2015/bb_2015-R044.pdf.

12. *Constitution & Canons*, General Convention Office, 2018, 13 (emphasis added), https://extranet.generalconvention.org/staff/files/download/23914.

13. You may see the legislation and follow its development here: "The Acts of Convention," Archives of the Episcopal Church, https://www.episcopalarchives.org/cgi-bin/acts/acts_search.pl.

14. Originally defined in the English Act of Uniformity 1662, which established the Book of Common Prayer for sole use in the Church of England, held statutory authority until the Worship and Measure of 1974 repealed all rubrics except the banns of marriage in the course of enacting an updated regime of public worship. The rubrics retain some measure of their original authority in The Episcopal Church, even as there is disagreement about the degree of that authority. Philip Jones, "The Rubrics of The Book of Common Prayer," Ecclesiastical Law, April 23, 2012, https://ecclesiasticallaw.wordpress.com/2012/04/23/the-rubrics-of-the-book-of-common-prayer.

15. *The Book of Common Prayer* (2007), 861.

16. Canon I.18.3(d)–(g), 2012. See *Constitution & Canons*, General Convention Office, 2012, https://www.episcopalarchives.org/sites/default/files/publications/2012_CandC.pdf

17. Canon I.18.4 (2015). See *Constitution & Canons*, General Convention Office, 2015, https://www.episcopalarchives.org/sites/default/files/publications/2015_CandC.pdf.

18. Nine dioceses are subject to non-US law in countries that had not extended marriage to same-sex couples at the time of the survey. Canon I.18.1 would prevent their authorization in deference to civil law restrictions.

19. Twenty bishops authorized use of the trial rites with conditions. Of those twenty, twelve required vestry approvals, two required vestry approval and permission of the bishop, one required approval of the bishop, two required a parish discernment process, and three authorized only one of the available rites. *Task Force on the Study of Marriage*, 2018, 795, https://www.episcopalarchives.org/e-archives/gc_reports/reports/2018/bb_2018-R036.pdf.

20. Ibid., 794.

21. "Caring for All the Churches: A Response of the House of Bishops of the Episcopal Church to an Expressed Need of the Church," March 20, 2012, http://images .acswebnetworks.com/1/3008/DEPOMarch2012HouseofBishops.pdf.

22. Canon 1.19(c). *Constitution & Canons 2015*, Episcopal Church Archives, accessed January 5, 2022, https://www.episcopalarchives.org/sites/default/files/pub lications/2015_CandC_ES.pdf.

23. Resolution 2015-A169 authorized the Standing Commission on Liturgy and Music to develop a plan for the revision of the Book of Common Prayer. The presiding officers appointed this legislative committee to receive both the proposals for prayer book revision and the report of the Task Force on the Study of Marriage and consider them together as liturgical revisions.

24. "Acts of Convention: Resolution #2018-A169," Episcopal Church Archives, https://www.episcopalarchives.org/cgi-bin/acts/acts_resolution.pl?resolution=2018 -B012.

25. Canon III.9.6(a). *Constitution & Canons 2015*, Episcopal Church Archives, https://www.episcopalarchives.org/sites/default/files/publications/2015_CandC.pdf.

26. Resolution 2015-A054, Seventh Resolve (emphasis added). "Acts of Convention: Resolution #2015-A054," Episcopal Church Archives, https://www.episcopalar chives.org/cgi-bin/acts/acts_resolution-complete.pl?resolution=2015-A054.

27. Resolution 2018-B012, Thirteenth Resolve. "Acts of Convention: Resolution #2018-B012," Episcopal Church Archives, https://www.episcopalarchives.org/cgi -bin/acts/acts_resolution-complete.pl?resolution=2018-B012.

28. "The Canons of the Diocese of Albany 2016," Episcopal Diocese of Albany, https://albanyepiscopaldiocese.org/wp-content/uploads/2021/08/The-Canons-of -the-Diocese-of-Albany-2016-version.pdf .

29. Emphasis added by the Hearing Panel, pp. 22–23. See "In the Title IV Disciplinary Matter Involving the Rt. Rev. William Love," Episcopal Diocese of Albany, https://albanyepiscopaldiocese.org/wp-content/uploads/2020/10/BpLoveSJOp 100220.pdf.

30. Ibid., 24–25.

31. Ibid., 25–26.

32. "Acts of Convention: Resolution #1994-B005," Episcopal Church Archives, 1995, https://www.episcopalarchives.org/cgi-bin/acts/acts_resolution-complete.pl?re solution=1994-B005.

33. *Constitution & Canons*, General Convention Office, 2018, https://www.episcopa larchives.org/sites/default/files/publications/2018_CandC.pdf.

NOTES TO CHAPTER 13

34. *Book of Common Prayer* (2007), 861.

35. "Liturgical Resources 2," General Convention, 6, https://extranet.generalconven
tion.org/staff/files/download/21226.

36. "Acts of Convention: Resolution #2018-B012," Episcopal Church Archives, 2019, https://www.episcopalarchives.org/cgi-bin/acts/acts_resolution-complete.pl?re
solution=2018-B012.

37. *Book of Common Prayer* (2007), 844.

38. *Constitution & Canons 2015*, Episcopal Church Archives, https://www.episcopa
larchives.org/sites/default/files/publications/2015_CandC.pdf.

39. Ibid. (emphasis added).

40. In January 1995, ten bishops of The Episcopal Church charged Ret. Asst. Bishop of Newark Walter Righter with heresy and violation of his ordination vows after he signed a statement supporting ordination of noncelibate homosexuals and ordained the Rev. Barry Stopfel, a partnered gay man, to the diaconate in 1990. In May 1996, the Court for the Trial of a Bishop, comprised of nine bishops, dismissed the charge in a 7–1 vote (one member, Bishop Borsch of Los Angeles, withdrew after objection to his participation by the presenting bishops after a noncelibate homosexual was ordained in his diocese after the first hearing). The court said, regarding the charge of heresy, there is "no core doctrine in this Church that prohibits the ordination of a non
-celibate, homosexual person living in a faithful and committed sexual relationship with a person of the same sex." Regarding the charge of violation of his ordination vows, the court held it was unable to find "sufficient clarity in the church's teaching at the present time concerning the morality of same-sex relationships" to support the charge. Gustav Niebuhr, "Hearing Begins for Bishop Who Ordained Gay Deacon," *New York Times*, February 28, 1996.

41. "Hearing Panel," note above, page 36. And citing *Book of Common Prayer* (2007), 861.

42. "Acts of Convention: Resolution #2018-B012," Episcopal Church Archives, 2019, https://www.episcopalarchives.org/cgi-bin/acts/acts_resolution-complete.pl?re
solution=2018-B012.

43. *Constitution & Canons*, General Convention Office, 2018, https://extranet.gener
alconvention.org/staff/files/download/23914.

44. Ibid.

45. *The Constitution of the Diocese of Albany (2011)*, https://albanyepiscopaldiocese
.org/wp-content/uploads/2021/12/Constitution-of-the-Episcopal-Diocese-of-Al
bany-Rev-2011.docx.pdf. See also Mary Frances Schjonberg, "ALBANY: Convention Pledges Loyalty to Church, but Disputes Role of General Convention," Episcopal

News Service, June 17, 2009 [061709-02], https://www.episcopalarchives.org/cgi
-bin/ENS/ENSpress_release.pl?pr_number=061709-02.

46. *Constitution & Canons*, General Convention Office, 2018. Bishop Love's Response Brief cites Canon II.12.3(3). The correct citation is Canon III.12.3(e).

47. Ibid.

48. Ibid.

49. Bishop Love's Response Brief. See Hearing Panel Report, 25.

50. Canon III.9.6(a)(1) (2018).

51. "Acts of Convention: Resolution #2018-B012," Episcopal Church Archives, 2019, https://www.episcopalarchives.org/cgi-bin/acts/acts_resolution-complete.pl?re solution=2018-B012.

52. Resolution 2018-B012 passed in the House of Bishops by a voice vote, making it difficult to say for sure how many bishops voted against passage. Following the close of the 2018 General Convention, ten bishops dissented from the passage of B012 in what has become known as "the Austin Statement," suggesting the number of bishops who may have voted against B012. In the House of Deputies, B012 passed twice on a vote by orders by wide margins. On the first vote to adopt and send it to the House of Bishops for concurrence, lay deputations voted 97 to 13 for passage, clergy deputations voting 96 to 14. On the second and final vote for adoption as amended in the House of Bishops, lay deputations voted 101 to 6 and clergy deputations 99 to 7 for passage.

53. "Cross Motion of Bishop Love and Brief in Support of Cross Motion and Opposition to the Church's Motion," The Episcopal Church, https://www.episcopalchurch.org/wp-content/uploads/sites/2/2020/11/bplove_brief_BISHOP-LOVE-RESPONSE-final-2.pdf. See also "Bishop Love Brief and Motion to Dismiss," The Episcopal Church, https://www.episcopalchurch.org/wp-content/uploads/sites/2/2020/11/bplove_brief_BISHOP-LOVE-RESPONSE-final-2.pdf.

54. "Opposition of the Church to Respondent's Cross Motion for Summary Judgment and Motion to Vacate Restriction on Ministry and Brief in Support," The Episcopal Church, 24, https://www.episcopalchurch.org/wp-content/uploads/sites/2/2020/11/bplove_decisions_tec_reply_-_final_033020_.pdf.

55. *Constitution & Canons*, General Convention Office, 2018, https://extranet.gener alconvention.org/staff/files/download/23914. See also https://www.episcopalarchives .org/sites/default/files/publications/2018_CandC.pdf.

56. "Acts of Convention: Resolution #2018-B012," Episcopal Church Archives, 2019, https://www.episcopalarchives.org/cgi-bin/acts/acts_resolution-complete.pl?re solution=2018-B012.

57. Resolution 2018-B012, Eighth Resolve. "Acts of Convention: Resolution #2018-B012," Episcopal Church Archives, 2019, https://www.episcopalarchives.org/cgi-bin/acts/acts_resolution-complete.pl?resolution=2018-B012.

58. Resolution 2018-B012, Third Resolve. "Acts of Convention: Resolution #2018-B012," Episcopal Church Archives, 2019, https://www.episcopalarchives.org/cgi-bin/acts/acts_resolution-complete.pl?resolution=2018-B012.

59. *Constitution & Canons*, General Convention Office, 2018, https://extranet.general convention.org/staff/files/download/23914. See also https://www.episcopalarchives.org/sites/default/files/publications/2018_CandC.pdf.

Chapter 14

1. The relatively new field of relational leadership theory offers a plethora of studies and hard data about leadership and interpersonal relationships. I commend the work and writings of Dr. Mary Uhl-Bien. My comments in this chapter are based on anecdotal experience and not this research-based social science framework, though they are undoubtedly related.

2. "2018 Diocesan Convention," The Episcopal Diocese of Indianapolis, accessed October 19, 2021, https://indydio.org/diocesan-convention/2018-diocesan-convention/.

3. "2019 Diocesan Convention," The Episcopal Diocese of Indianapolis, accessed October 19, 2021, https://indydio.org/diocesan-convention/2019-diocesan-convention.

4. "2020 Diocesan Convention," The Episcopal Diocese of Indianapolis, accessed October 19, 2021, https://indydio.org/diocesan-convention/2020-diocesan-convention.

5. Jordan Fischer, "The History of Hate in Indiana: How the Ku Klux Klan Took over Indiana's Halls of Power," WRTV, Scripps Media, December 8, 2016, https://www.wrtv.com/longform/the-ku-klux-klan-ran-indiana-once-could-it-happen-again.

6. David Whyte, "Half a Shade Braver: The Foundations of Conversational Leadership," accessed January 6, 2022, https://davidwhyte.com/products/half-a-shade-braver-the-foundations-of-conversational-leadership?_pos=1&_sid=84b09de84&_ss=r.

Chapter 15

1. "Religion: The Church & the Churches," *Time*, March 26, 1951.

2. Ibid.

3. Ibid.

4. Ibid.

5. Ibid.

6. "Welcome: The Church Awakens: African Americans and the Struggle for Justice," The Archives of the Episcopal Church, accessed January 6, 2022, https://www.episcopalarchives.org/church-awakens.

7. Ronald Heifetz, Alexander Grashow, and Marty Linsky, *The Practice of Adaptive Leadership: Tools and Tactics for Changing Your Organization and the World* (Boston: Harvard Business Press, 2009), 30.

8. E. H. Schein, *Organizational Culture and Leadership* (San Francisco: Jossey-Bass, 2009), 173.

9. Peter M. Senge, *The Fifth Discipline: The Art & Practice of the Learning Organization* (New York: Currency, 2006), 273.

Chapter 16

1. Joy Harjo, *Conflict Resolutions for Holy Beings* (New York: W. W. Norton, 2015), 77.

2. Robert Heaney, John Kafwanka, and Hilda Kabia, *God's Church for God's World: A Practical Approach to Partnership in Mission* (New York: Church Publishing Incorporated, 2020), 97.

3. "The Ship Rock Landform," New Mexico Bureau of Geology & Mineral Resources, https://geoinfo.nmt.edu/tour/landmarks/shiprock/home.html#.

4. Ibid.

5. Wati A. Longchar, *Returning to Mother Earth: Theology, Christian Witness and Theological Education: An Indigenous Perspective* (Tainan, Taiwan: PTCA/SCEPTRE, 2012), 96.

6. Randy S. Woodley, *Shalom and the Community of Creation: An Indigenous Vision* (Grand Rapids, MI: Eerdmans, 2012) 149.

7. Wesley Frensdorff, *The Dream: A Church Renewed* (Cincinnati, OH: Forward Movement Publications, 1995).

8. James Treat, *Native and Christian: Indigenous Voices on Religious Identity in the United States and Canada* (New York, NY: Routledge, 1996), 79–80.

9. Robert S. Heaney, *Post-Colonial Theology* (Eugene, OR: Cascade Books, 2019), 138.